CONTENTS

CW00692545

Cover Picture: View from the Savile Residence, Turkey (see page 334)

JOHANSENS
RECOMMENDED HOTEL

FOREWORD BY THE EDITOR

People who use Johansens guides often ask why we never say anything critical about a hotel which we recommend. The answer is easy. If we knew anything bad to say about one of our selections we would not recommend it.

We visit all establishments regularly, overtly or covertly – our professional inspectors non-stop, the rest of us ad hoc; but the many thousands of you who use our guides are really the best guardians of quality. Our recommendations must be reliable, so keep sending us those freepost Guest Survey Reports which you will find among the back pages of the guides or on separate sheets in four languages at hotel reception desks. They provide us with the first hint of any fall in standards, though, as you will be glad to read, the majority are entirely complimentary.

Johansens Recommended Hotels – Europe & the Mediterranean is now in its fourth year and, as the title indicates, the scope of the guide encompasses more than the geographical continent of Europe.

The picture on the cover is the magnificent view from the Savile Residence, a hotel in Turkey, while far to the west, in the Atlantic, are Johansens recommended hotels on the islands of Madeira and Tenerife. The latter, off the west coast of Africa, is on a line south of Cairo! Thanks to the jet engine, the holiday map of Europe has changed forever, but wherever you land, you can be sure of the warm welcome awaiting you at all of our recommendations.

Rodney Exton, Editor

Hotels, from top: **Albergo Pietrasanta – Palazzo Barsanti Bonetti** *Italy p211,* **Schlosshotel Igls** *Austria p24,* **Hotel de Arendshoeve** *The Netherlands p251,* **Hôtel de Crillion** *France, p140.*

Published by

Johansens Limited, Therese House, Glasshouse Yard, London EC1A 4JN

Tel: +44 171 566 9700 Fax: +44 171 251 6112

Find Johansens on the Internet at: http://www.johansens.com

Publisher:	Jolyon Harris
Editor:	Rodney Exton
Copy Editor:	Yasmin Razak
European Executive Inspectorate:	Carol Blench
	Stéphanie Court
	Pierre–Jérôme Degy
	Charlotte Evans
	Hilary Soul
Production Manager:	Daniel Barnett
Production Controller:	Kevin Bradbrook
Senior Designer:	Michael Tompsett
Designer:	Sue Dixon
Map Illustrations:	Linda Clark
Copywriters:	Norman Flack
	Yasmin Razak
	Jill Wyatt
Sales and Marketing Manager:	Laurent Martinez
Marketing Executive:	Emma Woods
Sales Executive:	Babita Sareen
P.A. to Managing Director:	Angela Willcox
Managing Director:	Andrew Warren

Copyright © 1998 Johansens Limited

Johansens is a member company of Harmsworth Publishing Ltd, a subsidiary of the Daily Mail & General Trust plc

ISBN 1 86017 504X

Printed in England by St Ives plc
Colour origination by Graphic Facilities

Distributed in the UK and Europe by Johnsons International Media Services Ltd, London (direct sales) & Biblios PDS Ltd, West Sussex (bookstores). In North America by general sales agent: ETL Group, New York, NY (direct sales) and The Cimino Publishing Group, INC. New York (bookstores). In Australia and New Zealand by Bookwise International, Findon, South Australia.

HOW TO USE THIS GUIDE

If you want to identify a Hotel whose name you already know, look for it in the indexes on pages 335–336.

These indexes are arranged by country.

If you want to find a Hotel in a particular area,

- Turn to the map of Europe on page 2, which will show you the countries in which there are Johansens Recommended Hotels.

- Turn to the title page of the country that you want, where you will find a Map. The location of each Hotel appears in red on the Map with a number corresponding to the page on which the Hotel entry is published.

The countries and place names appear in alphabetical order throughout the guide.

Mini Listings pages 337–340: The names, locations and telephone numbers of all Johansens recommendations in the British Isles and in North America are listed. A display of the Johansens guides in which these recommendations appear is on the outside back cover. Copies of these guides are obtainable direct from Johansens by calling +44 990 269397 or by using the order coupons on pages 341–352.

The prices, in most cases, are a guide to the cost of one night's accommodation with breakfast for two people. Prices are also shown for single occupancy. These rates are correct at the time of going to press but they should always be checked with the hotel.

We occasionally receive letters from guests who have been charged for accommodation booked in advance but later cancelled. Readers should be aware that by making a reservation with a hotel, either by telephone or in writing, they are entering into a legal contract. A hotelier under certain circumstances is entitled to make a charge for accommodation when guests fail to arrive, even if notice of cancellation is given.

(don't keep 'em waiting)

AT&T Direct® Service

AT&T Direct is a great way to reach those you care about back home. It provides quick access to English-speaking operators and fast connections with clear sound quality.

For easy dialing instructions and access numbers, please find a wallet guide in the back of this publication.

For more information, check out the AT&T Worldwide Traveler Web Site at http://www.att.com/traveler/

AT&T

It's all within your reach.

KEY TO SYMBOLS

14 rms — Total number of rooms	14 rms — Nombre de chambres	14 rms — Anzahl der Zimmer
MasterCard accepted	MasterCard accepté	MasterCard akzeptiert
Visa accepted	Visa accepté	Visa akzeptiert
American Express accepted	American Express accepté	American Express akzeptiert
Diners Club accepted	Diners Club accepté	Diners Club akzeptiert
JCB accepted	JCB accepté	JCB akzeptiert
Quiet location	Un lieu tranquille	Ruhige Lage
Access for wheelchairs to at least one bedroom and public rooms	Accès handicapé	Zugang für Behinderte

(The 'Access for wheelchairs' symbol does not necessarily indicate that the property fulfils National Accessible Scheme grading)

Chef-patron	Chef-patron	Chef-patron
Meeting/conference facilities with maximum number of delegates	Salle de conférences – capacité maximale	Konferenzraum-Höchstkapazität
Children welcome, with minimum age where applicable	Enfants bienvenus	Kinder willkommen
Dogs accommodated in rooms or kennels	Chiens autorisés	Hunde erlaubt
At least one room has a four-poster bed	Lit à baldaquin dans au moins une chambre	Himmelbett
Cable/satellite TV in all bedrooms	TV câblée/satellite dans les chambres	Satellit-und Kabelfernsehen in allen Zimmern
Fax available in rooms	Fax dans votre chambre	Fax im Schlafzimmern
No-smoking rooms (at least one no-smoking bedroom)	Chambres non-fumeur	Zimmer für Nichtraucher
Lift available for guests' use	Ascenseur	Fahrstuhl
Air Conditioning	Climatisation	Klimatisiert
Indoor swimming pool	Piscine couverte	Hallenbad
Outdoor swimming pool	Piscine de plein air	Freibad
Tennis court at hotel	Tennis à l'hôtel	Hoteleigener Tennisplatz
Croquet lawn at hotel	Croquet à l'hôtel	Krocketrasen
Fishing can be arranged	Pêche	Angeln
Golf course on site or nearby, which has an arrangement with the hotel allowing guests to play	Golf sur site ou à proximité	Golfplatz
Shooting can be arranged	Chasse / Tir	Jagd
Riding can be arranged	Équitation	Reitpferd
Skiing	Ski	Schilaufen
Hotel has a helicopter landing pad	Helipad	Hubschrauberlandplatz
Licensed for wedding ceremonies	Cérémonies de mariages	Konzession für Eheschliessungen

JOHANSENS AWARDS FOR EXCELLENCE
RECOMMENDED HOTELS – EUROPE & THE MEDITERRANEAN

The 1998 Johansens Awards were presented by Penny Junor at the Johansens Annual Dinner held at The Dorchester on November 3rd 1997. It was a happy occasion for everybody especially for the host hotel, winner of an award.

For the first time ever 3 awards were made to members of Johansens Recommended Hotels – Europe & The Mediterranean for their outstanding excellence. Their individual merits were recognised by the large number of guests from whom we received exceptionally complimentary Guest Survey Reports and letters during the year. In every case these high ratings were endorsed by our Inspectors and then confirmed, according to custom, by further enquiries.

The awards were made in 3 different categories according to location: In the City, In the Country, On the Water.

The Most Excellent City Hotel was deemed to be the Königshof in Munich, Germany, a famous hotel facing Stachus in the heart of the city with a restaurant whose renown extends far beyond Bavaria.

Mr & Mrs Petersson of Château des Vigiers receiving the European Country Hotel Award

Lorenzo Cattaneo of The Königshof receiving the European City Hotel Award

Carol Blench receiving the European Waterside Resort Hotel Award on behalf of Il Pellicano

The Most Excellent Country Hotel was Château des Vigiers at Monestier in South-West France in the Bordeaux area near St. Emilion. A mecca for sport lovers, the golf course is one of the best, equalling the quality of the local wine.

In the Waterside Resort category, the candidates included hotels on the lake, on the river and on the sea. The winner was a superb hotel in a beautiful position overlooking the Mediterranean: Il Pellicano at Porto Ercole, Italy.

Congratulations to these 3 winners and thank you to everyone who sent in Guest Survey Report forms.

Each year we rely on the appraisals of Johansens guests, alongside the nominations of our team of inspectors, as a basis for making all our awards, not only to our Recommended Hotels – Europe and the Mediterranean but also to our Recommended Hotels, Country Houses and Inns with Restaurants in Great Britain & Ireland. In these categories the award winners of 1998 were:

Johansens Most Excellent City Hotel Award:
The Royal Crescent, Bath, Somerset

Johansens Most Excellent Country Hotel Award:
Arisaig House, Inverness-shire, Scotland

Johansens Most Excellent London Hotel Award:
The Dorchester, Park Lane, Mayfair

Johansens Country House Award for Excellence:
Chippenhall Hall, Fressingfield, Suffolk

Johansens Inn Award for Excellence:
The Inn at Whitewell, Clitheroe, Lancashire

Johansens Most Excellent Value for Money Award:
Kingston House, Totnes, Devon

Johansens Most Excellent Restaurant Award:
The Sea Crest, Jersey, Channel Islands

Johansens Most Excellent Service Award:
Gilpin Lodge, Lake Windermere

J&H MARSH & McLENNAN

J&H Marsh & McLennan, the world's leading insurance broker, is proud to be appointed the Preferred Insurance Provider to Johansens Members Worldwide

ARE YOU A HOTELIER?

There is never a spare moment when you're running a Hotel, Inn, Restaurant or Country House. If you're not with a customer, your mind is on stocktaking. Sound familiar?

At J&H Marsh & McLennan, we realise you have little time to worry about your insurance policy, instead, you require peace of mind that you are covered.

That is why for over 20 years J&H Marsh & McLennan have been providing better cover for businesses like yours.

Our unique services are developed specifically for establishments meeting the high standards required for entry in a Johansens guide.

CONTACT US NOW FOR DETAILS OF THE INSURANCE POLICY FOR JOHANSENS
01892 553160 (UK)

ARE YOU AN INDEPENDENT TRAVELLER?

Insurance is probably the last thing on your mind. Especially when you are going on holiday or on a business trip. But are you protected when travelling? Is your home protected while you are away?

J&H Marsh & McLennan offer a wide range of insurances that gives you peace of mind when travelling.

FOR DETAILS ON THESE SERVICES RING (UK):

TRAVEL	**01462 428041**
PENSIONS & FINANCIAL SERVICE	**01892 553160**
HOUSEHOLD	**01462 428200**
MOTOR	**01462 428100**
HEALTHCARE	**01462 428000**

Insurance Policy for Johansens members arranged by:
J&H Marsh & McLennan (UK) Ltd.
Mount Pleasant House,
Lonsdale Gardens,
Tunbridge Wells, Kent TN1 1NY

INTRODUCTION

From The Königshof, Munich, Germany
Winner of the 1998 Johansens Most Excellent European City Hotel Award

The Hotel Königshof is delighted to have been given the Johansens 1998 European City Hotel Of The Year Award.

At the Hotel Königshof we pride ourselves in offering the very highest standards of service with a friendly, personal touch. Our staff are dedicated to ensuring that guests enjoy a quiet and relaxing stay where every need is catered for. To this end we are committed to providing our staff with training and development to motivate and equip them with the necessary skills.

We have a warm and friendly team here at the Hotel Königshof and this award could not have been achieved without the hard work and commitment of our staff. Their drive and enthusiasm is the secret of our success.

Lorenzo Cattaneo, General Manager

HILDON LTD.
Hildon House, Broughton, Hampshire SO20 8DG
☎ 01794-301 747, Fax 01794-301 718

INTRODUCTION

From Il Pellicano, Porto Ercole, Italy
Winner of the 1998 Johansens Most Excellent European Waterside Hotel Award

Il Pellicano was delighted to win the 1998 Johansens Most Excellent European Waterside Hotel Award presented last November at the Dorchester in London's Park Lane.

Harpers & Queen has said that Il Pellicano is one of the 300 best hotels in the World, the Sunday Telegraph has said it is the most tasteful and luxurious small hotel in the world, Time Magazine has said that it is one of the most luxurious hotels in Italy with a magnificent view over the water.

Our Johansens award is something new and different. We were honoured to receive it and we look forward to welcoming many more Johansens guests to Il Pellicano.

Paolo Sagina, Sales & Marketing Manager

WELL…DE GUSTIBUS
NON EST DISPUTANDUM

HILDON

AN ENGLISH
NATURAL MINERAL WATER
OF EXCEPTIONAL TASTE

DELIGHTFULLY STILL

Composition in accordance with the results of the officially
recognized analysis 26 March 1992.
Hildon Ltd., Broughton, Hampshire SO20 8DG. ☎01794-301 747

750 ml e

"FOR BEST BEFORE DATE SEE CAP"
Bottled at source, Broughton, Hampshire

Bottled at source, Broughton, Hampshire
"FOR BEST BEFORE DATE SEE CAP"

INTRODUCTION

From Château des Vigiers, Monestier, France
Winner of the 1998 Johansens Most Excellent European Countryside Hotel Award

We were delighted as well as honoured to receive Johansens European Countryside Hotel of the Year award. I take it as a tribute to our marvellous and friendly staff who work so hard to ensure that each of our guests has a memorable stay.

Our facilities are splendid with the 400 year old Château, known locally as "Little Versailles", 18 hole golf course, gourmet food and our own wine production, but it is good, friendly service that really makes the difference.

Add to all that a most beautiful region steeped in history, ideal for wine tasting and cultural excursions and you get what many of our guests describe as a "total experience".

So, many thanks to Johansens from all of us here at Château des Vigiers. We wish you the best of luck with your expansion plans, and know that you will impose strict quality criteria when you admit new properties into the family.

Lars Petersson, Owner

ERCOL

Furniture for living rooms

The first choice at
every Johansens
Recommended Hotel

Austria

LANDHAUS HUBERTUSHOF

PUCHEN 86 – 8992 ALTAUSSEE, STEIERMARK, AUSTRIA
TEL: +43 3622 71280 FAX: +43 3622 71280 80

This enchanting 19th century hunting lodge has a wonderful display of authentic memorabilia of the chase. Countess Strasoldo has transformed it into an elite hotel, welcoming guests into her private home. The attractive chalet-style Hubertshof has its own verdant parkland and spectacular surrounding scenery – mountains, the Altaussee, the village and pine forests. It is wonderfully peaceful, a sanctuary from the fast stream of city life. Pine panelling, a carved staircase, rustic furniture, colourful rugs and wooden floors enhance the idyllic country life ambience. There is also an exquisite south-facing suite. Guests awake to spectacular views of the lake and mountains. The Countess prepares breakfast herself and this is enjoyed in the morning room or on the sunny terrace. No other meals are offered, but there are many local inns and restaurants serving delicious dinners, beers and local wines. Altaussee is a cultural centre, home of artists and literary cognoscenti. It also offers sporting visitors tennis, golf, hiking, climbing, trout fishing, boat trips in summer and skiing in winter. It is convenient for the Salzburg Festival and the thermal spas nearby. **Directions:** A1, exit Gmunden. Follow directions to Bad Ischl, then Bad Aussee. At Altaussee, take second left and watch for signs to the Landhaus. Price guide: Double/twin ATS550–650; suite ATS700–850.

HOTEL & SPA HAUS HIRT

KAISERHOFSTRASSE 14, 5640 BAD GASTEIN, AUSTRIA
TEL: +43 64 34 27 97 FAX: +43 64 34 27 97 48

The Haus Hirt is ten minutes walk from the centre of the spa resort of Bad Gastein. It is in a lovely park, one of the sunniest places in the area, peaceful and verdant, with breathtaking views over the Gastein valley to the mountains. There are pleasant rooms in which to relax and a superb terrace frequented by sunbathers. Alfresco eating is also encouraged and many of the delightful bedrooms have balconies. A whole floor is dedicated to building up health and reducing stress. Guests indulge themselves with thermal cures, mud-baths, hydrotherapy, aromatherapy, sauna and steam bath, massage, solarium and the beauty salon with Maria Galland Cosmetics. The energetic take exercise classes or dive into the large, scenic indoor pool. The versatile restaurant, with attractive rustic furniture and overlooking the valley, prepares delicious, imaginative meals, both for those who are hungry and those on special diets. Fine wine is listed and there is a cocktail party once a week. The hotel is well-situated for first-class skiing, with many lifts and cable-cars and spectacular pistes. Après-ski includes a visit to the Casino. In summer, golf and riding are popular. **Directions:** From Salzburg, exit at Bischofshofen to Schwarzach and the Gastein Valley. On reaching the town centre, follow the Kaiserhofstrasse to the Haus Hirt. Price guide: Single ATS490–1040; double/twin ATS990–2780.

KUR–SPORT AND GOURMETHOTEL MOSER

KAISER–FRANZ–PLATZ 2, 5630 BAD HOFGASTEIN, AUSTRIA
TEL: + 43 6432 6209 FAX: +43 6432 6209 88 E-MAIL: info@gourmethotel–moser.com

The family-owned Moser Hotel had a special role in the history of the town of Bad Hofgastein. In the 13th century it belonged to rich and powerful families who had mined silver and gold in the Tauer mountains. They spent their wealth on castle-like buildings that have stood the test of time. This richly historical hotel is made out of two houses – one 15th and one 16th century – linked by attractive winding passages. The traditional 80-roomed hotel offers all the comforts of a well-groomed house, but personal touches are much in evidence and a family atmosphere pervades. There is a choice of three restaurants, providing a wide range of dining experiences – from the informality of a café to the set-piece dining room. The swimming pool area is a former gold cellar and here guests can also take advantage of the sauna, thermal bath and relaxation facilities. The hotel is in the centre of the aristocratic health resort of Bad Hofgastein and offers easy access to the extensive pleasures of the beautiful Gastein Valley with its alpine meadows, panoramic views of mountain peaks, rustic houses and farms. There are also plenty of opportunities for skiing, tobogganing and sleighing. **Directions**: The hotel is situated in the centre of Bad Hofgastein. Price guide: Double/ twin ATS800–1,250. Single supplement of ATS50 a day.

GRAND HOTEL SAUERHOF

WEILBURGSTRASSE 11–13, 2500 BADEN BEI WIEN, AUSTRIA
TEL: +43 2252 41251 0 FAX: +43 2252 48047 E-MAIL: sauerhof@rtk.at

Situated in the centre of the Baden spa, Grand Hotel Sauerhof resembles a Biedermeier Palace featuring both comfortable and stylish accommodation and a choice of modern amenities. Delicate pastel shades and soft fabrics dominate the public rooms whilst the 88 bedrooms are beautifully appointed and offer every modern convenience. The hotel is an ideal location for weddings as it has its own chapel. Business meetings and seminars may also be held in the various conference rooms, accommodating up to 150 delegates. The therapeutic sulphur spring forms the base of the hotel's health and beauty centre. There is a wide range of beauty and lifestyle treatments to choose from, including medical herb baths, massages and other methods of relaxation. Special packages are designed for guests and those wishing to visit for a weekend or benefit from the health and beauty offers. The beautiful town of Vienna, with its many attractions, is nearby. Popular excursions include trips to the Castle of Durnstein, where Richard Coeur de Lion was held. **Directions:** From Vienna, take the A2 in the direction of Baden, Bad Vöslau. Take the exit marked Baden and follow the signs to the hotel. Price guide: Single ATS1450–1900; double/twin ATS2200–2950; suites ATS3900–5400.

HOTEL SCHLOSS DÜRNSTEIN

3601 DÜRNSTEIN, AUSTRIA
TEL: +43 2711 212 FAX: +43 2711 351

A fairytale castle built for royalty in the 17th century, standing on the banks of the Danube, is today an exclusive hotel. It has an enviable position, with the river to the fore and the verdant Wachau Valley in the background. The guest rooms all differ yet are equally charming, reflecting the history of the castle through the Baroque, Biedermeier and Empire periods. The furnishings are magnificent, with elaborate drapes, and the bathrooms opulent. The salons are filled with antiques. The impeccable staff will bring superb coffee and irresistible Austrian patisseries. The intimate bar is an ideal rendezvous before entering the grand dining room with its lofty arches. The menu recommends regional and international dishes and the wine list includes a wide choice of wines, among them superb dessert wines. In summer, meals are served on the enchanting Danube Terrace. There are two pools, one in the flower-filled patio and the other indoors, part of the fitness centre. Tennis and golf are nearby, the hotel has bikes for exploring the Wachau valley, while the Danube offers waterskiing, fishing and boat trips. Vienna is just 1 hour away, with its galleries and concerts. **Directions:** A1 from Vienna, exit Melk, cross the Danube taking Road A3 towards Krems, following the Danube to Dürnstein. Price guide (halfboard): Single ATS1950–2150; double/twin ATS1250–2400; suites ATS2400.

SCHLOSSBERG HOTEL

KAISER-FRANZ-JOSEF-KAI 30, 8010 GRAZ, AUSTRIA
TEL: +43 316 80700 FAX: +43 316 807070

The first impression of this lovely hotel is one of surprise that so many comfortable and spacious rooms lie behind its attractive, blue front façade. Nestling against a wooded hillside it is a welcome oasis in the centre of a busy city. Consisting of three buildings surrounding a courtyard dating back to 1450, Schlossberg Hotel is a wealth of heavy oak beams and arched doorways. Each of the 54 en suite bedrooms is individually decorated and furnished with Austrian country antiques and rich brocade curtains. They have every facility for a guest's comfort, including soft, fluffy bathrobes and frottee slippers. The relaxing public rooms have polished stone or wooden floors with 20th century works of art from the owner's private collection decorating the walls. Buffet breakfast can be taken in the courtyard. Visitors are invited to enjoy the hotel's peaceful garden terraces which offer wonderful views over the rooftops and river, or sip cool drinks around the swimming pool during the warm summer months. The cable railway up the Schlossberg hill is popular, as is the opera house which hosts international companies. **Directions**: Leave autobahn A9/A2 at Graz/Graz West and follow signs to the railway station. Turn into Keplerstrasse towards the town, travel over the bridge and take the second right turn into Kaiser Franz Josef Kai. Price guide: Single ATS1,600–2,200; double/twin ATS2,400–3,000; suite ATS4,000–5,000.

SCHLOSSHOTEL IGLS

VILLER STEIG 2, 6080 IGLS, TIROL, AUSTRIA
TEL: +43 512 37 72 17 FAX: +43 512 37 86 79 E-MAIL: schlosshotel.igls@tyrol.at

Set in Igls, on a sunny terrace above Innsbruck, the Schlosshotel is an enchanting Tyrolean castle with turrets and spires surrounded by a beautiful tree-lined site. In the summer, the hotel parkland becomes flower-filled gardens leading out to brilliant green pastures whilst in the winter, the landscape glistens white with snow. The Schloss has truly earned its award of five stars. The interior of the hotel is exquisite, with lovely festooned curtains and co-ordinating wallpapers, graceful period furniture, clever use of colour and discreet lighting. The bedrooms and suites are charming, with views across the countryside to the Patscherkofel Mountains. The spacious reception area is welcoming and the bar, with its baroque fireplace is very convivial. Guests linger in the elegant dining room, appreciating the fine food and wines served by attentive staff. The hotel has both an indoor and outdoor swimming pool, steam room, sauna and solarium. Skiing is for Olympians, families, beginners and those who enjoy cross-country. Bobsleigh, skating and curling are alternative winter sports. In summer, tennis, walking in the 'old park' and golf on nearby courses are the principal activities. Nearby Innsbruck has theatres, concerts, exhibitions and museums. **Directions:** Leave Innsbruck on the Inntal highway, following signs to Igls. Price guide: Single ATS2,000–2,550; Double/twin ATS3,600–4,700; suites ATS4,200–5,300.

SPORTHOTEL IGLS

HILBERSTRASSE 17, 6080 IGLS, TIROL, AUSTRIA
TEL: +43 512 37 72 41 FAX: +43 512 37 86 79 E-MAIL: sporthotel.igls@tyrol.at

In Igls, on its sunny terrace above Innsbruck, stands this élite chalet-style hotel offering traditional Austrian hospitality all year round – during the winter, when Igls is a premier ski resort and in summer when visitors enjoy the many sporting activities and walking through the scenic countryside. It is also an exceptional venue for conferences. Fine pieces of Austrian period furniture can be found in the hall and the spacious elegant salon with an open fire–place. The bedrooms, suites and apartments are very comfortable. Guests relax in the winter garden, drink apéritifs in the lounge or join friends in the Tyrolean dance-bar. Dinner is by candlelight in the handsome restaurant which serves a feast of new award-winning Austrian cuisine. Marvellous buffets appear for occasions and conference guests enjoy superb banquets in the private dining hall. The excellent wine list is cosmopolitan. The leisure centre is magnificent – a large indoor/outdoor pool (60ft) with a poolside bar, saunas, solariums, gymnasium with modern equipment, whirlpools and a beauty parlour. Winter sports include skiing, skating, curling and tobogganing. In the summer, guests play golf, tennis and bowls, explore the countryside on bikes or on foot and climb the mountains. Innsbruck offers theatres, music, and museums. **Directions:** Leaving Innsbruck on the Inntal highway, follow signs to Igls. Price guide: Single ATS1,080–1,430; double/twin ATS1,760–2,460; suites ATS2,500–3,220.

ROMANTIK HOTEL SCHWARZER ADLER

KAISERJÄGERSTRASSE 2, 6020 INNSBRUCK, AUSTRIA
TEL: +43 512 58 71 09 FAX: +43 512 56 16 97

Surrounded by lofty mountains and over 1000 years old, Innsbruck is one of the most fascinating places in Austria, and close to the romantic Old Town is the successful Hotel Schwarzer Adler, which has been in the hands of the Ultsch family for four generations. Careful modernisation of the 16th century building has preserved its Tyrolean charm, and the panelled walls, beamed ceilings and staff in national dress enhance the atmosphere. The bedrooms, decorated in soft relaxing colours, have simple period furniture from the region, and many have balconies. The bar is very convivial, open to the locals. In fine weather drinks are served in the courtyard. Diners choose between two restaurants, one elegant with a sophisticated menu, the other rustic, offering succulent local specialities. Fine wines are listed. Breakfast is a fabulous buffet. This is a popular base for winter sports enthusiasts, in summer walkers enjoy the countryside, maybe visiting the Alpine Zoo. Those exploring the town will find many historic buildings and museums. Night-life includes theatres, clubs and the casino. **Directions:** From Salzburg leave A12 at Innsbruck Ost exit. Follow signs to the main station, turn left into Museumstrasse then right into Sillgasse, finding the hotel on the right. Price guide: Single ATS950–1500; double/twin ATS1600–2300; suites ATS2700–3200.

120

ROMANTIK HOTEL TENNERHOF

6370 KITZBÜHEL, GRIESENAUWEG 26, AUSTRIA
TEL: +43 5356 6 3181 FAX: +43 5356 6 318170 E-MAIL: tennerhof@netway.at

Once a farmhouse, now a first-class hotel, the Tennerhof is a most attractive chalet-style building, with flower bedecked balconies, standing in beautifully kept grounds – snow-covered in winter and much enjoyed by summer guests. The reception rooms are charming, the spacious lounge with its elegant furnishings and the more traditional stone-floored sitting-room with its fireplace. Bridge players have their own corner and there is a smart, well-stocked bar. The bedrooms, many with panelled walls, beamed ceilings and traditional painted furniture include highly romantic suites. There are two restaurants, one slightly more formal where jackets are requested, and a popular terrace for alfresco dining. The restaurant has been awarded two toques. The chefs prepare gourmet international specialities, using home-grown vegetables. Well-chosen wines are listed. Other facilities within the hotel are a well-equipped conference room, and a leisure complex with a palatial pool surrounded by plants and spectacular murals, a sauna and steam-room. A second, outdoor pool is a focal point in summer. In winter Kitzbühel is a famous ski-resort, and when the snows go there are three golf courses. The hotel also arranges excursions with wonderful picnics. **Directions:** Take A12 from Innsbruck, exit at Wörgl, take the B312, then B161 to Kitzbühel. Price guide: ATS1480 2250; double/twin ATS2340–4500; suites ATS3380–6680.

27

HOTEL PALAIS PORCIA

NEUER PLATZ 13, 9020 KLAGENFURT, AUSTRIA
TEL: +43 463 51 15 90 FAX: +43 463 51 15 90 30 E-MAIL: schlosshotel@mail.palais-porcia.co.at

A unique town house in the very heart of Klagenfurt, Hotel Palais Porcia has great style. Immediately on entering the hotel, guests are aware they have come to somewhere very special, far from the ultra-modern large hotels of the 20th century. The house was built in the 17th century and has been decorated appropriately. The reception area is glamorous, with its marble, mirrors and blackamoor lamps. The salon, which has the bar at one end, is very handsome, with wonderful big period chairs, magnificent wall-covering and rich Persian rugs. A superb meeting place! The guest rooms are stunning, the furnishings baroque and the colour schemes glorious. The beds are ornately carved - they are also extremely comfortable.

The opulent marble bathrooms, by contrast, are modern in design. The hotel has no restaurant, but it has a magnificent breakfast room, again with mirrors used to great effect. The walls are hung in red and gold, the chairs elegant and there is fine porcelain on the table. In summer, residents appreciate the hotel's private beach on the Wörthersee. Golf is 20 km away, whilst tennis is close by. The museums and castle are fascinating and there is a vibrant nightlife in the town. **Directions:** From the A2 take Viktringer Ring, turning left into Oktoberstrasse, finding the hotel on the Neuer Platz. Valet car-parking is available. Price guide: Single ATS950; double/twin ATS1350–4800; suites ATS2500–4800.

LANDHAUS KELLERWAND

MAUTHEN 24, 9640 KÖTSCHACH – MAUTHEN, AUSTRIA
TEL: +43 4715 269 / 378 FAX: +43 4715 37816

To visit here is to stay in the private home of Sissy Sonnleitner, one of Austria's most famous chefs, such is the ambience of the Landhaus Kellerwand – a restaurant where connoisseurs of fine food and good wines may reside in great comfort! The hotel's architecture is typical of the neighbourhood, with its little turret, tall windows and colourful window boxes. There are pleasant gardens behind the house. The drawing room is delightful, big chairs covered in rose chintz, where guests relax by the fireside, with a drink and canapés, perhaps listening to the piano. The apartments and suites are luxurious, with whirlpool baths and separate living rooms and the bedrooms are charming, with their rustic furnishings. There is also a fitness room and spa with its own waterfall! The pièce de résistance is the restaurant, an elegant and sophisticated setting for the magnificent dishes prepared by Sissy, accompanied by superb wines. On warm days visitors enjoy apéritifs on the terrace. The hotel offers several special packages – one includes Cookery Seminars; others are for golfers, wild flower and nature lovers or include the local cheese festival and Advent ceremonies. **Directions:** A10 motorway, following signs to Seeboden, then take E66 at Oberdrauburg and follow signs to Kötschach-Mauthen. Price guide: Single ATS735–890; double/twin ATS850–1005; suites ATS1000–1155.

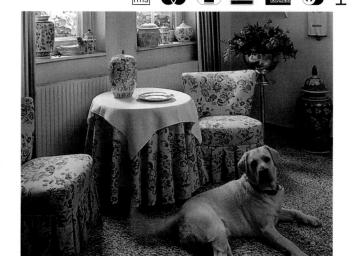

SPORTHOTEL KRISTIANIA

OMESBERG 331, 6764 LECH AM ARLBERG
TEL: +43 5583 25 610 FAX: +43 5583 3550 E-MAIL: kristiania@lech.at

This enchanting chalet hotel on the outskirts of Lech is only open in the winter-sports season. It is owned by Olympic slalom champion Othmar Schneider, who has named it after the Kristiania ski turn. The surrounding scenery is magical – snowclad mountains, pine forests and the picturesque village. The Schneider family have created a warm and colourful ambience. The bedrooms are delightful, furnished with comfortable modern chairs, fine old rugs and local antiques. Some have balconies opening onto spectacular views. All amenities are provided. Après-ski guests relax in the cheerful bar before indulging in delicious dishes listed in the sophisticated buffet and dinner menus, presented with appropriate wine suggestions. The restaurant is charming and part of the Schneider's fine modern art collection is exhibited on its pine-clad walls. Another showpiece which fascinates visitors is the impressive display of trophies won by their host. The Kristiania is ideally situated, five minutes from the slopes, next to the cross country run. Non-skiers sunbathe on the terrace. Lech offers skating, curling, tobogganing, sleigh rides and ski kindergarten. It has a lively night life. **Directions:** First right after Arlberg tunnel, following signs to Lech, finding the hotel on left just before entering the village. Price guide: Single ATS1450–2700; double/twin ATS2900–5600; suites ATS3400–6100.

HOTEL SCHLOSS LEONSTAIN

LEONSTEINSTR 1, PÖRTSCHACH AM WÖRTHER SEE, AUSTRIA
TEL: +43 4272 28160 FAX: +43 4272 2823

A sophisticated hotel in a 14th century castle near a sparkling lake! The charming village of Pörtschach is on the Wörther See, one of Austria's larger lakes, surrounded by mountains and forests. The castle has been imaginatively restored, and the focal point is the central courtyard. The gardens are pretty, with fountains, pools, statues and fine old trees. Many original features of the castle have been retained, carved doors, painted ceilings, graceful archways, tiled floors – a background for the many fine antiques. The guest rooms are pleasant, decorated in soft colours, furnished with period pieces and having all modern comforts. The spacious salons are elegant and the smart bar is well stocked. The Leonstain

is proud of its cooking and guests feast on Austrian specialities in the splendid dining hall which opens onto the courtyard on sunny days. The Leonstain has a private beach on the lake, just minutes away, rowing boats, table tennis and children's playground. Water-sking, windsurfing, sailing, tennis and golf can be arranged. Boat trips are fun and Klagenfurt should be explored. **Directions:** Leave motorway between Villach and Klagenfurt at Pörtschach exit, follow signs to the lake, and on leaving town centre find the Schloss behind white walls on the right. Price guide (including breakfast and dinner, per person per day): Single ATS1100–1510; double/twin AT5S850–1500; suites ATS1250–1940.

HOTEL ALTSTADT RADISSON SAS

RUDOLFSKAI 28 / JUDENGASSE 15, 5020 SALZBURG, AUSTRIA
TEL: +43 662 84 85 71 0 FAX: +43 662 84 85 71 6

This hotel, with its graceful architecture, has a long history which can be traced back to 1377. Originally an inn, one of the oldest in historic Salzburg, it is now an elite and luxurious hotel offering immaculate and personal service. The elegant facade tells new arrivals that the Hotel Altstadt is very special; once inside, the enchanting interior rooms with low stone archways, fine antiques, and the fascinating glass atrium confirm this impression. The bedrooms are individual, some large and some small. They offer a choice of views over the Salzach River with the Kapuzner Monastery on the far bank, the Fortress or the old town. The bar is a popular rendezvous. The enchanting Restaurant Symphonie with its verandah-style wall, providing a spectacular view across the river, serves the finest food and wine, while special occasions in the beamed Renaissance Saal are memorable. Small conferences can also be accommodated. Salzburg, the birth place of Mozart, is famous for its music festivals. It has many places of historic interest, theatres and opera to explore. River trips are possible and leaving the city, the famous White Horse Inn on the Wolfgangsee is not too far away. **Directions:** Follow signs to the centre of Salzburg. The hotel is adjacent to the river, opposite the monastery. Garage service can be arranged. Price guide: Single ATS1850–3900; double/twin ATS2700–6500; suites ATS4950–9700.

HOTEL AUERSPERG

AUERSPERGSTRASSE 61, 5027 SALZBURG, AUSTRIA
TEL: +43 662 88 944 FAX: +43 662 88 944 55

The Hotel Auersperg is a traditional family-run hotel near the right bank of the River Salzach. Just five minutes walk from the fascinating Old City in which Mozart was born. The hotel has beautiful green and sunny gardens, a wonderful place to relax after a long day's sightseeing. The guest rooms and suites are delightful, with comfortable modern furniture, big windows and chintz covers – each individually decorated in harmonious colours. A fitness centre with a sauna and steam bath occupies the top floor, together with a roof terrace which has spectacular views. The welcoming spacious reception hall, with its marble floor and 19th century moulded ceiling, leads into the drawing room, filled with antiques

and period furniture. The smart library bar is convivial, informal meals being available in the dining area. International dishes and local specialities are served in the restaurant and some of the wine is from the region. Salzburg is famous for its music, major festivals taking place regularly. Many historic old buildings, museums and the castles wait to be explored. Pleasant days can be spent driving to the mountains and lakes, including the famous Wolfgangsee. **Directions:** Take the Salzburg North exit from the Autobahn. Auerspergstrasse runs east off Schwarzstrasse by Kongress Haus. The hotel has car parking. Price guide: Single ATS1090–1490; double/twin ATS1440–2140; suites ATS1940–2640.

HOTEL SCHLOSS MÖNCHSTEIN

MÖNCHSBERG PARK 26, 5020 SALZBURG–CITY CENTER, AUSTRIA
TEL: +43 662 84 85 55 0 FAX: +43 662 84 85 59 E-MAIL: salzburg@monchstein.at

This enchanting castle, described as 'The urban sanctuary of the world' by Hideaway Report, has offered hospitality since the 14th century. It stands on the Mönchsberg, a hill in the heart of Salzburg, the centre of the festival city and can be reached via "Mönchstein Panorama Path" and lift within 7 minutes. The intimate Paris Lodron Restaurant, "Restaurant of the year" – CLL-D, has the finest reputation in Salzburg, founded on the exquisite table settings with the view over the old city, impeccable staff and above all, the imaginative presentation of Austrian dishes and a connoisseurs' wine list. Guests meet in the friendly Cocktail Bar "P.L." or on the garden terrace "Apollo" and enjoy divine pastries in the Castle-Café 'Maria Theresia'. Romantics exchange vows in the Wedding Chapel followed by a banquet. A sign on 'Salzburg's Wedding Wall' keeps this special event in the memory forever. Music is very important in Salzburg and there is a rich programme throughout the year. The castle itself holds harp concerts every Saturday and Sunday. Conference facilities in unique atmosphere; Royal and Princely suite. **Directions:** On reaching Salzburg, take the Müllner Hauptstrasse, the Augustiner Gasse and follow the signs for the Hotel Schloss Mönchstein. Price guide: Single ATS2900–3900; double/twin ATS2900–6500; suite ATS5400–30000.

72

SCHLOSS HAUNSPERG

5411 OBERALM BEI HALLEIN (SALZBURG), AUSTRIA
TEL: +43 6245 80 662 FAX: +43 6245 85 680

To stay at this bewitching castle, just fifteen minutes drive from Salzburg, is a unique and unforgettable experience. Built in the 14th century, it has the most lovely architecture – a graceful ivy-clad mansion with wrought iron balconies and a splendid tall tower. Its own Baroque chapel has painted ceilings and an ornate gold altar. Eike and Georg von Gernerth are splendid hosts. Both multilingual, they welcome guests into their magnificent home with great enthusiasm. The salons are treasure-troves, filled with priceless antiques, fine Persian rugs, brilliant chandeliers, yet comfortable and lived-in. There is a strong emphasis on music and a Black Bösendorfer grand piano is in the dramatic music room. The guest rooms, some enormous, are filled with period furniture and objets d'art – it is a privilege to stay here. Breakfast comprising fruit, eggs, cheese, meat and breads, is a joy with starched linen, gleaming silver and fresh flowers completing the picture. At dusk, the Gernerths invite guests to join them for glasses of Austrian wine in the parlour. They will prepare light meals on request, but there is an excellent restaurant nearby. Sporting guests play tennis, golf or squash, others enjoy Salzburg and its music festivals, visit nearby lakes or wander in the castle grounds. **Directions:** A10 exit 16 Hallein, follow directions to Oberalm then signs to the hotel. Price guide: Single ATS 950–1300; double/twin ATS 1530–1900; suite ATS 2100–2500.

ROMANTIK HOTEL GASTHOF HIRSCHEN

HOF 14, 6867 SCHWARZENBERG, AUSTRIA
TEL: +43 55 12 29 44 0 FAX: +43 55 12 29 44 20 E-MAIL: romantikhotel@hirschen.vol.at

The Gasthof Hirschen, in Schwarzenberg, one of the prettiest villages in the Vorarlberg, has offered hospitality since 1757. Still with baroque detail, it is now a delightful hotel in surroundings that are snow-clad in winter and verdant in summer. The spacious and elegant lounge, with its big fireplace, is also the bar. The restaurant, with its carved ceiling, stone floors and traditional furniture, faces an attractive courtyard with a fountain. The menu is Austrian /cosmopolitan and the wine list extensive. Bedrooms in the Gasthaus are cosy and rustic, with fabulous views across to the Arlberg. A second house, once the old farmhouse, just 30 metres from the hotel, has been converted into a contemporary annex.

Other facilities include a sauna, steam room and underground parking. In winter this is a skiers' hotel, with superb skiing made especially pleasant by the many ski huts along the pistes. Summer is the time for walkers and climbers to explore the Bregenzerwald. Nearby Bregenz has many attractions, the old town with historic buildings and the new with its shops and casinos, boat trips on Lake Constance and superb music at festival time and during the Schubertiade festival in Feldkirch and Schwarzenberg. **Directions:** Leave the A14 at the Dornbirn Nord exit, driving through Dornbirn to Bödele and Schwarzenberg, the Gasthof is in the square. Price guide: Double/twin ATS1280– 1800; suites ATS1900–2850.

HOTEL VIKTORIA

GEIGENBÜHELWEG 589, 6100 SEEFELD/TIROL, AUSTRIA
TEL: +43 5212 4441 FAX: +43 5212 4443 E-MAIL: hotel.viktoria@happynet.at

Visitors enjoy a stay in Seefeld, both in winter and summer. Perhaps best known as a ski-resort, it is also a marvellous centre for summer holidays. The Hotel Viktoria is a very modern chalet, utterly luxurious, the interior designers having used an enormous amount of glass and marble, creating an impression of immense space and reaching towards the Millennium. The bedrooms are categorised as suites, apartments or duplexes, all rooms have separate bath and toilet, hair–dryer, bathrobe, minibar, roomsafe, telephone, cable-TV, CD player and a large balcony. All are individually decorated and very modern with spectacular views over the mountains. The cosmopolitan dining room, with its impeccable staff, serves superb food and has an impressive wine list. The bar is very friendly and well-stocked. Leisure facilities include a well-equipped gymnasium, sauna, solarium and steam room. There is also an enormous Jacuzzi but no pool as yet. Winter sports occupy guests from December to March, and when the snows have gone in April the Viktoria re-opens for tourists coming up from Innsbruck, perhaps en route for Salzburg. They enjoy walking in the flower-filled meadows, mountaineering, fishing in the lake or playing the nearby golf courses. **Directions:** A12 from Innsbruck to the centre of Seefeld, then turn left at the station. Car parking is available. Price guide per person: Single/double/twin ATS990–1980; suites ATS1280–2550 per person.

HOTEL KLOSTERBRÄU

6100 SEEFELD, TIROL, AUSTRIA
TEL: +43 5212 26210 FAX: +43 5212 3885 E-MAIL: info@klosterbrau.com

Seefeld is a superb holiday resort all the year round. In its centre there is an enchanting chalet – the 5 star Hotel Klosterbräu – with its fairy-tale architecture and background of mountains in the quiet pedestrian area, Once a monastery, today the hotel is vibrant yet traditional. Friendly staff in national costume, historic rooms with stone walls, magnificent wooden ceilings and panelled walls, all contribute to the superb ambience. The spacious bedrooms are charming and the bathrooms efficient. The Klosterbräu has four restaurants offering gourmet food and regional specialities. The old Kapuziner Keller hosts small gatherings – in summer dine in the old monastery courtyard. Breakfasts in the dining room are served late for all night revellers!

Inspecting the incredible wine cellar in the vaults is a must. High life includes the piano bar, the night club (après ski tea dances in winter), Tyrolean Bräukeller, the live music Siglu-Bar and disco. Additionally the hotel has conference rooms and a pool area in the extensive leisure and beauty centre. Hotel Klosterbräu is an ideal point of departure for many sports activities: the hotel has it's own tennis courts and putting-green with a championship golf course nearby and only a few minutes away from the skiing pistes. **Directions:** Leaving Innsbruck on A12, take Seefeld exit then follow signs to the Zentrum. Hotel has valet parking. Price guide: Single ATS1,380–1,840; double/twin ATS1,380–1,840; suites ATS1,950–3,500.

ROMANTIK HOTEL IM WEISSEN RÖSSL

5360 ST WOLFGANG AM SEE, SALZKAMMERGUT, AUSTRIA
TEL: +43 6138 23060 FAX: +43 6138 2306 41 E-MAIL: hpeter@weissesroessl.co.at

This magical hotel became legendary through "The White Horse Inn" operetta, and has retained its refreshing Austrian charm. It stands on the edge of Lake St Wolfgang, a delightful building with its terraces and flower-filled window boxes, overlooking the waterfront, adjacent to the church spire and set against a background of the village, mountains and pine forests. It has benefited from being in the hands of the Peter family for three generations. The bedrooms are pleasant and comfortable and both they and the bathrooms are pristine. The reception rooms are delightful and there are sunny terraces for warm weather. Guests soon relax in the inviting bar. The restaurant serves gorgeous Salzkammergut dishes and delicious Austrian wines. Leisure activities abound: swimming in the pool or lake, windsurfing and other water sports, boat trips, tennis, golf, fishing and in winter downhill or cross country skiing or sledging. There are also activities for children. At night there is dancing, occasionally operettas or marvellous music in Salzburg. **Directions:** From Salzburg City Centre take A-Road 158 for St Gilgen, then follow signs to St Wolfgang. The Weissen Rossl is in St Wolfgang See. Price guide: Single ATS950–1400; double/twin ATS1400–2400; apts ATS2100–2800.

SEESCHLÖSSL VELDEN

KLAGENFURTER STRASSE 34, 9220 VELDEN, AUSTRIA
TEL: +43 4274 2824 FAX: +43 4274 2824 44

This beautiful, sun-yellow painted lakeside hotel is just a five minutes' walk from the bustling town centre and tucked away behind a thick protective roadside shield of tall trees. Similar in style to many of the area's holiday villas built at the turn of the century its unusual, attractive features include two corner towers whose bedrooms are favourites among visitors for their unique design and scenic views. Each of the hotel's 14 bedrooms are extremely comfortable, have spacious bathrooms, all modern amenities and are delightfully furnished with period pieces. Some have balconies opening on to magnificent views. The lounges, with their panelled walls, polished wooden floors, soft colourings and delightful rustic furnishings, have a warm, comfortable and relaxing ambience. On warmer mornings, breakfast is served on the terrace which overlooks the garden leading down to the waters edge. The hotel has a private water front, complete with a small pier and a wooden bathing hut. There is a tennis court and golf enthusiasts have the choice of a number of courses within easy reach. For those who enjoy a little "flutter" there is a casino in the town. Closed from November until Easter. **Directions**: Exit Autobahn E66 at Velden-Ost for the town centre. The hotel is on the left. Price guide: Double/twin ATS700–1,300; suites: ATS1,000–1,500.

HOTEL IM PALAIS SCHWARZENBERG

SCHWARZENBERGPLATZ 9, 1030 VIENNA, AUSTRIA
TEL: +43 1 798 4515 FAX: +43 1 798 4714 E-MAIL: palais@schwarzenberg.via.at

This grand hotel is palatial and nostalgic of imperial Austria when baroque architecture was in fashion. It stands in enchanting gardens with famous roses, ornamental ponds and acclaimed sculptures. The guest rooms are spacious and luxurious, with their graceful period furniture, harmonious colour schemes and views over the courtyard. The bathrooms are in marble. Six new designer suites and rooms have been added in theleft side wing of the palais. The reception rooms, several of which are ideal for conferences and meetings, are sumptuous – the Kuppelsaal (entrance hall) has a superb domed ceiling, there is a circular gilded lounge and the spectacular Marble Hall with its exquisite frescoes transforms into the most spectacular private dining hall. The Palais Bar is perfect for cocktails and the Viennese rendezvous in the elegant Terrace Restaurant looking out over the park, while enjoying classical French or Austrian cuisine and superb wines. Lighter, more informal meals can be found in the Kaminzimmer or on the coffee terrace. Guests can play croquet on the lawns or follow the jogging trail. The nearby tennis club is available and golf is just 5km away. Vienna is renowned for its music and art. **Directions:** From the airport, follow A4 to the centre of Vienna. There is a large private car park. Price guide: Double/twin ATS3400–5600; suites ATS5600–12000.

PrimaHotels

THURNHERS ALPENHOF

6763, ZÜRS/ARLBERG, AUSTRIA
TEL: +43 5583 2191 FAX: +43 5583 3330

The Thurnhers Alpenhof is a luxury family-owned chalet hotel, high up in the Alps. Dedicated to winter sports enthusiasts of all ages, it is only open in the ski season. New arrivals are instantly aware of the professionalism of the staff and the warmth projected by the owners' interest in antiques and other delightful memorabilia. The roomy bedrooms are light and very pretty, floral fabrics covering the comfortable chairs by the window, looking out over the snow. The bathrooms are sophisticated! Guests mingle in the piano bar throughout the evening and dine well by candlelight in the Restaurant – the gourmet menu includes local specialities and international cuisine. Every week there is a Gala Dinner, Fondue Evening and a Heurigen Buffet. The cellar is impressive with wines for all budgets. The skiing is marvellous with direct access from the hotel to the graded pistes for novices and experts, cross country or downhill. Après-ski is important and exotic cocktails or warming gluhwein are always waiting at the end of the day. Guests may relax in the pool, enjoy a sauna, steam bath or solarium or have their weary muscles massaged. The hotel has an in-house ski instructor, who organises ski trips and excursions. Children have their own ski school and programme. **Directions:** The nearest airport is Zürich. Leave motorway at Bludenz, follow signs to Zürs/Arlberg. Price guide (per person): Single ATS2700–3200; double/twin ATS2200–3200; suites ATS2300–4500.

Belgium

BELGIUM (Antwerp)

FIREAN HOTEL

KAREL OOMSSTRAAT 6, 2018 ANTWERPEN, BELGIUM
TEL: +32 3 237 02 60 FAX: +32 3 238 11 68

This exclusive and prestigious town house hotel in a quiet residential street close to the centre of Antwerp was built in preparation for the 1930 World Exhibition. Today its exquisite Art Deco style ensures an appreciative clientele, who travel worldwide and are weary of large standardised chain hotels. The Art Deco theme is evident throughout The Firean, from its stunning entrance, through the unique doors leading into the salon, with authentic Tiffany enamel and glass and in the furnishings of the comfortable bedrooms. The bathrooms are modern and efficient. The high standards of courtesy of that era are maintained by the proprietors who like to welcome guests personally, ascertaining any special needs. Breakfast is served and drinks are available in the small, friendly bar or enjoyed on the patio in good weather. The new Minerva restaurant, located 50m away from the hotel, combines excellent standards of service and fine cuisine with good value for money. Antwerp has many museums and excellent shopping. **Directions:** From Brussels, (A1-E19) Antwerp exit through tunnel, over bridge, following signs for Antwerpen Centrum; 3rd traffic light find hotel on left. From UK/Paris/Bruges(A14–E.17) 2nd exit after Kennedy Tunnel, left over bridge into Karel Oomsstraat. The hotel has a private garage. Price guide: Single BF4250–4700; double/twin BF5150–5900; suites BF7800.

44

HOTEL RUBENS

OUDE BEURS 29, 2000 ANTWERP, BELGIUM
TEL: +32 3 222 48 48 FAX: +32 3 225 19 40 E-MAIL: hotel.rubens@glo.be

Antwerp – a busy port and the centre of the diamond market over many centuries – has a fascinating Old Town, and this is where business people and tourists alike are delighted to find the Hotel Rubens, close to the Grande Place. The Rubens dates back to the sixteenth century but inside its graceful old exterior it has been completely renovated. The reception hall, with the bar at one end, is smart, but on fine days guests tend to congregate in the attractive plant-filled inner courtyard. There is also a secluded flower garden at the rear of the hotel. The colourful bedrooms are beautifully decorated and quiet, many overlooking picturesque old houses. The luxurious Rubens Suite, with a lovely view of the cathedral, has a spacious sitting room, perfect for meetings. The hotel has no formal restaurant, although a substantial breakfast buffet and room service are available. However there are many good restaurants and interesting bistros in walking distance. The Cathedral, Rubens' House and the Diamond Museum should be visited, and boat trips are a pleasant way to sightsee. **Directions:** The hotel is in a street called Oude Beurs (the old stock exchange) just North of the cathedral. When reserving a room obtain detailed advice. Parking facilities available. Price guide: Single BF4500–5500; double/twin BF4500–7500; suites BF7000–18,000.

DIE SWAENE

STEENHOUWERSDIJK, 8000 BRUGES, BELGIUM
TEL: +32 50 34 27 98 FAX: +32 50 33 66 74

Swans are legendary symbols in Bruges. Die Swaene, dating back to the 15th century, once the home of city elders, has been brilliantly transformed into the most magnificent hotel, romantically situated by a pretty canal and surrounded by historic buildings. Guests enter into luxury on a grand scale – lovely antiques, gleaming chandeliers, large mirrors, baskets of fruit and bowls of fresh flowers, indoor plants and statuary abound. The drawing room is reminiscent of Louis XV. There is a terraced garden where guests enjoy apéritifs on fine evenings and gracious dining areas where spectacular candlelit dinners and champagne lunches take place. The menu offers classical and contemporary dishes and the large cellar houses some rare vintage wines. The bedrooms are opulent, with exotic festoons over ornately carved beds, although there are some simpler rooms available. Facilities include a well-equipped conference room, fitness centre, indoor pool and private car park. Guests enjoy exploring Bruges, taking the canal tours arranged by the hotel. **Directions:** Enter Bruges from Katelijnepoort, taking Katelijnestraat, turn right along Gruuthusestraat and follow the canal, keeping it on the left, along Dyver and then left at Vismarkt into Steenhouversdijk. Price guide: Single BF4800; double/twin BF5950–8950; suite BF11500.

HOTEL ACACIA

KORTE ZILVERSTRAAT 3A, 8000 BRUGES, BELGIUM
TEL: +32 50 34 44 11 FAX: +32 50 33 88 17

The central location of Hotel Acacia makes it an ideal choice for anyone wanting to explore the historic city of Bruges. It provides an excellent standard of accommodation and hospitality, with tastefully furnished and decorated bedrooms providing every modern comfort and convenience. Indulgence in generously-portioned breakfasts, which can be served either in the bedrooms or the breakfast room, can be worked off in the indoor health and leisure centre. This features a swimming pool, Jacuzzi and sauna. The intimate bar is the perfect place to relax and enjoy a quiet drink before dinner and there is also a small living room. Although there is no restaurant, there are plenty of excellent restaurants within easy reach. The hotel has a private underground car park, which offers direct access to the ground floor and reception. The city is the lace-making capital of Europe and shops selling exquisite lace, made according to the traditions of this ancient craft, abound. Bruges is also renowned for its wealth of art treasures, which includes many fine masterpieces of Flemish painting. Among its many attractions is the presence of Michel Angelo's beautiful marble statue of Madonna. **Directions**: Enter Bruges through Boeveriepoort and then follow signs to public car park Zilverpand. The hotel is just 100m away. Price guide: Single BF4450; double/twin/suite BF4950–5450.

HOTEL DE ORANGERIE

KARTUIZERINNENSTRAAT 10, 8000, BRUGES, BELGIUM
TEL: +32 50 34 16 49 FAX: +32 50 33 30 16

The nuns who lived in this 15th century convent would envy today's residents; today it is a small, attractive hotel with a big sunny terrace overlooking the canal, on the other side of which is its bigger and elegant sister, Hotel De Tuilerieen. Both are owned by vivacious Madame Beatrice Geeraert, legendary for her hospitality. The exterior is delightful, with long tall windows at the front and flower bedecked balconies at the back. Guests relax in the generous sized bedrooms, appreciating the warm, welcoming colour schemes, the comfortable furnishings and the marble bathrooms. A pleasant lounge awaits guests and there is an inviting small bar but only breakfast (very substantial) is served in the dining room, with its pretty china and flowers on every table. Residents, however, enjoy eating in the neighbouring bistros and restaurants. The Tuilerieen hosts many conferences and the Orangerie is often used to accommodate delegates. The fitness facilities are shared by visitors from both hotels. Bruges is a marvellous city to explore, with its many historic buildings and fascinating waterways – special walks have been identified for the benefit of tourists. **Directions:** E40/Exit 8 (St Michaels), take Koning Albertlaan, 't Zand, Zuidzandstraat, Steenstraat, Markt, Wollestraat, then turn into Kartuizererinnenstraat Price guide: Single BF6950; double/twin BF7950; junior suites BF8950.

HOTEL HANSA

N. DESPARSSTRAAT, NO.11, 8000 BRUGES, BELGIUM
TEL: +32 50 33 84 44 FAX: +32 50 33 42 05 E-MAIL: information@hansa.be

Bruges is very easy to get to, especially by rail and it is linked to the Eurostar. It has some mid-19th century mansions, one of which has been meticulously renovated and is now an excellent value hotel close to the Market Square in the very centre of the city. The Hansa has a fine façade and the talents of a skilled interior decorator are evident in the decorations and furnishings throughout the hotel. It is a small hotel, with just twenty bedrooms, all in soft colours and extremely comfortable and equipped with all modern amenities. The bathrooms are efficient. A small bar in the reception area is adjacent to a pleasant, welcoming lounge, which in turn leads through attractive glass doors into the charming breakfast room which reflects the Hansa's elegant past. It has an ornate ceiling and gilded cornice, marble fireplace and gilded mirrors. The hotel does not have a restaurant, but there are many places to dine in the locality, to suit all tastes and budgets. Small seminars can be held in the conference room. Audio-visual systems can be arranged. Bruges is fascinating and canal trips are a favourite way to explore the historic city. **Directions:** E40, exit 8, head for Brugge Centrum, through Ezelstraat and St Jacobstraat to Eiermarkt. At junction, left into Niklaas Desparsstraat. Price guide: Single BF3200–5300; double/twin BF3500–5600.

BELGIUM (Bruges)

HOTEL JAN BRITO

FREREN FONTEINSTRAAT 1, 8000 BRUGES, BELGIUM
TEL: +32 50 33 06 01 FAX: +32 50 33 06 52 E-MAIL: Hotelbrito@unicall.be

The Hotel Jan Brito, a 16th century listed building, offers a unique balance of opulence, comfort and tranquillity. The owners have made service an important criterion and as a result the standard is excellent. Many vestiges of the hotel's past are scattered around the rooms and include the marble chimneys, oak staircases and fine 18th century paintings. The beautifully appointed bedrooms feature many modern facilities and include hairdryer, television and minibar. Several thoughtful extras can be found in the marbled bathrooms such as soft towels and large mirrors. The elegant breakfast room serves an extensive buffet of fresh fruits and other delights and is located downstairs, adjacent to the cosy, intimate bar. Although there is no dining room, some of Bruges finest restaurants are only minutes away. The city of Bruges itself is a pleasure to explore with historic buildings, old churches and a plethora of cafés and bars. Many distractions are clustered around the area such as the picturesque canals and the market place. **Directions:** Enter Bruges from Katelijnepoort, taking Katelijnestraat. Turn right along Gruuthusestraat and follow the canal, veering to the left, along Dyver. Then take the first right after the fish market into Freren Fonteinstraat. Price guide: Single BF3,450–5,450; double/twin BF3,800–5,900; suites BF6,900–7,600.

HOTEL MONTANUS

NIEUWE GENTWEG 76, 8000 BRUGES, BELGIUM
TEL: +32 50 33 11 76 FAX: +32 50 34 09 38

In the quarter of Bruges dominated by its many canals and the "minne water" lake, lies the Hotel Montanus, which reflects the atmosphere of serenity that characterises this district. The hotel occupies a fine 18th century grand house, with an imposing exterior and an interior packed with aesthetic pleasures. As visitors enter the hall, they are immediately struck by the quality of the décor and furnishings and the many works of art which are judiciously arranged. Notable features on the ground floor include a very large library, a light and airy dining room and a bar whose atmosphere is conducive for imbibing the world's finest wines. Another particularly charming feature is a great window overlooking a terrace into the lovely gardens. This is an ideal family hotel, with 25 very spacious rooms with minibars and en suite facilities. A romantic suite is available for honeymooners. Each bedroom is equipped with a full range of modern amenities, including satellite television. Three restaurants close by and four others within easy reach are recommended by the hotel. **Directions:** Enter Bruges from the Katelijnepoort, taking Visspaanstraat on the right. Follow the road and take the second turning on the left which is called "Nieuwe Gentweg". Price guide: Single BF2950–3400; double/twin BF3400–4800; suites BF5600–6500.

HOTEL PRINSENHOF

ONTVANGERSSTRAAT 9, 8000 BRUGES, BELGIUM
TEL: +32 50 34 26 90 FAX: +32 50 34 23 21 E-MAIL: prinsenhof@unicall.be

This 20th century Flemish mansion, in the very heart of Bruges, having been renovated with great flair, is now a superb small hotel hidden down a side street. A member of Relais du Silence, it is family run, the ambience is warm, with a feeling that guests are all-important. The interior decoration, in the style of Burgundy, is rich with chandeliers, moulded ceilings and antiques, polished floors and marvellous rugs. The breakfast room is charming, where an excellent buffet is served in the mornings, but there is no restaurant, although drinks are available from the licensed bar. Many interesting places to dine can be found nearby. The bedrooms are peaceful, double glazing keeping out noise, beautifully furnished in traditional style and having particularly elegant drapery. A discreet mini-bar completes the many comforts provided. Businessmen find the central location ideal and tourists enjoy wandering through the maze of small streets, along the canal banks and exploring the many museums and fascinating shops. **Directions:** Approaching Bruges from Zeebrugge or Ostend, leave the ring road at Ezelpoort, taking Ezelstraat, forking left into St Jakobstraat, right into Geldmunstraat to Noordzandstraat, with a right turn into Ontvangersstraat. Price guide: Single BF3300–3700; double/twin BF4200–5000; suite BF7000.

       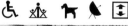

ART HOTEL SIRU

1 PLACE ROGIER, 1210 BRUSSELS, BELGIUM
TEL: +32 2 203 35 80 FAX: +32 2 203 33 03

Built in 1932, on the spot of a former hotel where Verlaine and Rimbaud stayed at the height of their romantic tryst in Brussels, Art Hotel Siru is a unique art deco property, dedicated to the promotion of Belgium artists, architects and designers. The impressive building is dominated by an imposing dome topped with stars, spirals and twists. The concept of 'sleeping with art' was created by the owner Jacques Hollander, who commissioned 101 artists to design each guest room in their individual style. The result is a hotel where, in the words of the owner, "guests can brush their teeth, make love or do business, all in the presence of art". A ceiling fresco of grazing sheep, entitled 'Valium', a bright Warholian mural of Marilyn Monroe, an immense sculpture of a steel bow and arrow and plastic grey rocks suspended from the ceiling are some of the many visual delights. Every room offers a wide range of amenities and is supplied with water from a natural spring. Guests may choose their room from the selection of photographs at the front desk. Brasserie Le Saint-Germain has an exciting menu comprising typically Belgian produce such as endives, game and freshwater fish. The hotel is in an ideal location for those wishing to discover the city of Brussels with its museums, boutiques, galleries and lively night-life. **Directions:** The hotel is situated close to the 'Jardin du Botanique' and is within easy walking distance of the Grand Place. Price guide: Single BF5200; double/twin BF5900.

L'AMIGO

1-3 RUE L'AMIGO, 1000 BRUSSELS, BELGIUM
TEL: +32 2 547 47 47 FAX: +32 2 513 52 77 E-MAIL: hotelamigo@compuserve.com

Just off the Grand'Place, visitors to Brussels will be delighted to find this friendly hotel. A corner building, enlivened by colourful flowers and shrubs in window boxes on the many balconies, the reception rooms are charming, very light, spacious and comfortably furnished. Handsome paintings hang on the walls, and big bowls of flowers add to the welcoming ambience. The bedrooms are enchanting, with small chandeliers, wonderful brocades used to create harmonious colour schemes, tall windows letting in the morning sun and luxurious marble bathrooms. The suites are particularly splendid, some having terraces looking out across the city. The small well-stocked bar is congenial, an ideal meeting place before dining in the excellent restaurant, which has a fine wine list including a 1986 Grand Cru Bordeaux! The hotel has superb meeting rooms and an elegant banqueting hall, where corporate functions can be hosted in great style. The Bourse is nearby, also the Theatre Royal and the Palais Royal. Prestigious boutiques and cafés help pass the day and the hotel arranges tours around Brussels and to Bruges. **Directions:** Leave Autoroute E42 at Exit 6, following signs to the Grand'Place (Grote Markt). The hotel has parking for 50 cars. Price Guide: Single BF7.300; double BF7750–9.000; suite BF16.500–21.300; executive BF12.450.

THE STANHOPE

9, RUE DU COMMERCE, 1000, BRUSSELS, BELGIUM
TEL: +32 2 506 91 11 FAX: +32 2 512 17 08

This recherché hotel, retreat of the cognoscenti in this busy city, has maintained its aura of a fin de siècle private residence. It was built round a courtyard, today laid out as an attractive garden where guests can relax. The many salons, intercommunicating and varying in size, are exquisite, furnished with fine antiques, traditional chairs, brilliant chandeliers, handsome portraits, silk curtains and Oriental rugs. Bowls of fruit and tall vases of flowers add to its charisma – there is no ordinary bar but a table of cut crystal decanters and elegant glasses, where guests can enjoy their favourite drink. The Library is a quiet refuge after a stressful day. The guest rooms are enticing, with their lovely period pieces, gilt mirrors, beautiful fabrics and wall hangings and the luxurious suites in the old annex open out onto the private garden. The bathrooms are lavish, having many indulgent accessories. The restaurant is enchanting, with murals, columns and candelabra. The tables are laid with crisp linen, fine porcelain and sparkling silver. The chef creates Ambrosian dishes which should be accompanied by vintage French wines. The superb fitness centre is much frequented by guests as tennis, golf and swimming are all some distance away. **Directions:** The Stanhope is in the centre of the business quarter, close to the Palais Royal. Garage parking. Price guide: Single BF9,900; double/twin BF12,900; junior suite BF17,500; suite BF22,500.

HOSTELLERIE LE PRIEURÉ DE CONQUES

RUE DE CONQUES 2, 6820 FLORENVILLE, BELGIUM
TEL: +32 61 41 14 17 FAX: +32 61 41 27 03

In magnificent surroundings, far removed from the frantic pace of modern life, guests of the Hostellerie le Prieuré de Conques are offered a taste of a past life. The building's history dates back to 648, when it was a monastery. In 1173, the Priory was given as a gift to the Cistercian monks of Orval, who transformed it into a place of study and convalescence. Today, peace still reigns supreme throughout the Priory, where 11 bedrooms are situated. Each is individually designed and decorated with careful consideration given to retaining and enhancing original features. A further eight bedrooms, opening onto the park, are located in the Residence, which was built in 1990. The culinary delights prepared by the hotel's owner and his son are guaranteed to meet the approval of the most discerning palate. The menu makes excellent use of seasonal specialities and local produce, while over 200 vintage wines provide an extensive and impressive wine list to complement every dish. This region of Belgium is steeped in history and overflowing with cultural sites. Nature lovers will enjoy the numerous signposted walks in the near vicinity, while other opportunities for relaxation include golf and fishing. **Directions**: Take exit 25 from E411, follow sign to Bertrix then Herbeumont. The hotel is located 3 km after Herbeumont towards Florenville. Price guide: Single: BF3600; double/twin BF4,400–5,700.

HOTEL MANOIR DU DRAGON

ALBERTLAAN 73, 8300 KNOKKE, BELGIUM
TEL: +32 50 63 05 80 FAX: +32 50 63 05 90

"One of the 5 hotels of the Family Vanhollebeke". Standing in acres of magnificent gardens, this four-star country house hotel is ideally situated for those seeking tranquillity. The interior of the hotel is the essence of comfort, with plush furnishings and spacious rooms. A warm welcome is extended to all guests as the proprietors strive to create a homely atmosphere within the hotel. The superb bedrooms enjoy glorious views of the lawns and offer every modern amenity. They are individually decorated, with some rooms offering a balcony, terrace or small garden. The beautiful bathrooms have a large selection of beauty products and include bathrobes and slippers. An extensive menu comprising imaginative and healthy dishes is served at breakfast. Although there is no dining room, there is an extensive choice of gourmet restaurants within the locality. Golf enthusiasts will be delighted with the location; the hotel is set on the edge of the Royal Zoute Golf Course. Other sports include biking, tennis at the nearby court and local walks. Knokke is an interesting town to explore with its beaches, casino, nature reserve and butterfly garden. **Directions:** The hotel is situated just 15km from Bruges. Take the E40 from Bruges, follow signs to Zeebrugge and then follow the coast road towards Knokke. Price guide: Double/twin BF5750–9900; suites BF9900–15.000.

LA BUTTE AUX BOIS

PAALSTEENLAAN 90, 3620 LANAKEN, BELGIUM
TEL: +32 89 72 12 86 FAX: +32 89 72 16 47

This twentieth century château, built in 1924, only became a hotel in 1986. Much work has taken place since then and today it is sophisticated, with extensive conference and exhibition facilities. Geographically, it is well-situated, in the Euro-Region of Maastricht, Hasselt, Liège and Aachen. A verdant estate surrounds La Butte aux Bois, providing the peace and privacy sought by weary executives. The terraces and pools are floodlit at night, to spectacular effect. The ambience is English country house. The salons are spacious and comfortable, with fires in winter and tasteful flower decorations. The bedrooms are roomy, with harmonious colour schemes, thoughtfully furnished and equipped to meet the demands of today's traveller. Guests gather in the lounge or on the terrace for drinks before adjourning to the palatial restaurant. The Chef prepares inspired interpretations of traditional dishes and the cellar holds fine wines. Corporate functions are frequently hosted in private rooms or in the grounds. The hotel has a pool, beauty spa and cycles for exploring the countryside. Tennis and golf can be arranged. Cultural activities abound. **Directions:** Leave E25 for Antwerp (E314). Cross border, take first turning,N78 towards Lanaken. After 5 km, right into Paalsteenlaan, finding the hotel 1km later. Three car parks. Price guide: Single BF3400–5700; double/twin BF4100–6400.

420

HOSTELLERIE TRÔS MARETS

ROUTE DES TRÔS MARETS, 4960 MALMÉDY, BELGIUM
TEL: +32 80 33 79 17 FAX: +32 80 33 79 10

This delightful hotel, surrounded by forest, atop a small mountain, is close to Germany, Luxembourg and Holland. In winter the snow-clad terrain attracts skiers and in summer visitors enjoy the sunshine and fresh air. The Trôs Marets has modern comfort and style. The lounge and dining room have spectacular views. The furnishings are elegant while creating a relaxing ambience and the same theme has been applied in the bedrooms, well-equipped for today's traveller. The annexe houses four superb suites, with balconies off the drawing rooms and luxurious bedrooms – the bathrooms have sunbeds! There is a small conference room. The pretty indoor swimming pool is in this part of the hotel and opens onto the garden in fine weather. There is an attractive terrace for alfresco dining, but serious eating is in the outstanding restaurant where succulent meals are served, including many fish dishes. Perfectly cooked vegetables, immaculate service and wine served at the correct temperature complete a memorable occasion. Nearby are the Ardennes and Bastogne, where the Americans victoriously battled in 1944. Energetic guests explore the forest but others unwind in the tranquil atmosphere. **Directions:** From Liège follow the E40 over the scenic viaduct to the Malmédy exit, then follow the N68 uphill for 5 kilometres. Price guide: Double/twin BF3900–8500; suite BF9000–18,000. Special midweek price -25%.

CHÂTEAU D'HASSONVILLE

MARCHE-EN-FAMENNE, 6900, BELGIUM
TEL: +32 84 31 10 25 FAX: +32 84 31 60 27

This is a fairytale 17th century château, with turrets, spires and pinnacles and peacocks strutting on the lawns. It is owned by the Rodrigues family, ideal for a long stay or for an overnight stop when travelling. The interior is sumptuous and the decoration very grand – brilliant chandeliers, swagged silk curtains in jewel colours and exquisite antiques. The bedrooms facing the park have wonderful views, furnished for a sybaritic lifestyle, the bathrooms are appointed in a contemporary style. Guests start their day with breakfast in the graceful conservatory, filled with exotic plants. Later in the day, after relaxing with apéritifs in the bar, they feast in the elegant restaurant amidst candles, sparkling crystal and gleaming silver. The menu is sophisticated and the award-winning sommelier advises on the choice of wine. There are museums and caves nearby or residents explore the countryside on the house bicycles or in hot-air balloons. Others fish, take boats out on the river, play snooker, try clay-pigeon shooting and watch falconry displays, while golfers use the hotel's practice ground before playing the three local courses. **Directions:** From Brussels take the outway No: 18 (Marche) on the E 411 Bruxelles–Namur. On the N4 go out on Km 98 (Aye) and follow 6km the castle indications. Price guide: Single BF4500; double/twin BF5200–7200.

HOTEL CHÂTEAU DE PALOGNE

ROUTE DU PALOGNE, 3, 4190 VIEUXVILLE, BELGIUM
TEL: +32 86 21 38 74 FAX: +32 86 21 38 76

The Château de Palogne was built in the last century – its beauty is magical – and the surrounding parkland filled with centuries' old trees is bordered by two rivers, the Lambree and the Ourthe. It is on the outskirts of the attractive village of Vieuxville, not far from Lieges. It is an elite hotel, with just eleven guest rooms – each named after a different flower and having its own appropriate colour scheme. The period furniture is handsome and all have fine views over the estate. They have been thoughtfully equipped to meet the demands of today's travellers. Breakfast always includes a delicious platter of fruit. Guests relax in the elegant salon, filled with fine antiques and big bowls of flowers,

or enjoy apéritifs in the bar, or in warm weather on the terrace, while waiting for the car service which will take them just 1 km away to the Restaurant au Vieux Logis where they can dine in splendour and drink the finest wines. Daniel and Dely Pauwels are superb hosts and have created a tranquil and welcoming ambience. They will arrange golf, tennis, cycle hire, riding and canoeing for energetic guests and recommend lovely walks. **Directions:** From Brussels take Highway E411 towards Namur and N4 through Durbuy after which follow signs to Barvaux, Bomal and Vieuxville. Price guide: Double/twin BF2500–5500.

HONDA

First man, then machine.

When we first set out to design the CR-V, we approached it with the same philosophy that Sochiro Honda, our founder, encouraged.

He insisted that everything done in his name be done for a reason, rather than developing technology for technology's sake. Everything has to have a purpose, a relevance, a benefit.

For example, with the CR-V, we bore in mind that the vast majority of journeys it would undertake would be on tarmac. So instead of giving it permanent 4-wheel drive, we developed a system that could detect when 4-wheel drive was needed and immediately engage it.

It's this kind of thinking that's evident across the Honda range, whether in major pieces of technology, or in the more considered placing of switchgear.

For dealers and details, phone **0345 159 159** and find out why we try to follow our founder's example.

Technology you can enjoy, from Honda.

Some places are
more accessible
than others.

The British Isles

SHETLAND ISLANDS

ORKNEY ISLANDS

JOHN 'O' GROATS

ABERDEEN

CHANNEL ISLANDS

ALDERNEY

GUERNSEY

ST PETER

JERSEY

DUNDEE

EDINBURGH

GLASGOW

67

CARLISLE NEWCASTLE-UPON-TYNE

BELFAST

ISLE OF MAN

72
93

LEEDS

KINGSTON-UPON-HULL

BLACKPOOL

LIVERPOOL

MANCHESTER
SHEFFIELD

DUBLIN

68

90

LIMERICK

BIRMINGHAM

KINGS LYNN   NORWICH

WATERFORD

CAMBRIDGE

IPSWICH

WEXFORD

OXFORD

CORK

SWANSEA

LONDON

SOUTHEND-ON-SEA

69

NEWPORT

92 91

70 65

BRISTOL

71

GATWICK

DOVER

SOUTHAMPTON

66

64

BRIGHTON

TORBAY

LANDS END

ISLES OF SCILLY

CHANNEL ISLANDS

ALDERNEY

GUERNSEY

ST PETER

JERSEY

94

AMBERLEY CASTLE

AMBERLEY, NR ARUNDEL, WEST SUSSEX BN18 9ND
TEL: + 44 1798 831992 FAX: + 44 1798 831998

Winner of the Johansens 1995 Country Hotel Award, Amberley Castle is over 900 years old and is set between the rolling South Downs and the peaceful expanse of the Amberley Wildbrooks. Its towering battlements give breathtaking views while its massive, 14th-century curtain walls and mighty portcullis bear silent testimony to its fascinating history. Resident proprietors, Joy and Martin Cummings, have transformed this medieval fortress into a unique country castle hotel. They offer a warm, personal welcome and their hotel provides the ultimate in contemporary luxury, while retaining an atmosphere of timelessness. Guests can choose from four-poster, twin four-poster or brass double-bedded rooms. Each room is individually designed and has its own Jacuzzi bath. The exquisite 12th-century Queen's Room Restaurant is the perfect setting for the creative cuisine of head chef Sam Mahoney and his team. Amberley Castle is a natural first choice for romantic or cultural weekends, sporting breaks or confidential executive meetings. Roman ruins, antiques, stately homes, castle gardens, horse racing and history 'everywhere' you look, all within a short distance. It is easily accessible from London and the major air and channel ports. **Directions:** Amberley Castle is on the B2139, off the A29 between Fontwell and Bury. Price guide Double/twin £145–£300.

EASTWELL MANOR

BOUGHTON LEES, ASHFORD, KENT TN25 4HR
TEL: + 44 1233 219955 FAX: + 44 1233 635530

In the midst of a 3,000 acre estate, set in 62 acres of lovely grounds, lies Eastwell Manor. It was once the home of Queen Victoria's second son, Prince Alfred, and his wife. The Queen and her elder son, later to become Edward VII, were frequent visitors here. The elegant bedrooms are named after past owners, lords, ladies and gentlemen, bearing witness to the hotel's rich history. Each room is individually and gracefully furnished and offers every modern comfort. Huge open fireplaces with stone mantles, carved panelling, leather Chesterfield sofas and fine antique furniture are features of the lounges, billiard room and bar. Modern British cuisine is served in the handsome wood

panelled dining room, matched by an excellent cellar of carefully chosen wines. Guests are invited to take advantage of the hotel's tennis court and croquet lawn, while a variety of other leisure pursuits are available locally. The Manor is conveniently located for visiting the historic cathedral city of Canterbury, Leeds Castle and a number of charming market towns. It is also situated near to the Ashford stop for the Eurostar. **Directions:** M20 junction 9. A28 towards Canterbury, then A251 signed Faversham. Hotel is three miles north of Ashford in the village of Boughton Lees. Price guide: Single £130–£170; double/twin £170–£220; suites £240–£330.

POWDERMILLS HOTEL

POWDERMILL LANE, BATTLE, EAST SUSSEX TN33 0SP
TEL: + 44 1424 775511 FAX: + 44 1424 774540 E-MAIL: powdc@aol.com

Situated outside the historic Sussex town famous for the 1066 battle, PowderMills is an 18th century listed country house which has been skilfully converted into an elegant hotel. Nestling in 150 acres of parks and woodland, the beautiful and tranquil grounds feature a 7-acre specimen fishing lake. Wild geese, swans, ducks, kingfishers and herons abound. Privately owned and run by Douglas and Julie Cowpland, the hotel has been carefully furnished with locally acquired antiques. On cooler days, log fires burn in the entrance hall and drawing room. The bedrooms – five with four-posters – are all individually furnished and decorated. The Orangery Restaurant has 2 AA rosettes and offers fine classical cooking by chef Daniel Ayton. Guests may dine on the terrace in summer, looking out over the swimming pool and grounds. Light meals and snacks are available in the library. The location an is ideal base from which to explore the beautiful Sussex and Kent countryside and there are many villages and small towns in the area. **Directions:** From centre of Battle take the Hastings road south. After $\frac{1}{4}$ mile turn right into Powdermill Lane. After a sharp bend, the entrance is on the right; cross over the bridge and lakes to reach the hotel. Price guide: Single from £70; double/twin £95–£150.

TILLMOUTH PARK

CORNHILL-ON-TWEED, NEAR BERWICK-UPON-TWEED, NORTHUMBERLAND TD12 4UU
TEL: + 44 1890 882255 FAX: +44 1890 882540

Designed by Charles Barry, the son of the famous Victorian architect of the Houses of Parliament in Westminster, Tillmouth Park offers the same warm welcome today as it did when it was an exclusive private country house. It is situated in a rich countryside farmland of deciduous woodland and moor. The generously sized bedrooms have been recently refurbished in a distinctive old fashioned style with period furniture, although all offer modern day amenities. The kitchen prides itself on traditional country fare, with the chef using fresh local produce to create imaginative and well-presented dishes. The restaurant serves a fine table d'hôte menu, while the Bistro is less formal. Fresh salmon and game are always available with 24 hours' notice. A well chosen wine list and a vast selection of malt whiskies complement the cuisine. Tillmouth Park is an ideal centre for country pursuits including field sports, fishing, hill-walking, shooting, riding, bird-watching and golf. For the spectator there is rugby, curling and horse-racing during the season. Places of interest nearby include stately homes such as Floors, Manderston and Paxton. Flodden Field, Lindisfarne and Holy Island are all within easy reach and the coast is just 15 minutes away. **Directions:** Tillmouth Park is on the A698 Cornhill-on-Tweed to Berwick-on-Tweed road. Price guide: Single £85–£100; twin/double £120–£160.

 # THE CHESTER GROSVENOR

EASTGATE, CHESTER CH1 1LT
TEL: +44 1244 324024 FAX: + 44 1244 313246

The Chester Grosvenor is in the heart of the historic city of Chester beneath the famous Queen Victoria Clock. The hotel is owned by the Duke of Westminster's Grosvenor Estate. It is renowned for its fabulous cuisine and has two restaurants – the Arkle and La Brasserie. The Arkle is an award winning gourmet restaurant, named after the famous racehorse Arkle. La Brasserie is an informal Parisian style restaurant which is open all day, every day. The Chester Grosvenor has an extensive cellar with over 600 bins of fine wine. There are 85 bedrooms of which 11 are suites. All are beautifully appointed, fully air-conditioned with 24 hour room service provided and each room is equipped with all the amenities expected in a de luxe hotel awarded 5 AA Stars and RAC. The hotel has its own leisure suite with a multi-gymnasium, sauna and solarium and membership of an exclusive local country club which has indoor and outdoor swimming pools, tennis and gymnasium. Adjacent are the famous Roman Walls and the Chester Rows with their boutiques and exclusive shops. A short stroll away is Chester Cathedral, Chester race course and the River Dee. **Directions:** In the centre of Chester on Eastgate. 24-hour NCP car parking – follow signs to Grosvenor Precinct Car Park. Price guide: Single from £165; double/twin from £260; suites £425. Weekend break rates available on request.

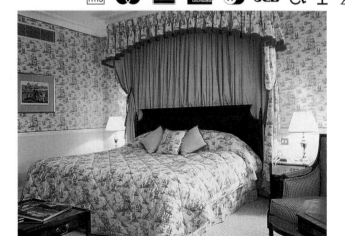

THE PLOUGH AT CLANFIELD

BOURTON ROAD, CLANFIELD, OXFORDSHIRE OX18 2RB
TEL: + 44 1367 810222 FAX: + 44 1367 810596

The Plough at Clanfield is an idyllic hideaway for the romantic at heart. Set on the edge of the village of Clanfield, typical of the Oxfordshire Cotswolds, The Plough dates from 1560 and is a fine example of well-preserved Elizabethan architecture. The hotel is owned and personally run by John and Rosemary Hodges, who have taken great care to preserve the charm and character of this historic building. As there are only six bedrooms, guests can enjoy an intimate atmosphere and attentive, personal service. All the bedrooms are beautifully appointed to the highest standard and all have en suite bathrooms. At the heart of the hotel is the two AA Rosette Restaurant, regarded as one of the finest in the area. The cuisine is superbly prepared and impeccably served, with an interesting selection of wines. Two additional dining rooms are available for private entertaining. The hotel is an ideal base from which to explore the Cotswolds or the Thames Valley. There are many historic houses and gardens in the area, as well as racing at Newbury and Cheltenham. Hotel closed 27th, 28th & 29th December. **Directions:** The hotel is located on the edge of the village of Clanfield, at the junction of the A4095 and B4020, between the towns of Witney and Faringdon, some 15 miles to the west of the city of Oxford. Price guide: Single £70; Double £105–£120.

LANGSHOTT MANOR

LANGSHOTT, HORLEY, SURREY RH6 9LN
TEL: + 44 1293 786680 FAX: + 44 1293 783905

The peace and seclusion of this beautiful Manor House belies its close proximity to London's Gatwick Airport, 8 minutes away by taxi or Hotel car. Retaining the essential feel of a fine Elizabethan home, Langshott offers stylish bedrooms and an intimate dining room with every provision for your comfort. The Manor becomes the perfect beginning or end to your holiday in Britain. Free car parking is offered at a local secure compound for one week and complimentary taxis are made available to guests travelling to Gatwick. Although Langshott Manor is situated near to the airport, the house is tucked away down a quiet country lane amidst 3 acres of beautiful gardens and enchanting ponds. A peaceful ambience pervades the manor, ensuring complete relaxation for all its guests. The property is not under the flight path. For a longer stay, the area is also a haven for sport enthusiasts with racing at Epsom and Goodwood and polo at Cowdray and Gaurds. Many National Trust gardens and properties are clustered around Langshott Manor such as Hever Castle, Chartwell and Knole Park. Central London is 30 minutes away via the Gatwick/Victoria Express. **Directions:** From A23 in Horley take Ladbroke Road (Chequers Hotel roundabout) to Langshott. The manor is three quarters of a mile (one kilometre) on the right. Price guide: Single from £125; double/twin from £155.

LYTHE HILL HOTEL

PETWORTH ROAD, HASLEMERE, SURREY GU27 3BQ
TEL: + 44 1428 651251 FAX: + 44 1428 644131 E-MAIL: lythe@lythehill.co.uk

Cradled by the Surrey foothills in a tranquil setting is the enchanting Lythe Hill Hotel. It is an unusual cluster of ancient buildings – parts of which date from the 14th century. While most of the beautifully appointed accommodation is in the more recently converted part of the hotel, there are five charming bedrooms in the Tudor House, including the Henry VIII room with a four-poster bed dated 1614! There are two delightful restaurants, the Auberge de France offers classic French cuisine in the oak-panelled room which overlooks the lake and parklands, and the 'Dining Room' has the choice of imaginative English fare. An exceptional wine list offers over 200 wines from more than a dozen countries.

Its situation, easily accessible from London, Gatwick and Heathrow. An excellent train service at Haslemere makes both central London and Portsmouth less than one hour away. National Trust hillside adjoining the hotel grounds provides interesting walking and views over the surrounding countryside. The area is steeped in history, with the country houses of Petworth, Clandon and Uppark to visit as well as racing at Goodwood and polo at Cowdray Park. Brighton and the south coast are only a few miles away. **Directions:** Lythe Hill lies about $1^1/_2$ miles from the centre of Haslemere, east on the B2131. Price guide (excluding breakfast): Single from £98; double/twin from £115; suite from £140.

SHARROW BAY COUNTRY HOUSE HOTEL

HOWTOWN, LAKE ULLSWATER, PENRITH, CUMBRIA CA10 2LZ
TEL: + 44 17684 86301/86483 FAX: + 44 17684 86349

Now in its 51st year, Sharrow Bay is known to discerning travellers the world over, who return again and again to this magnificent lakeside hotel. It wasn't always so. Francis Coulson arrived in 1948. He was joined by Brian Sack in 1952 and the partnership flourished, to make Sharrow Bay what it is today. Recently they have been joined by Nigel Lawrence and Nigel Lightburn who carry on the tradition. All the bedrooms are elegantly furnished and guests are guaranteed the utmost comfort. In addition to the main hotel, there are four cottages nearby which offer similarly luxurious accommodation. All the reception rooms are delightfully decorated. Sharrow Bay is universally renowned for its wonderful cuisine. The team of chefs led by Johnnie Martin and Colin Akrigg ensure that each meal is a special occasion, a mouth-watering adventure! With its private jetty and 12 acres of lakeside gardens Sharrow Bay offers guests boating, swimming and fishing. Fell-walking is a challenge for the upwardly mobile. Sharrow Bay is the oldest British member of Relais et Châteaux. Closed in December and January. **Directions:** M6 junction 40, A592 to Lake Ullswater, into Pooley Bridge, then take Howtown road for 2 miles. Price guide: (including 7-course dinner and full English breakfast) Single £120–£270; double/twin £230–£350; suite £340–£380.

London

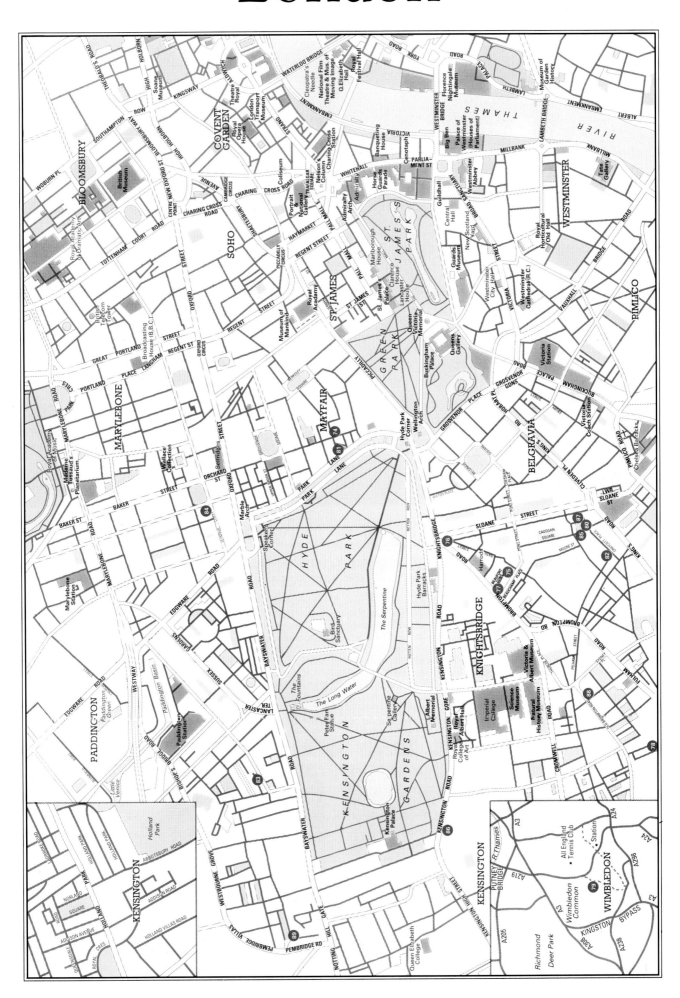

THE ASCOTT MAYFAIR

49 HILL STREET, LONDON W1X 7FQ
TEL: + 44 171 499 6868 FAX: + 44 171 499 0705 E-MAIL: ascottmf@scotts.com.sg

This, the latest concept in city centre accommodation, offers all the benefits of a hotel and yet also privacy and space in what the brochure describes as "residences", with one, two or three bedrooms, in a spectacular art deco building. The apartments have a 24 hour concierge for security and assistance. A maid will be assigned to you for the full duration of your stay. There is no restaurant; however, a complimentary Continental breakfast is served in The Terrace, overlooking the private gardens. There is an Honour Bar in The Club where guests can mingle or entertain. The Hothouse offers a gym, sauna, steam room and solarium. The Business Service includes the use of a private boardroom. A marvellous kitchen is provided in each apartment with everything necessary for entertaining in the versatile lounge. The study area has fax and computer links. The sitting room is extremely comfortable and beautifully decorated. It has satellite television, a music system and video. The luxurious bedrooms have amazing en suite bathrooms, full of soft white towels. The Ascott is in the heart of London – Mayfair being close to all the major shopping centres and best restaurants, theatre-land and sightseeing. **Directions:** Hill Street is off Berkeley Square, near Green Park Underground Station. Price guide: 1 bed £164–£247 daily, £1,095–£1,645 weekly; 2 beds from £375daily–£2,495 weekly. (All rates are subject to VAT).

THE BEAUFORT

33 BEAUFORT GARDENS, KNIGHTSBRIDGE, LONDON SW3 1PP
TEL: + 44 171 584 5252 FAX: + 44 171 589 2834 E–MAIL: thebeaufort@nol.co.uk.

The Beaufort offers the sophisticated traveller all the style and comfort of home – combining warm contempory colourings with the highest possible personal attention. The owner Diana Wallis (pictured below) believes that much of the success of the hotel is due to the charming, attentive staff – a feeling happily endorsed by guests. The Beaufort is situated in a quiet tree-lined square only 100 yards from Harrods and as guests arrive they are all greeted at the front door and given their own door key to come and go as they please. The closed front door gives added security and completes that feeling of home. All the bedrooms are individually decorated, with air conditioning and a great many extras such as shortbread, Swiss chocolates and brandy. The hotel owns a video and cassette library and is home to a magnificent collection of original English floral watercolours. Breakfast is brought to the bedroom – hot rolls and croissants, freshly squeezed orange juice and home-made preserves, tea and coffee. In the drawing room there is a 24-hour bar (all drinks including champagne are free) and between 4–5pm every day a free cream tea is served with scones, clotted cream and home-made jams. There is a complimentary airport transfer to or from the hotel by chauffeur driven car. The hotel is proud of its no tipping policy and is open all year. **Directions:** From Harrods exit at Knightsbridge underground station take third left turn left. Price guide: Single £150; double/twin from £180; junior suite £295 (rates excl. 17.5% VAT).

BASIL STREET HOTEL

BASIL STREET, LONDON SW3 1AH

TEL: + 44 171 581 3311 FAX: + 44 171 581 3693 FROM USA TOLL FREE: UTELL 1 800 448 8355 E-MAIL: thebasil@aol.com

The Basil feels more like an English home than a hotel. Privately owned by the same family for three generations, this traditional Edwardian hotel is situated in a quiet corner of Knightsbridge, on the threshold of London's most exclusive residential and shopping area. Harrods, Harvey Nichols and other famous stores are only minutes away. It is close to museums and theatres. The spacious public rooms are furnished with antiques, paintings, mirrors and *objets d'art*. The lounge, bar and dining room are on the first floor, reached by the distinctive staircase that dominates the front hall. Bedrooms, all individually furnished, vary in size, style and décor. The Hotel's Dining Room is an ideal venue either for unhurried, civilised lunch or dinner by candlelight with piano music. The Parrot Club, a lounge for the exclusive use of ladies, is a haven of rest in delightful surroundings. The Basil combines tradition and caring individual service with the comfort of a modern, cosmopolitan hotel. There is a discount scheme for regular guests, for weekends and stays of five nights or more. Garage parking space available on request. E-mail: thebasil@aol.com **Directions:** Close to Pavilion Road car park. Basil Street runs off Sloane Street in the direction of Harrods. Near Knightsbridge underground and bus routes. Price guide: Single from £120; double/twin from £179; family room from £239. (Excluding VAT).

BEAUFORT HOUSE APARTMENTS

45 BEAUFORT GARDENS, KNIGHTSBRIDGE, LONDON SW3 1PN
TEL: + 44 171 584 2600 FAX: + 44 171 584 6532 US TOLL FREE: 1 800 23 5463 E-MAIL: info@beauforthouse.co.uk

Situated in Beaufort Gardens, a quiet tree-lined Regency cul-de-sac in the heart of Knightsbridge, 250 yards from Harrods, Beaufort House is an exclusive establishment comprising 22 self-contained fully serviced luxury apartments. All the comforts of a first-class hotel are combined with the privacy and discretion and the relaxed atmosphere of home. Accommodation ranges in size from an intimate one-bedroomed suite to a spacious, four-bedroomed apartment. Each apartment has been individually decorated in a traditional style to a standard which is rigorously maintained. All apartments have direct dial telephones, personal safes, satellite TV and video systems. Most bedrooms benefit from en suite bathrooms and several have west facing balconies. The fully fitted and equipped kitchens include washers/dryers; many have dishwashers. A daily maid service is included at no additional charge. Full laundry/dry cleaning services are available. For your added security, a concierge is on call 24 hours a day, through whom taxis, theatre tickets, restaurant reservations and other services are also available. Executive support services are provided with confidentiality assured at all times. Complimentary membership at the nearby Aquilla Club is offered to all guests during their stay. Awarded 4 Keys Highly Commended by the English Tourist Board. **Directions:** Beaufort Gardens leads off Brompton road near Knightsbridge Tube. 24hr car park down the road. Price Guide: £160–£430 per night (excl. VAT).

BLAKES HOTEL

33 ROLAND GARDENS, LONDON SW7 3PF

TEL: + 44 171 370 6701 FAX: + 44 171 373 0442 FROM USA CALL FREE: 1 800 926 3173 E-MAIL: blakes@easynet.co.uk

Created by Anouska Hempel, designer, hotelier and couturière, Blakes is unique – a connoisseur's refuge. Each room has been individually designed, the colour schemes are daring, stunning and dramatic – black and mustard, rich cardinal reds, lavender, vanilla washes of tea rose and a room that is white on white on white offering style and elegance to the discerning traveller. "If ever dreams can become reality, then Blakes is where it will happen". The bedrooms and suites have been described as each being a fantasy. A full 24 hour room service is provided and if a guest is travelling on business the hotel will provide a room fax machine, full secretarial services and a courier service if required.

Blakes intimate restaurant is recognised as one of the finest in the capital and is open until midnight. Breakfast, summer lunches and candlelit dinners can be enjoyed on the Garden Terrace which overlooks the private and secluded courtyard – an explosion of greenery all year round. The smart, fashionable shops of Brompton Cross are only a short stroll away through the leafy streets of South Kensington and Harrods can be reached by taxi in five minutes. **Directions:** Roland Gardens is a turning off Old Brompton Road. The nearest underground tube station is South Kensington. Price guide: Single £130; double/twin £155–£300; suite £475–£695 (excluding VAT).

CANNIZARO HOUSE

WEST SIDE, WIMBLEDON COMMON, LONDON SW19 4UE
TEL: + 44 181 879 1464 FAX: + 44 181 879 7338

Cannizaro House, an elegant Georgian country house, occupies a tranquil position on the edge of Wimbledon Common, yet is only 18 minutes by train from London Waterloo and the Eurostar terminal. Cannizaro House restored as a superb hotel has, throughout its history, welcomed Royalty and celebrities such as George III, Oscar Wilde and William Pitt. The 18th century is reflected in the ornate fireplaces and mouldings, gilded mirrors and many antiques. All the hotel's 46 bedrooms are individually designed, with many overlooking beautiful Cannizaro Park. Several intimate rooms are available for meetings and private dining, including the elegant Queen Elizabeth Room – a popular venue for wedding ceremonies. The newly refurbished Viscount Melville Room offers air-conditioned comfort for up to 100 guests. Ray Slade, General Manager of Cannizaro House for many years, ensures the high standards of excellence for which the hotel is renowned are consistently met, which has earned the hotel the coveted AA courtesy and care award. The award-winning kitchen, under the leadership of Christopher Harper, produces the finest modern and classical cuisine, complemented by an impressive list of wines. **Directions:** The nearest tube and British Rail station is Wimbledon. Price guide: (room only) Single from £168; double/twin from £194; suite from £310. Special weekend rates and celebratory packages available.

THE CLIVEDEN TOWN HOUSE

26 CADOGAN GARDENS, LONDON SW3 2RP
TEL: + 44 171 730 6466 FAX: + 44 171 730 0236 FROM USA TOLL FREE 1 800 747 4942

The Cliveden Town House offers the perfect balance of luxury, service, privacy and location. Tucked discreetly away in a tranquil, tree-lined garden square between Harrods and Kings Road it is at the very centre of fashionable London and is the epitome of stylish good taste and elegance. Like its gracious country cousin at Cliveden, one of England's most famous stately homes, The Cliveden Town House combines the grandeur of the past with the luxuries and conveniences of today, offering the sophisticated traveller all the exclusive comforts and ambience of a grand private residence. The Town House has enhanced its charm with the addition of 9 opulent suites with a fully-equipped kitchen and/or a separate sitting room. Exclusive use of the 9 suites, boardroom and dining room can be arranged creating the atmosphere of a private home. The full-time services of the steward are included. The spacious rooms are splendidly decorated, reflecting the Edwardian period, and combine the highest 24-hour service with state-of-the-art technology. The fashionable shops and restaurants of Knightsbridge, Chelsea and Belgravia, West End theatres and the City are all within easy reach and the gym is accessible 24 hours a day. The chauffeur is available for airport transfers and personalised tours. Enjoy complimentary afternoon tea or a glass of Champagne each evening in the Drawing Room. **Directions:** Nearest tube station is Sloane Square. Price guide: Single from £125; double/twin £215–£260; suite £320–£840.

THE DORCHESTER

PARK LANE, MAYFAIR, LONDON W1A 2HJ

TEL: + 44 171 629 8888 FAX: + 44 171 409 0114 TELEX: 887704 E-MAIL: info@dorchesterhotel.com

The Dorchester first opened its doors in 1931, offering a unique experience which almost instantly became legendary. Its reopening in November 1990 after an extensive refurbishment marked the renaissance of one of the world's grand hotels. Its history has been consistently glamorous; from the early days a host of outstanding figures has been welcomed, including monarchs, statesmen and celebrities. The architectural features have been restored to their original splendour and remain at the heart of The Dorchester's heritage. The 192 bedrooms and 52 suites have been luxuriously designed in a variety of materials, furnishings and lay-outs. All bedrooms are fully air-conditioned and have spectacular Italian marble bathrooms. There are rooms for non-smokers and some equipped for the disabled. In addition to The Grill Room, there is The Oriental Restaurant where the accent is on Cantonese cuisine. Specialised health and beauty treatments are offered in The Dorchester Spa with its statues, Lalique-style glass and water fountain. A series of meeting rooms, with full supporting services, is available for business clientèle. As ever, personalised care is a pillar of The Dorchester's fine reputation. **Directions:** Toward the Hyde Park Corner/Piccadilly end of Park Lane. Price guide excluding VAT: Single £255–£775; double/twin £285 £315, suite £400–£1,900.

DRAYCOTT HOUSE APARTMENTS

10 DRAYCOTT AVENUE, CHELSEA, LONDON SW3 3AA
TEL: + 44 171-584 4659 FAX: + 44 171-225 3694 E-MAIL: sales@draycotthouse.co.uk

Draycott House stands in a quiet, tree-lined avenue in the heart of Chelsea. Housed in an attractive period building, the apartments have been designed in individual styles to provide the ideal surroundings for a private or business visit, combining comfort, privacy and security with a convenient location. All are spacious, luxury, serviced apartments, with three, two or one bedrooms. Some have private balconies, a roof terrace and overlook the private courtyard garden. Each apartment is fully equipped with all home comforts; cable television, video, radio/cassette, a private direct line for telephone/fax/answer machine. Complimentary provisions on arrival, milk and newspapers delivered. Daily maid service Monday to Friday. In-house laundry room and covered garage parking. Additional services, laundry and dry cleaning services. On request cars, airport transfers, catering, travel and theatre arrangements, child-minders and an introduction to an exclusive health club. The West End is within easy reach. Knightsbridge within walking distance. **Directions:** Draycott House is situated on the corner of Draycott Avenue and Draycott Place, close to Sloane Square. Price guide: from £1089–£2648 +VAT per week: £172–£416 +VAT per night. Long term reservations may attract preferential terms. Contact: Jane Renton, General Manager.

PrimaHotels

THE HEMPEL

31-35 CRAVEN HILL GARDENS, LONDON W2 3EA
TEL: + 44 171 298 9000; FAX: + 44 171 402 4666 E-MAIL: the–hempel@easynet.co.uk

Designer Anouska Hempel has created The Hempel to be elegant, redefining space for the traveller. Situated within easy reach of London's many attractions, the hotel with its immaculately preserved Georgian façade houses 46 individually designed rooms and six fully serviced apartments. Influenced by the peace and simplicity of the Orient, the structure of Ancient Egypt with up to the minute technology from the Western World for the business connoisseur. The Hempel is innovative, monochromatic and full of surprises – tap water that is lit at night, an open fireplace that appears to float, a mix of light and shadow that can keep guests guessing how and pondering on just how this can all be real. The huge atrium within the lobby is astounding. A delicious mix of Italian-Thai and Japanese food, devised by Anouska Hempel is presented with style and flair in the I-Thai restaurant. Guests enjoying a pre-dinner drink in The Shadow Bar are surrounded by illusion and fantasy as The Hempel aims to take them out of this world and make their dreams a reality. **Directions:** The Hempel is situated in Lancaster Gate with a short walk to Kensington Gardens and Hyde Park. Paddington Heathrow Link railway station with Lancaster Gate and Queensway underground railway stations nearby. Price guide: Room/suite/apartment: from £220–£775 (excluding VAT).

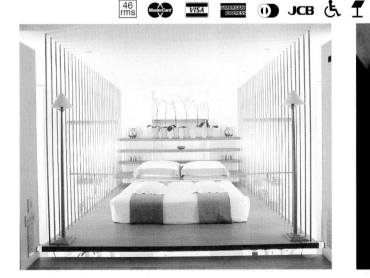

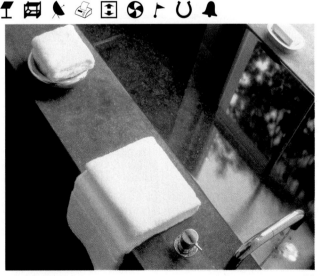

THE LEONARD

15 SEYMOUR STREET, LONDON W1H 5AA
TEL: + 44 171 935 2010 FAX: + 44 171 935 6700 E-MAIL: the.leonard@dial.pipex.com

Four late 18th century Georgian town houses set the character of this exciting new property which opened in 1996 and has already proved to be extremely popular with Johansens guests, being winner of the Johansens Recommended London Hotel of the Year Award 1997. Imaginative reconstruction has created nine rooms and twenty suites decorated individually to a very high standard. Wall coverings present striking colours, complemented by exquisite French furnishing fabrics creating a warm luxurious atmosphere. All rooms are fully air-conditioned and include a private safe, mini-bar, hi-fi system and provision for a modem/fax. Bathrooms are finished in marble and some of the larger suites have a butler's pantry or fully-equipped kitchen. For physical fitness and stress reductions there is a compact exercise room. "Can do" staff ensure that guests can enjoy the highest level of attention and service. Breakfast is available in the café bar and light meals are served throughout the day. 24-hour room service is also available. There are, of course, many good restaurants nearby, a restaurant guide is available on request. The Wallace Collection is just a short walk away and one of London's premier department stores, Selfridges, is round the corner in Oxford Street. **Directions:** The Leonard is on the south side of Seymour Street which is just north of Marble Arch and runs west off Portman Square. Car parking in Bryanston Street. Price guide: Double £180; suites £225–£370.

84

THE LONDON OUTPOST OF THE CARNEGIE CLUB

69 CADOGAN GARDENS, LONDON SW3 2RB
TEL: + 44 171 589 7333 FAX: + 44 171 581 4958 E-MAIL: londonoutpost@dial.pipex.com

This elite town house hotel is in a unique position in Knightsbridge – close to the prestigious shops and yet away from the bustle and noise in quiet Cadogan Gardens. It is a lovely building and skilful restoration has transformed it into a beautiful residence where guests can relax and the staff will attend to their every need. Incidentally, it is not mandatory to be a member of the Carnegie Club to stay here. The Entrance Hall is graceful, with high ceilings, handsome paintings on the walls, antiques and bowls of flowers and this elegance is echoed in the Drawing Room, a peaceful retreat, the Library – perfect for pre-dinner drinks or a nightcap – and the convivial Snooker Room. The bedrooms are luxurious, with lovely drapes across the tall windows and comfortable period furniture. A drinks tray is on the table. Room service will deliver delicious light lunches, suppers and a traditional breakfast – although the latter can also be enjoyed in the attractive Conservatory. In the evening the staff will recommend good restaurants in walking distance. Theatre tickets can be booked, chauffeurs ordered or riding in Rotten Row can be arranged. Exclusive stores and fascinating museums are all 'round the corner'. **Directions:** Sloane Square is the nearest underground station. Price guide (excluding VAT): Single from £150; suite from £235.

THE MILESTONE

1–2 KENSINGTON COURT, LONDON W8 5DL

TEL: + 44 171 917 1000 FAX: + 44 171 917 1010 FROM USA TOLL FREE: 1 800 854 7092 E-MAIL: res@themilestone.com

The beautifully appointed Milestone Hotel is situated opposite Kensington Palace with uninterrupted views over Kensington Gardens and the remarkable Royal parklands. A Victorian showpiece, this unique hotel has been carefully restored to its original splendour whilst incorporating every modern facility. The 53 bedrooms including 12 suites are all individually designed with antiques, elegant furnishings and some have private balconies. Guests may relax in the comfortable, panelled Park Lounge which, in company with all other rooms, provides a 24-hour service. The hotel's original Dining Room has an elaborately carved ceiling, original fireplace, ornate windows and an oratory, which can also be used for small private parties. The health and fitness centre offers guests the use of a solarium, sauna and gymnasium. The traditional bar on the ground floor is an ideal place for meeting and entertaining friends. The Milestone is within walking distance of some of the finest shopping in Kensington and a little further away in Knightsbridge and is a short taxi ride to the West End, the heart of London's Theatreland. The Albert Hall and all the museums in Exhibition Road are nearby. **Directions:** At the end of Kensington High Street, at the junction with Princes Gate. Price guide: Single from £220; double/twin £270; suites from £330.

NUMBER ELEVEN CADOGAN GARDENS

11 CADOGAN GARDENS, SLOANE SQUARE, KNIGHTSBRIDGE, LONDON SW3 2RJ
TEL: + 44 171 730 7000 FAX: + 44 171 730 5217 E-MAIL: reservations@number–eleven.co.uk

Number Eleven Cadogan Gardens was the first of the exclusive private town house hotels in London and now, with the addition of its own in-house gymnasium and beauty rooms it continues to take the lead. Number Eleven remains traditional; no reception desk, no endless signing of bills, total privacy and security. It also offers the services you have a right to expect in the 1990s: round-the-clock room service, a chauffeur-driven Mercedes for airport collection and sightseeing and a private room which can accommodate 12 for a meeting. Another attraction is the Garden Suite, with a large double bedroom and a spacious drawing room overlooking the gardens. The hotel occupies four stately Victorian houses tucked away between Harrods and Kings Road in a quiet, tree-lined square. Wood-panelled rooms, hung with oil-paintings, are furnished with antiques and oriental rugs in a traditional understated style. The fashionable shops and first-class restaurants of Knightsbridge, Chelsea and Belgravia are within easy walking distance. Theatre tickets can be arranged. **Directions:** Off Sloane Street. Nearest underground is Sloane Square. Price guide: Single from £133; double/twin from £170; suite from £250. (Excluding VAT)

NUMBER SIXTEEN

16 SUMNER PLACE, LONDON SW7 3EG

TEL: + 44 171 589 5232 FAX: + 44 171 584 8615 US TOLL FREE: 1 800 592 5387 E-MAIL: reservations@numbersixteenhotel.co.uk

On entering Number Sixteen with its immaculate pillared façade visitors find themselves in an atmosphere of seclusion and comfort which has remained virtually unaltered in style since its early Victorian origins. The staff are friendly and attentive, regarding each visitor as a guest in a private home. The relaxed atmosphere of the library is the perfect place to pour a drink from the honour bar and meet friends or business associates. A fire blazing in the drawing room in cooler months creates an inviting warmth, whilst the conservatory opens on to a beautiful secluded walled garden which once again has won many accolades and awards for its floral displays. Each spacious bedroom is decorated with a discreet combination of antiques and traditional furnishings. The rooms are fully appointed with every facility that the discerning traveller would expect. A light breakfast is served in the privacy of guests' rooms and a tea and coffee service is available throughout the day. Although there is no dining room at Number Sixteen, some of London's finest restaurants are just round the corner. The hotel has membership of Aquilla Health and Fitness Club, 5 minutes away. The hotel is close to the West End, Knightsbridge and Hyde Park. **Directions:** Sumner Place is off Old Brompton Road near Onslow Square. South Kensington Tube Station is a 2 minute walk. Price guide: Single £90–£125; double/twin £160–£190; junior suite £200.

PEMBRIDGE COURT HOTEL

34 PEMBRIDGE GARDENS, LONDON W2 4DX
TEL: + 44 171 229 9977 FAX: + 44 171 727 4982 E-MAIL: reservations@pemct.co.uk

This gracious Victorian town house has been lovingly restored to its former glory whilst providing all the modern facilities demanded by today's discerning traveller. The 20 rooms some of which have air conditioning and are individually decorated with pretty fabrics and the walls adorned with an unusual collection of framed fans and Victoriana. The Pembridge Court is renowned for the devotion and humour with which it is run. Its long serving staff and its two famous cats "Spencer" and "Churchill" assure you of an immensely warm welcome and the very best in friendly, personal service. Over the years the hotel has built up a loyal following amongst its guests, many of whom regard it as their genuine 'home from home' in London. Previous Winner of the RAC Award for Best Small Hotel in the South East of England, the Hotel is situated in quiet tree-lined gardens just off Notting Hill Gate, an area described by Travel & Leisure magazine as 'one of the liveliest, most prosperous corners of the city'. "The Gate" as is affectionately known, is certainly lively, colourful and full of life with lots of great pubs and restaurants and the biggest antiques market in the world at nearby Portobello Road. **Directions:** Pembridge Gardens is a small turning off Notting Hill Gate/Bayswater Road, just 2 minutes from Portobello Road Antiques Market. Price guide: Single £115–£150; double/twin £170–£185 (inclusive of both English breakfast & VAT).

STAPLEFORD PARK, AN OUTPOST OF THE CARNEGIE CLUB

NR MELTON MOWBRAY, LEICESTERSHIRE LE14 2EF
TEL: + 44 1572 787 522 FAX: + 44 1572 787 651

A Stately Home and Sporting Estate where casual luxury is the byword. This pre-eminent 16th century house was once coveted by Edward, The Prince of Wales, but his mother Queen Victoria forbade him to buy it for fear that his morals would be corrupted by the Leicestershire hunting society! Today, Stapleford Park offers house guests and club members a "lifestyle experience" to transcend all others in supremely elegant surroundings with panoramic views over 500 acres of parkland. Described as "The Best Country House Hotel in the World" in Andrew Harper's Hideaway Report, Stapleford has received innumerable awards for its unique style and hospitality. Individually designed bedrooms and a four-bedroom cottage have been created by famous names such as Mulberry, Wedgewood, Liberty and Crabtree & Evelyn. English cuisine with regional specialities is carefully prepared to the highest standards and complemented by an adventurous wine list. Sporting pursuits include fishing, falconry, riding, tennis and golf for all levels at The Stapleford Golf Academy. The Carnegie Clarins Spa with indoor pool, Jacuzzi, sauna and fitness room is a luxurious oasis offering an array of health therapies. Eleven elegant function and dining rooms are eminently suited to private dinners, special occasions and corporate hospitality. **Directions:** By train Kings Cross/Grantham in one hour. A1 north to Colsterworth then B676 via Saxby. Price guide (excl VAT): Double/twin £165–£245; suites from £250.

THE SWAN DIPLOMAT

STREATLEY-ON-THAMES, BERKSHIRE RG8 9HR
TEL: + 44 1491 873737 FAX: + 44 1491 872554 E-MAIL: sales@swan–diplomat.co.uk

In a beautiful setting on the bank of the River Thames, this hotel offers visitors comfortable accommodation. All of the 46 bedrooms, many of which have balconies overlooking the river, are appointed to high standards with individual décor and furnishings. The elegant Dining Room, with its relaxing waterside views, serves fine food complemented by a good choice of wines. Guests may also choose to dine in the informal Club Room. Moored alongside the restaurant is the Magdalen College Barge, which is a stylish venue for meetings and cocktail parties. Business guests are well catered for – the hotel has six attractive conference suites. Reflexions Leisure Club is superbly equipped for fitness programmes and beauty treatments, with facilities that include a heated 'fit' pool; rowing boats and bicycles may be hired. Squash, riding and clay pigeon shooting can all be arranged. Special theme weekends are offered, such as bridge weekends. Events in the locality include Henley Regatta, Ascot and Newbury races, while Windsor Castle, Blenheim Palace, Oxford and London's airports are easily accessible. **Directions:** The hotel lies just off the A329 in Streatley village. Price guide: Single from £74–£140; double/twin from £112–£174.

THE SPRINGS HOTEL & GOLF CLUB

NORTH STOKE, WALLINGFORD, OXFORDSHIRE OX10 6BE
TEL: + 44 1491 836687 FAX: + 4401491 836877 E-MAIL: SpringsUK@aol.com

The Springs is a grand old country house which dates from 1874 and is set deep in the heart of the beautiful Thames valley. One of the first houses in England to be built in the Mock Tudor style, it stands in six acres of grounds. The hotel's large south windows overlook a spring fed lake, from which it takes its name. Many of the luxurious bedrooms and suites offer beautiful views over the lake and lawns, while others overlook the quiet woodland that surrounds the hotel. Private balconies provide patios for summer relaxation. The Lakeside restaurant has an intimate atmosphere inspired by its gentle décor and the lovely view of the lake. The award winning restaurant's menu takes advantage of fresh local produce and a well stocked cellar of international wines provides the perfect accompaniment to a splendid meal. Leisure facilities include a new 18 hole par 72 golf course, Clubhouse and putting green, a swimming pool, sauna and touring bicycles. Oxford, Blenheim Palace and Windsor are nearby and the hotel is convenient for racing at Newbury and Ascot and the Royal Henley Regatta. **Directions:** From the M40, take exit 6 onto the B4009, through Watlington to Benson; turn left onto A4074 towards Reading. After $1/2$ mile go right onto B4009. The hotel is $1/2$ mile further, on the right. Price guide: Single from £84; double/twin £128–£154; suite from £160.

MILLER HOWE

RAYRIGG ROAD, WINDERMERE, CUMBRIA LA23 1EY
TEL: + 44 15394 42536 FAX: + 44 14594 45664 E-MAIL: lakeview@millerhowe.com

One of the finest views in the entire Lake District is from the restaurant, conservatory and terrace of this lovely hotel which stands high on the shores of Lake Windermere. Lawned gardens bedded with mature shrubs, trees and borders of colour sweep down to the water's edge. It is a spectacular scene. Visitors receive warm hospitality from this well-run and splendidly decorated hotel now owned by Charles Garside, the former Editor-in-Chief of the international newspaper 'The European'. Previous owner John Tovey, the celebrated chef and author, remains as a consultant and Miller Howe retains the homely ambience he created. All 12 en suite bedrooms are tastefully furnished, the majority of which have views over the lake to the mountains beyond. Chef Susan Elliott's imaginative menus will delight the most discerning guest, while the panoramic tableau across England's largest lake as the sun sets, presents an unforgettable dining experience. Guests can enjoy a range of water sports or boat trips on Lake Windermere and there are many interesting fell walks close by. **Directions:** From the M6 junction 36 follow the A591 through Windermere, then turn left onto the A592 towards Bowness. Miller Howe is ½ mile on the right. Price guide (including 4-course dinner): Single £95–£175; double/twin £140–£250.

THE ATLANTIC HOTEL

MONT DE LA PULENTE, ST BRELADE, JERSEY JE3 8HE
TEL: + 44 1534 44101 FAX: + 44 1534 44102 E–MAIL: atlantic@itl.net

A major refurbishment programme in 1994 has transformed this modern building into one with classical warmth and style internally. Privately owned and supervised, every aspect of the four-star service matches its location overlooking the five-mile sweep of St Ouen's Bay. Situated in three acres of private grounds alongside La Moye Golf Course, there is something here for everyone. General Manager, Simon Dufty and his team provide the highest standards of welcome and service. The 50 bedrooms are furnished in the style of the 18th century and like the public rooms, all have co-ordinated colours and fabrics. All have picture windows with views of the sea or the golf course. There are luxury suites and garden studios within the hotel as well. The award-winning restaurant, beautifully situated overlooking the open air pool and terrace, specialises in modern British cooking created by Head Chef, Ken Healy. For the more energetic guest, or those wishing to lose excess calories, The Atlantic has extensive indoor health and leisure facilities in The Palm Club including an indoor ozone treated pool. The hotel is an ideal spot from which to walk on the beach or coast paths, to play golf, go riding or just relax. There are comprehensive meeting facilities. **Directions:** Off a private drive off the A13 at La Pulente, two miles from the airport. Price guide: Single £95; double/twin £120; suite £195.

HIGHLAND.
An almost feminine charm and character all of its own. Light and aromatic, the Gentle Spirit is rich in body with a soft heather honey finish.

ISLE OF SKYE.
Assertive but not heavy. Fully flavoured with a pungent, peaty ruggedness. It explodes on the palate and lingers on. Well balanced. A sweetish seaweedy aroma.

SPEYSIDE.
Finely balanced with a dry, rather delicate aroma, good firm body and a smoky finish. A pleasantly austere malt of great distinction with a character all its own.

WEST HIGHLAND.
Oban is the West Highland malt. A singular, rich and complex malt with the merest suggestion of peat in the aroma, slightly smoky with a long smooth finish.

ISLE OF ISLAY.
Seaweed, peat, smoke and earth are all elements of the assertive Islay character. Pungent, an intensely dry 16 year old malt with a firm robust body and powerful aroma.

LOWLAND.
Typically soft, restrained and with a touch of sweetness. An exceptionally pale smooth malt which, experts agree, reaches perfection at 10 years maturity.

DALWHINNIE	TALISKER	CRAGGANMORE	OBAN	LAGAVULIN	GLENKINCHIE
15 YEARS OLD	10 YEARS OLD	12 YEARS OLD	14 YEARS OLD	16 YEARS OLD	10 YEARS OLD
HIGHLAND	SKYE	SPEYSIDE	WEST HIGHLAND	ISLAY	LOWLAND

Les grands crus de Scotland.

In the great wine-growing regions, there are certain growths from a single estate that are inevitably superior.

For the Scots, there are the single malts. Subtle variations in water, weather, peat and the distilling process itself lend each single malt its singular character. The Classic Malts are the finest examples of the main malt producing regions. To savour them, one by one, is a rare journey of discovery.

SIX OF SCOTLAND'S FINEST MALT WHISKIES

You'll also find that when your customers taste The Classic Malts, their appreciation will almost certainly increase your sales of malt whisky – in itself a discovery worth making.

To find out more, contact our Customer Services team on 0345 444 111, or contact your local wholesaler.

Cyprus

FOUR SEASONS HOTEL

PO BOX 7222, LIMASSOL, CYPRUS
TEL: +357 5 310 222 FAX: +357 5 310 887

Luxurious amenities and elegant decor are hallmarks of this superior hotel, located in the Amathus area just outside cosmopolitan Limassol. An excellent choice of bedrooms includes double rooms, studios, beach studios, honeymoon and executive suites and theme suites. Features of this varied accommodation are an abundance of natural light, beautiful décor and panoramic views of the Mediterranean. The bedrooms, many of which have balconies, are decorated in a modern style with comfortable furnishings. There are three restaurants, each marked by its own distinctive style and cuisine. 'The Palace' resembles an ancient Greek palace and serves international dishes whilst the 'Cafe Tropical' offers a wide selection

of local and exotic dishes. In 'Seasons Oriental' guests have a menu which provides a choice of Chinese specialities and Japanese Teppan-Yai cuisine in a formal, yet intimate setting. The excellent children's facilities include a supervised kindergarten and daily activity programme. Fitness enthusiasts enjoy the indoor pool, high-tech gym, Jacuzzis and sauna. Treatments in the Thalasso Spa include hydromassage, jet massage, steam bath and Swiss needle shower. The beautiful island of Cyprus is a delight to explore with many tavernas, shops and lively night spots close by. **Directions**: The hotel is located just outside Limassol. Price guide: Single CY£117–133; double/twin CY£143–164; studio room; CY£143–173; suites CY£196–750.

PREFERRED PARTNERS

Preferred partners are those organisations specifically chosen and exclusively recommended by Johansens for the quality and excellence of their products and services for the mutual benefit of Johansens members, readers and independent travellers.

 AT&T Global Services

 Classic Malts of Scotland

 Diners Club International

 Dunhill Tobacco

 Ercol Furniture Ltd

 Hildon Ltd

 J&H Marsh & McLennan

 Knight Frank International

 Honda UK Ltd

 Moët Hennessy

 NPI

 Pacific Direct

Czech Republic

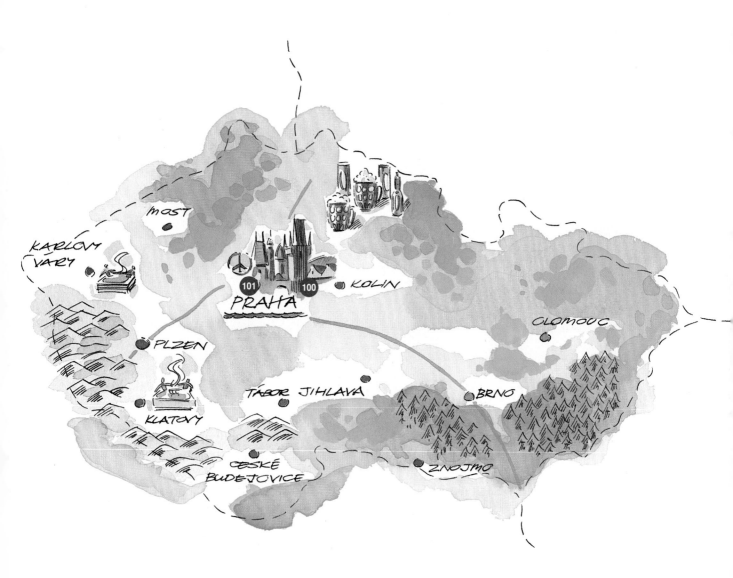

HOTEL HOFFMEISTER

POD BRUSKOU 7, MALA STRANA, 11800 PRAGUE 1, CZECH REPUBLIC
TEL: +420 2 57 31 09 42 FAX: +420 2 57 32 09 06 E-MAIL: hotel@hoffmeister.ct

This first class hotel is in a historic location. Above is the castle, below is the river and the magical city of Prague. The buildings are a blend of old and new, creating a combination of traditional comfort and modern luxurious efficiency. An original feature which adds personal character to the distinctive interiors is the unique collection of paintings and portraits depicted by the owner's famous late father, Adolf Hoffmeister, thinker, artist and patriot. Among them are contemporary pictures of celebrities such as Charlie Chaplin, Virginia Woolf and Salvador Dali. The colourful bedrooms and suites have every modern amenity including satellite television and minibar. The public rooms include a café on the terrace, ideal for summer and a cellar bar snug in winter. In the restaurant, Head Chef Vaclav Kosnár produces exceptional menus: international dishes and also the specialities of the region. On the cosmopolitan wine list are classic wines, also Bohemian and Moravian vintages, lovingly selected by the owner. Golf and hunting can be arranged. Concerts, museums, theatres and shopping are close by. **Directions:** From Mánesur Bridge ascend Pod Bruskou, hotel is on the left. Transport to and from airport by arrangement. Good parking facilities. Price guide (plus 22% tax): Single $125–197; double/twin $149–223; suites $205–395.

SIEBER HOTEL & APARTMENTS

SLEZSKÁ 55, 130 00 PRAGUE 3, CZECH REPUBLIC
TEL: +420 2 24 25 00 25 FAX: +420 2 24 25 00 27 E-MAIL: sieber@comp.cz

This intimate town house hotel is in a quiet one-way street close to Wenceslas Square in the centre of Prague. Its nearest landmark is the impressive National Museum. It is ideal for those visiting the city on business, immaculate and very civilised, yet having a warm ambience achieved by an understanding host. Modern lines have been softened by clever use of wood panelling and Alfons Mucha prints. The bedrooms are spacious and comfortable, thoughtfully designed and supplied with today's requisite amenities. There is one floor dedicated to non-smoking. The three duplex suites are luxurious, with handsome open staircases connecting the living area with the sleeping quarters, perfect for those making a long stay, as the Sieber has no sitting-room nor patio. The small bar leads into the restaurant, an attractively lit room where diners can indulge in Czech specialities or familiar international dishes prepared by the well-known chef. An excellent selection of wines is available. The hotel will arrange tours of Prague with its famous castle, river and museums, organise tickets for concerts and direct guests to the nearby fitness centre, tennis and city night life. **Directions:** The hotel is close to Jiriho Z Podebrad Metro. For those driving, from Wenceslas Square, follow Vinohradska, turning right down Perunova, then right again into Slezska. Overnight parking is 500m away. Price guide: Single £83; double/twin £88; suites £104.

The Historical Hotels
your First, Best and only Choice in Scandinavia

We would like to welcome you to The Historical Hotels. The group comprises 35 well-run and long-established hotels built between 1380 and 1939, all of which have their own character and style. The architecture of each hotel ranges from pseudo Swiss and empire to Jugendstil. Interest for The Historical Hotels has increased beyond expectations. This has meant that several of the hotels have become more conscious of their cultural heritage and have carried out extensive restoration work. This is a unique opportunity for visitors to experience the beauty of Scandinavian nature with its extreme contrasts, combined with a stay at a hotel steeped in tradition.

De Historiske Hotel

Denmark

STEENSGAARD HERREGÅRDSPENSION

MILLINGE, STEENSGAARD, 5600 FAABORG, DENMARK
TEL: +45 62 61 94 90 FAX: +45 62 61 78 61

This hotel stands on the delightful island of Fyn, in 24 acres of parkland with its own game reserve. A 14th century manor house, it has been carefully restored to provide modern amenities without diminishing its historic appeal. Guests arriving find an attractive low stone and brick building, with marvellous old chimneys and oak beams, surrounding a cobbled courtyard. Inside are superbly panelled rooms with handsome oil paintings, lovely antiques, chandeliers and comfortable sofas in harmonious colours. A grand mahogany staircase leads to the bedrooms, decorated in peaceful colours, looking out over the estate. All bedrooms have period furniture and up-to-date bathrooms. The library is a venue for pre-dinner drinks before entering the dining room with its tiled floor, family crests above the fireplace, ornately carved chairs and tables gleaming with silver. The restaurant offers an exceptional standard of Danish and French cuisine; the wines are international. It is essential for guests to make reservations as it has a fine reputation in the neighbourhood. Guests can use the tennis court or stroll in the well-tended gardens, row on the moat or go for a walk in the Funen Alps or along the beaches. Golf is 2km and riding is ½km away. **Directions:** 2½ hours drive from Copenhagen. Nearest major airport is Billund. Price guide: Single Kr815–1250; double/twin Kr990–1250.

HOTEL HESSELET

CHRISTIANSLUNDSVEJ 119, 5800 NYBORG, DENMARK
TEL: +45 65 31 30 29 FAX: +45 65 31 29 58

Situated on the garden Island of Funen, surrounded by woods and adjacent to the beach, is the renowned Hotel Hesselet, a member of Small Luxury Hotels of the World. The distinctive Japanese – Scandinavian architecture, combined with the tasteful decor of the interior and the panoramic views, gives the hotel a special atmosphere. Antiques and beautiful paintings contribute to the "home away from home" feeling that makes the hotel a favourite country retreat. Spacious well-decorated rooms and suites with well-fitted en suite granite bathrooms together with beautiful reception rooms and the candle lit Tranquebar Restaurant offer a restful stay. Active guests will appreciate the indoor pool with fitness equipment or may prefer to swim from the hotel jetty, play tennis on artificial grass, see the countryside on the hotel's bikes, play golf on the 8 nearby courses or visit Odense, the town of Hans Christian Andersen. Driving in Denmark on the excellent roads is easy and pleasant. You can travel by Scandinavian Seaways from Harwich to Esbjerg (distance to hotel approx. 100 miles) or by air to Billund in Jutland (approx. 75miles) or to Copenhagen (approx. 75 miles). **Directions:** Leave the E20 at Exit 45 and the hotel is 3 minutes away, just north of Nyborg. Price guide: Single Kr990–1090; double/twin Kr1360–1560; Suite Kr2000–2500.

Estonia

PARK CONSUL SCHLÖSSLE

PÜHAVAIMU 13–15, 10123 TALLINN, ESTONIA
TEL: +372 699 7700 FAX: +372 699 7777

Set in the centre of Tallinn's beautiful and historic old town, just steps away from the main shopping streets and the town hall square, is the Park Consul Hotel. Its present site is on the narrow cobblestone street where numerous storage buildings and merchants houses were located in the 13th century when this fortified medieval village was a thriving trading centre. Today's hotel is based on twin storehouses which have been restored and changed throughout the years. In spite of the extensive alterations, the sturdy medieval base walls still stand and Park Consul has preserved all the structural details and exposed them in their original splendour. The result is a beautiful hotel which, with its portals of cut stone, small spiral staircases and irregular chambers, seems untouched by the passing centuries. In this baronial manor house setting, there are 23 rooms and suites, all spacious and boasting state-of-the-art facilities and comfortable bathrooms. Delicious and imaginative breakfasts and special meals are served in style in the vaulted cellar of the historic buildings. In the Great Hall, with its cosy fireplace and many ancient features, an extensive range of light meals and drinks are served. Tallinn's nearby attractions include several mansions, Guildhalls and museums that echo its rich past. **Directions:** The hotel is located in the centre of Tallinn. Price guide: Single $161–$189; double/twin $204–$232; suites $268–$354.

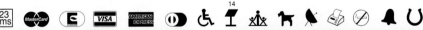

ERCOL
Furniture for living rooms

France

CALAIS
BOULOGNE
LILLE
CHERBOURG
LE HAVRE
128 127 129 119
BAYEUX
126 REIMS
123
BREST
ST MALO 150
NANCY
161 STRASBOURG
PARIS
VITTEL
114
LE MANS
125
NANTES 117 136
118
110
DIJON
POITIERS
112
LA ROCHEFORT
CLERMONT-FERRAND MÂCON
122 159
LYON
132
133
PÉRIGUEUX 158
142 116
120
135
121
GRENOBLE
134
BORDEAUX
AVIGNON
113 BIARRITZ
AIX-EN-PROVENCE
152 151
LOURDES
TOULOUSE MONTPELLIER
124 NTE CARLO
111
157
115 ANNES
MARSEILLE
153 154 137 . TROPEZ
155 156 130
PERPIGNAN

CALVI BASTIA
AJACCIO
PORTO VECCHIO
CORSE

CHÂTEAU DE VAULT DE LUGNY

11 RUE DU CHÂTEAU, 89200 AVALLON, FRANCE
TEL: +33 3 86 34 07 86 FAX: +33 3 86 34 16 36 E-MAIL: lugny@transco.fr

First sight of this magnificent domaine is magical – there is an authentic moat encircling the verdant estate, a 13th century watch tower – the château itself is 16th century – and there are proud peacocks and gaggles of geese in front of the historic farm buildings. This elite hotel is run by two marvellous hostesses, Madame Audan and her daughter, who have created a unique blend of sophistication and history. The interior is dramatic – marvellous panelling, superb antiques, big elaborate fireplaces and ornate ceilings. The luxurious guest rooms have romantic four poster beds. There is one large family suite. All the amenities of the hotel and the restaurant are exclusively for resident guests. On

Saturday evenings residents are invited to apéritifs. Three interesting menus, Seasonal, Burgundian and Gourmet, ensure that dining is memorable, whether alfresco or seated amiably around the kitchen table. The wines are exquisite. Picnics can be arranged for those exploring the countryside, although it is fascinating to see the estate from an air balloon! Tennis, trout-fishing, riding, exploring medieval Vézelay and wine-tasting are suggested recreations – gently strolling in the gardens is idyllic. There is a special games area for children. **Directions:** A6, exit Avallon, taking road for Vézelay until Pontaubert. Turn right, watching for signs to the Château. Price guide: Double/twin FF750–2400.

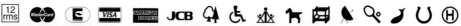

LA RÉSERVE DE BEAULIEU

5 BOULEVARD GÉNÉRAL LECLERC, 06310 BEAULIEU-SUR-MER, FRANCE
TEL: +33 4 93 01 00 01 FAX: +33 4 93 01 28 99

A glimpse at the guest book will reveal that royalty, politicians, comedians, poets, lords and actresses have all mingled at La Réserve de Beaulieu to experience the splendour of this palatial residence. Set on the riviera between Nice and Monte-Carlo, the rose-coloured building was constructed in 1880 inspired by the Florentine Renaissance style. A complete refurbishment in 1994 has resulted in this fine property where a refined ambience pervades every room and modern comforts fuse with traditional nuances. The opulent bedrooms are tastefully decorated with soft fabrics and restored furniture, whilst the bathrooms feature Sarrancolin marble and attractive woodwork. Guests relax in the informal bar, enjoying the tuneful sounds of the pianist, before dining in the exquisite restaurant, decorated in shades of ochre and red. Gastronomic delights feature on the classic menu, awarded a Michelin star and the talented chef adapts the dishes to incorporate the best of the fresh seasonal produce. The hotel has its own private port, accessible by boat. Fitness facilities include a superb sea water swimming pool, sauna and massage whilst a beautician is available on request. The diverse pastimes include glass blowing in Biot, strolling in exotic gardens and exploring the many villas nearby. **Directions:** Take A8 towards Nice. The hotel is equidistant from Monaco and Nice and only 30 minutes from the airport. Price guide: Double/twin FF1500–3850; suites FF3100–7400.

FRANCE (Beaune)

ERMITAGE DE CORTON

R.N. 74, 21200 CHOREY-LES-BEAUNE, FRANCE
TEL: +33 3 80 22 05 28 FAX: +33 3 80 24 64 51

Set in acres of glorious vineyards the Ermitage de Corton is an old burgundy-style mansion offering comfortable accommodation in fine surroundings. The Parra family extend a friendly and hospitable welcome to all the guests and pride themselves in an excellent standard of service. The 10 rooms are individually decorated in a diverse range of styles: some are grandiose whilst others are simple yet elegant. Their names form a tribute to the many prestigious wines in France such as 'Savigny' or 'Romanée Conti'. The superb restaurant is the centrepiece of the hotel and boasts André Parra as its chef. A maitre Cuisinier de France, the chef has created an imaginative menu, designed to satisfy the most discriminating palate. The exquisite French cuisine is complemented by a fine selection of wine accompaniments. Guests wishing to recreate the sumptuous delights will be pleased with the cooking lessons, taught in English, by the chef himself. Sport activities may be enjoyed within the vicinity and these include golf and tennis. Several wine cellars, particularly those offering burgundy vintages are nestled around the surrounding area. Other attractions include the Hospices de Beaune, Musée du Vin and the animated city of Dijon. **Directions:** Take the A6 motorway towards Beaune, leaving at exit 24. Then take the RN74 towards Dijon. The hotel is situated just 500m away. Price guide: Double/twin FF850–1500; suites FF950–1800.

HÔTEL DU PALAIS

AVENUE DE L'IMPÉRATRICE, 64200 BIARRITZ, FRANCE
TEL: +33 5 59 41 64 00 FAX: +33 5 59 41 67 99 E-MAIL: palais@cotebasque.tm.fr

This is a true palace, having been the summer haunt of royalty since 1855 – balls, receptions, charades, picnics and fireworks were the programme then (as they are now!). It became a hotel in the fabulous Belle Epoque, the 1880s, when the guest list included Queen Victoria. In 1950, a famous decorator undertook the complete renovation of the Palais, maintaining its grand style and today it is a sumptuous residence overlooking the waterfront. The richly furnished foyer has marble pillars, glistening chandeliers, superb antiques and a dramatic staircase. The bedrooms are luxurious, many with balconies facing the sea and access is easy for those with mobility problems. Sophisticated bars, cool in the hotel or on the terraces, are appreciated by guests before feasting in the elegant Michelin star restaurant, with a spectacular view across the sea. Lighter meals in an informal ambience are also served, including a buffet beside the pool. Families use the private beach huts between the pool and the sand. Sporting guests enjoy tennis, squash, 10 golf-courses, scuba-diving, riding or watching pelota, the Basque national game. Others explore the countryside, right up into the Pyrenees. At night, the casino is a great attraction. **Directions:** Biarritz is signed from the A63 and N10. Price guide: Single FF1200–2100; double/twin FF1500–2850; suites FF2000–6350.

DOMAINE DE ROCHEVILAINE

POINTE DE PEN LAN, 56190 BILLIERS, FRANCE
TEL: +33 2 97 41 61 61 FAX: +33 2 97 41 44 85

With its many 15th and 16th century 'manoirs', the Domaine de Rochevilaine resembles a picturesque village surrounded by magnificent gardens and terraces. Nestling on the edge of the rocky Pointe de Pen Lan, the manor house affords a panoramic vista across the waterfront. The 38 bedrooms are furnished in a stylish manner with soft furnishings and delicate patterns. Aubusson tapestries adorn the walls of the comfortable lounge where guests recline and enjoy a preprandial drink. Gastronomes will be delighted with the creations of Head Chef, Patrice Caillault, made using the finest of fresh, local ingredients. The menu comprises typically French flavours and is served in the elegant restaurant, overlooking the sea. The superb Centre de Balnéothérapie offers a vast array of beauty and lifestyle treatments including hydrotherapy, massages and seaweed wraps. Fitness facilities include an indoor swimming pool, salt-water pool on the rocks, spa, Hammam and gymnasium. Popular excursions include boat trips to the beautiful islands in the Gulf of Morbihan and exploring the historic villages nearby such as Rochefort-en-Terre. **Directions:** From Nantes, take the E60 in the direction of Vannes and exit at Muzillac. Then follow the signs to Billiers and then Pen Lan. Price guide: Double/twin FF535–1650; suites FF1500–2300.

50

HÔTEL SAVOY

5 RUE FRANÇOIS EINESY, 06400 CANNES, FRANCE
TEL: +33 4 92 99 72 00 FAX: +33 4 93 68 25 59

This modern hotel with elegant balconies and terraces, is just off the famous Boulevard de la Croisette, giving easy access to the beach and to the town centre. Bedrooms provide modern comfort for the business or pleasure guest. The barman mixes cocktails in the intimate bar before diners enter La Roseraie, the terraced restaurant in front of the hotel with its own waterfall. The menu offers good choices from the region including grilled seabass and rack of lamb, provençal style. A more modest menu reflects the best local market produce. Many of the wines listed are from the region. The Blue Beach on the 6th floor has a wonderful terrace alongside the swimming pool, serving drinks and buffet lunches to sun-worshippers. A private beach is ready for those who prefer sea and sand. Not far from the Palais des Congrès, The Savoy has its own well equipped conference suites, ideal for receptions and banquets. Exploring old Cannes and the modern shops is fascinating, as is the delightful countryside behind the coast. The Museum of Perfumery at Grasse, tennis and water sports are available, and golf is not far away. **Directions:** 24km from the Nice Airport, driving take the N7 or leave the A8 motorway at the Cannes exit. There is parking under the hotel. Price guide: Single FF620–1305; double/twin FF750–1455; suites FF1900–5000.

CHÂTEAU DE CANDIE

RUE DU BOIS DE CANDIE, 73000 CHAMBÉRY-LE-VIEUX, FRANCE
TEL: +33 4 79 966300 FAX: +33 4 79 966310

The history of this magical château dates back to the 14th century when it was built as a fortress by Knights returning from the Crusades. Almost at the Millennium, it is a comfortable and friendly hotel, its fine Savoyard architecture undiminished by the years. The Château reflects the talents and passions of its distinguished owner, Didier Lhostis. It is a connoisseur's paradise, filled with priceless antiques and collections of paintings; trompe l'oeil enhances the salons. To visit here is to stay in a magnificent private mansion with echoes of each past generation. Statues lurk in corridors, intriguing bibelots are on display. The meeting rooms are pleasant. The gorgeous bedrooms and suites are named after historical personalities and furnished accordingly. The bathrooms are opulent – one bath is carved out of a block of 19th century marble! The kitchen is in the hands of Chef Gilles Hérard who, having trained under famous Parisian chefs, has returned home to Chambéry, where his impeccable presentation and innovative cooking of Savoyan dishes excite the most discerning guests in the three exquisite dining rooms. The wines are superlative. Stroll through the idyllic park, relax on the terrace, explore the region, play golf or tennis and enjoy marvellous winter sports resorts nearby. **Directions:** Leave A43 Exit 15 for Chambéry Le Haut. Price guide: double/twin FF500–950; duplex FF1200.

CHÂTEAU DES BRIOTTIÈRES

49330 CHAMPIGNÉ, FRANCE
TEL: +33 2 41 42 00 02 FAX: +33 2 41 42 01 55 E-MAIL: briottieres@wanadoo.fr

This enchanting château, surrounded by well-kept lawns and 360 acres of parkland 'à l'anglaise', has been in the same family for over 200 years. Indeed this is not a hotel, but a stately home in which guests are graciously received. It is in Anjou, an unspoilt corner of France. The interior is lovely, filled with Louis XV antiques and memorabilia, family portraits and a pervading air of serenity. This château was used as the setting for the film "Impromptu" starring Emma Thompson and Hugh Grant. The bedrooms have windows looking out over the estate, letting in the fragrant perfumes of herbs and flowers. It is a joy to awake here in the mornings. Breakfast may be taken in the bedrooms or at separate tables downstairs. Lunch is

not available and everyone meets again for apéritifs with the owner of the property, François de Valbray, before a convivial dinner (served at 8.30pm) in the impressive dining room – traditional family recipes accompanied by delicious Anjou wines. The château offers swimming in summer, fishing in the lake and billiards in the evenings; golf and riding are nearby. Nearby attractions include the Loire châteaux and the Anjou wine trail, further west Brittany fishing ports. **Directions:** From Paris, take the A11 towards Nantes, exit 11 Durtal, then Daumeray on the D859 then Châteauneuf /Sarthe to Champigné, then follow the signs for 4 km. Price guide: Double/twin FF600–750; suites FF900–1100.

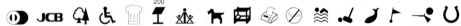

FRANCE (Chinon)

CHÂTEAU DE DANZAY

RD 749, 37420 CHINON, FRANCE
TEL: +33 2 47 58 46 86 FAX: +33 2 47 58 84 35

Nestling in acres of beautiful parkland, this 15th century castle exudes charm and a warm ambience reigns throughout the interior. The spacious bedrooms are decorated in an authentic medieval style with antique furniture, mullioned windows and canopied beds. All are located within the château itself and afford fine views across the park. The restaurant is beautifully appointed and guests dine by candlelight, indulging in creative recipes and regional specialities, served alongside the very best of Loire wines. The terraces surrounding the heated outdoor swimming pool are perfect for relaxing in the sunshine. A wide range of sporting activities may be practised nearby including hot-air ballooning, helicopter rides, tennis, golf, horse-riding and exploring the surrounding countryside on foot or bike. Guests will appreciate the glorious location of the property which lies within easy reach of the picturesque Châteaux de la Loire: Azay-le-Rideau, Ussé, Langeais, Saumur, Amboise, Villandry, Chenonceaux, Blois, Chambord, Cheverny. **Directions:** Leave the A10 at the exit signposted Saint-Avertin/Chinon and then take the D749 towards Bourgeuil. The Château de Danzay is situated only 5 kilometres away from Chinon. Price guide: Double/twin FF900–1400; suites FF1500–1600.

LE MOULIN DE CONNELLES

40 ROUTE D'AMFREVILLE-SOUS-LES-MONTS, 27430 CONNELLES, FRANCE
TEL: +33 2 32 59 53 33 FAX: +33 2 32 59 21 83

On an island of its own in a by-water of the Seine a few miles above Rouen stands Le Moulin de Connelles, a fabulously beautiful old manor house and water mill. This is the part of the river that so appealed to Monet and his fellow impressionists. There are six luxurious suites and seven luxurious bedrooms. Antiques and fine décor perpetuate the ambience of charming seclusion – the latest modern equipment provides, if audio-visual is required, immediate contacts with the outer world. Comfort is similarly assured by the up-to-date amenities. The manor's lounge and bar welcome guests with furnishings that induce that sense of well-being that can be heightened only by a glass of calvados. The restaurant poised above the water is famed for the skill of its young chef. As early guide books might have said: Le Moulin is worth more than a détour. The manor's swimming pool, pool house and tennis courts, nearby international golf courses, riding school and sailing or water skiing on the lake are the breathtaking choice of sporting pursuits. **Directions:** 110Km from Paris motorway A13 exit 18; 28Km from Rouen motorway A13 exit 19; 15Km from Louviers. Price guide: Single FF550–700; double/twin FF650–800; suites FF800–950.

HÔTEL ANNAPURNA

73120 COURCHEVEL (1850), FRANCE
TEL: +33 4 79 08 04 60 FAX: +33 4 79 08 15 31

Hotel Annapurna is a sophisticated hotel in the midst of the Alps. Built this century, it has recognised the needs of its sporting guests when they leave the pistes. The interior is spacious and elegant, reflecting the designer's savoir-faire. There are relaxing lounges, with comfortable modern furnishings. The bedrooms are luxurious, with panelled walls and ceilings, all with a south-facing balcony. The piano bar is an ideal après-ski rendezvous, perhaps after taking advantage of the leisure centre. This has a magnificent pool, looking out to the snowfields, a Jacuzzi, sauna, gymnasium, UVA, turkish bath masseur, table-tennis and billiards. After an exotic cocktail or two, studying the menu of the handsome restaurant, with its spectacular view of the mountains, the superb French food, beautifully served, is greatly appreciated, especially when accompanied by connoisseur wines. An orchestra plays on Thursday evenings. The Annapurna is a fantastic place for small seminars and conferences and all appropriate facilities are available. Every form of winter sports is possible in Courchevel, 600kms wonderful runs, Langlauf, skating, curling and tobogganing. At night there are discothèques, cinemas and clubs. **Directions:** A41 to Montmelian, then A43 to Albertville, then N90 to Moutiers, after which Courchevel is signed. Price guide per person: Single FF980–2165; double/twin FF980–1620; suites FF2690–3200.

LE BYBLOS DES NEIGES

BP 98, 73122 COURCHEVEL, FRANCE
TEL: +33 4 79 00 98 00 FAX: +33 4 79 00 98 01 E-MAIL: courchevel@byblos.com

Courchevel is a prestigious ski resort, made more so by hosting the Olympic Games in 1992 and Le Byblos Des Neiges has an unparalleled situation in the Jardin Alpin, in the midst of the pistes, close to ski-lifts and cable cars. From the exterior it resembles a modern hotel, inside new arrivals find the immaculate service and luxurious furnishings of the great chalets of earlier this century. The reception rooms are splendid, with tall larch pillars and big, comfortable chairs. Wonderful glowing fabrics give the spacious bedrooms a special warmth. Rustic yet contemporary furniture, balconies with spectacular views over the snow and lavish modern bathrooms add to the pleasure of staying here. La Clairière

Restaurant is famous for its buffets and regional dishes; skiers enjoy lunch on its sunny terrace. At night, guests can also dine in the L'Écailler, an elegant venue renowned for its fabulous fish specialities. The lounge bar is the meeting place in Courchevel, soft piano music and a big fire adding to its charm. Backgammon is played in the games room. Children have their own territory. After the day's exertions, the large pool and health centre are ideal, a wide range of treatments being offered. **Directions:** From Lyon A43, then A90 to Moutiers, follow signs to Courchevel. The hotel has a heated garage. Price guide (half-board per person): Single FF2070–2410; double/twin FF1650–2540; suites FF3020–5150.

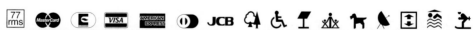

LE GRAND HOTEL DU DOMAINE DE DIVONNE

AVENUE DES THERMES, 01220 DIVONNE LES BAINS, FRANCE
TEL: +33 4 50 40 34 34 FAX: +33 4 50 40 34 24

Prima Hotels

The Domaine de Divonne is a vast estate in sight of Mont Blanc, close to the Swiss border, just fifteen minutes drive from Geneva The Domaine has Le Grand Hotel, Le Golf and Le Casino. The Grand Hotel is a dramatic Art Deco residence – decorated mirrors, exotic fireplaces, tasselled lampshades, stained glass, vibrant colours and a pianist playing Duke Ellington! The bedrooms are inviting, and guests should laze on the balcony gazing at the Alps. The marble bathrooms have gold fittings! Informal meals are enjoyed in La Brasserie de Léman. The pièce de résistance is La Terrasse, an romantic restaurant which stretches into the enchanting gardens. The chef is legendary, the cuisine cosmopolitan. Le Golf has Le Pavillon restaurant in the Clubhouse, with 1930s decor and views of Mont Blanc. The challenging course is immaculate. At night guests seek Le Casino, with its magnificent collection of early slot machines. Traditional gambling tables are busy. Its Four Seasons Restaurant serves French and Lebanese specialities. Dancing through the night at Le Club is fantastic. The countryside offers mountains, lakes, rivers – explore them by bike, otherwise relax after tennis and sunbathe by the pool. **Directions:** N1 from Geneva, exit Coppet/Divonne. Surveillance car parking. Price guide: Single FF750–1200; double/twin FF1150–1650; suites FF2700–9000.

HOSTELLERIE LA BRIQUETERIE

4 ROUTE DE SÉZANNE, 51530, VINAY – ÉPERNAY, FRANCE
TEL: +33 3 26 59 99 99 FAX: +33 3 26 59 92 10

La Briqueterie, standing at the foot of the Côte des Blancs, is surrounded by beautiful flower-filled grounds in the heart of the champagne country. It is owned by the Trouillard family, whose interest in vintage cars is evident from the distinctive works of art in the informal reception area. The salons are elegant and the quiet countryside even pervades the enchanting bedrooms and suites, identified by floral panels on the doors, the colours of which are echoed in the décor inside. The bathrooms are large and luxurious. The family have their own Champagne House and their vintages are among the prestigious champagnes imbibed in the attractive conservatory bar in the garden summer house. A wonderful buffet is served in the Breakfast Room, overlooking the pool. At night in the handsome, beamed restaurant diners have a choice of Regional and Dégustation menus or they select succulent dishes from the à la carte suggestions. The wines are superb. A splendid private dining room and conference facilities are also available. Visitors explore Reims Cathedral, tour champagne cellars or cruise on the Marne. Others relax at the hotel, in the gorgeous pool or the gymnasium. **Directions:** Drive 6km along the Route de Sézanne, signposted from the centre of Épernay, or land on the helipad. Price guide: Single FF620–780; double/twin FF730–890; suites FF1150.

CHÂTEAU EZA

RUE DE LA PISE, O6360 EZE VILLAGE, FRANCE
TEL: +33 4 93 41 12 24 FAX: +33 4 93 41 16 64

Eze Village is medieval, a total contrast to the sophisticated towns along the Côte d'Azur. The Château Eza is 1300 feet high on the great rock above the Mediterranean and was the residence of Prince William of Sweden from 1927 to 1957. Several 13th century houses have been transformed into this élite hotel, with its incredible view over the coast. The original stone walls and ancient oak beams are still evident in the graceful salons and magnificent suites. Log fires, unexpected alcoves, tapestries, superb rugs on tiled floors and fine antiques are part of the unique ambience of this historic hotel. Guests approach the château along a cobbled path, while their cars, when unloaded, are driven by hotel staff to a parking area at the foot of the village. Lunch and dinner is served on the elegant terrace, weather permitting, with its fantastic outlook over the sea to the horizon. It is a charming place for guests to watch a brilliant sunset and at dusk the scenery becomes a mass of flickering lights. Dinner is also served in the lovely panoramic restaurant which is renowned for its unique ambience and superb dishes created by the Chef de Cuisine. 400 great wines are listed. Guests explore Eze Village, visit perfume houses and wine caves, or tour the exotic Riviera with its beaches and casinos. **Directions:** Eze village is on the Moyenne Corniche between Nice and Monaco. Price guide: Single FF2000–3300; double/twin FF2000–3300; suites FF3300–3800.

HOSTELLERIE LES BAS RUPTS

88400 GÉRARDMER, VOSGES, FRANCE
TEL: +33 3 29 63 09 25 FAX: +33 3 29 63 00 40

The Vosges Mountains region is enchanting and Lake Gérardmer, just off the Routes des Vins, has its own magical retreat, the Hostellerie Les Bas Rupts with its adjacent Le Chalet Fleuri – appropriately named, for flowers are the theme of this pretty building with its exquisitely painted doors and friezes along the walls and colourful window boxes along the balconies. The Hostellerie is idyllic and welcoming, surrounded by lovingly tended gardens. The bedrooms are charming, peaceful and comfortable, with elegant period furniture. Delightful small salons provide a romantic ambience. Michel Philippe is a Maître Cuisinier de France, supported by a talented team – and connoisseurs of good food will be in heaven. A superb breakfast starts the day on the terrace in summer and it ends with a feast of inspirational interpretations of local specialities, accompanied by carefully selected wines. The view from the restaurant adds to the joy. In winter, guests work up their appetites skiing and in summer, they cycle, explore the countryside, go boating or play tennis – and in the evenings share their experiences in the bar, perhaps before visiting the village casino! **Directions:** From Paris, take the Nancy, Epinal road, N57 to Remiremont, left onto D417 to Gérardmer and right for 3km towards Bresse. Price guide: Double/twin FF780–900.

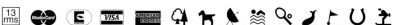

LE MANOIR DE GRESSY

77410 GRESSY EN FRANCE, ROISSY CDG, NR PARIS, FRANCE
TEL: +33 1 60 26 68 00 FAX: +33 1 60 26 45 46

Constructed on the site of the 17th manor house of Seigneur Robert de Frémont, le Manoir is situated in the peaceful village of Gressy-en-France, just 15 minutes from Roissy Charles de Gaulle airport and 30 minutes from Paris. Built around an attractive courtyard with landscaped gardens, le Manoir provides a relaxing venue for both business and leisure. A handsome staircase leads from the welcoming reception area. The enchanting meeting rooms and salons feature harmonising colour schemes and period furniture. The bedrooms echo this warm country house ambience. Guests can enjoy superb French cuisine and fine wines in the splendid le Cellier du Manoir whilst alfresco dining is enjoyed on the terrace overlooking the heated pool.

With 7 meeting rooms, 5 syndicate rooms and dedicated spacious reception areas, le Manoir's extensive conference facilities make it an ideal business venue, suitable for up to 120 delegates. Sports facilities comprise a fitness room, cycling, table tennis and billiards. Excursions include trips to Disneyland Paris, Parc Asterix and the Ile de France area. Special incentive packages are available on request for groups. **Directions:** A1 or A3 from Central Paris, then A104 and N2 towards Soissons, then right onto D212 towards Claye-Souilly and Gressy en France. Free shuttle service to and from the airport and nearby subway station to Paris. Price guide: Single/double FF990–1250. Contact hotel for details about monthly promotions such as weekend packages.

LA CHAUMIÈRE

ROUTE DU LITTORAL, 14600 HONFLEUR, FRANCE
TEL: +33 2 31 81 63 20 FAX: +33 2 31 89 59 23

A historic Norman house has been transformed into this intimate hotel with spectacular views of the coast. It is wonderfully peaceful, surrounded by verdant gardens. Today it is difficult to remember that the D-day landings were not far from here and envisage the turmoil of those days. The sitting room is authentic old Normandy country house style, with its tiled floor, enormous fireplace, elegant chairs and fine antiques. The quiet guest rooms are delightful, with pretty drapes and wallpapers, period furniture and scented with lavender. The modern marble bathrooms are well designed. Sipping apéritifs on the terrace watching the yachts approaching Honfleur and bigger ships heading for Le Havre is a pleasant recreation. Dining in the small but lively restaurant is memorable, from the tasty amusettes to the petits fours. Being close to the sea, the Prix Fixé menu usually includes delicious fish and puddings. The wine list is excellent. Strolling in the fragrant hotel gardens is therapeutic. Challenging golf courses are nearby. Honfleur itself is fascinating and also offers sailing, tennis, museums and boat trips. Bikes are available for exploring the countryside. Those wanting a casino or other activities drive to Deauville, 15km away. **Directions:** A13, exit 28 taking D180 for Honfleur, then D513 along coast road towards Trouville. Price guide: Double/twin FF990–2400.

LA FERME SAINT-SIMÉON

RUE ADOLPHE–MARAIS, 14600 HONFLEUR, FRANCE
TEL: +33 2 31 81 78 00 FAX: +33 2 31 89 48 48

Honfleur is an enchanting small port, much loved by the great impressionist painters, Monet and Boudin especially. Its yacht basin is always busy with boats flying flags from all parts of the globe. It is surrounded by magnificent countryside and just a mile away the Boelen family have created this elite and beautiful hotel. The half-timbered traditional Normandy farmhouse is most attractive, flanked by delightful cottages with decorative brickwork and colourful window boxes. The gardens are glorious. The salon has a beamed ceiling, a big fireplace filled with flowers in summer, fine antiques and comfortable sofas, with fascinating bibelots adding to its charm. The smart meeting room is well equipped. The bedrooms and apartments,

some in Le Pressoir, are luxurious, with wonderful wall coverings, warm colour schemes and graceful furniture. The marble bathrooms combine elegance with opulence. The semi-circular bar is stylish and the terrace with its pretty striped parasols and chairs and spectacular view over the estuary has 'joie de vivre'. The exquisite restaurant is another gem with artistic menus listing sophisticated dishes. The cellar holds over 1000 items. The dramatic fitness area resembles a Roman temple, with murals, pillars, exotic plants, statues and an azure blue pool. **Directions:** Take D180 to Honfleur, then D513 along the coast. Turn left at the lighthouse and follow the signs. Price guide: Double/twin FF790–3510; suites FF4400–5100.

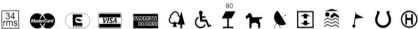

LE MANOIR DU BUTIN

PHARE DU BUTIN, 14600 HONFLEUR, FRANCE
TEL: +33 2 31 81 63 00 FAX: +33 2 31 89 59 23

Honfleur, on the estuary of the Seine, is a fascinating and historic port, with many narrow streets that have changed little over the centuries. Impressionist painters gathered here in the 19th century, friends and pupils of Eugène Boudin – Monet among them. A short drive from the centre, Le Manoir du Butin – a magnificent example of 18th century architecture with its distinctive half-timbering and graceful eaves – is now an idyllic retreat for those seeking tranquillity. It is surrounded by formal gardens and parkland. The guest rooms, just nine, are exquisite, with delicate fabrics on the walls and by the windows and local period furniture. Luxurious accoutrements add to guests' pleasure and the marble bathrooms are lavishly equipped. At night dinner is served in the romantic dining room, which has unique frescoes over its Palladiun fireplace. Intriguing ornaments and small statues add to its charm and the traditional bar has a fine array of bottles, surely including good Calvados. Normandy cooking is fabulous and fish caught that day by local trawlers is superb. Visitors wander along the quay, drink with the yachtsmen, play golf, tennis, take boat trips, explore the D-Day beaches or just relax in the hotel gardens. **Directions:** A13, exit 28 to Honfleur, follow D513 along the coast and turn left at Phare du Butin. Price guide: Double/twin FF640–1970

VILLA SAINT-ELME

CORNICHE DES ISSAMBRES, 83380 LES ISSAMBRES, FRANCE
TEL: +33 4 94 49 52 52 FAX: +33 4 94 49 63 18 E-MAIL: Saintelme@csi.com

This gorgeous 1930s villa is in an enviable and secluded position just off the Corniche between Saint Tropez and Saint Raphael. It is evocative of the past, when the guest list included Maurice Chevalier and Edith Piaf. The hotel is on the sea front, the garden filled with exotic trees and the air fragrant with jasmine. The luxurious bedrooms are pristine, beautifully decorated, air-conditioned and have well-equipped bathrooms. Suites with a definite Provençal influence are in the Bastide, across the road on the waters edge. There is a pleasant ground floor room for those with mobility problems. The Art Deco salons are joyous. Guests enjoy the 'Cocktail Maison' on the terrace. Painters exhibit in the bar and a pianist plays at weekends. The summer restaurant is alfresco, serving aromatic Mediterranean dishes and regional wines; in winter the dining room, overlooking the sea, has an unusual glass dome, the light creating a unique atmosphere. The Villa has a heated and covered sea water pool, private beach, fitness facilities and a Beauty Centre. Nearby are tennis, excellent golf and water sports. Visit the markets, perfumeries at Grasse, Saint Paul de Vence and the many islands. Excellent Provençal wines can be found at local châteaux and domaines. **Directions:** 45 minutes from Nice International Airport. Autoroute 8, exit Fréjus, take N98 towards St Tropez reaching Les Issambres. Security parking is available. Price guide: Single/double/twin FF850–2900; suites FF1700–3100.

LA TOUR ROSE

22 RUE DE BOEUF, 69005 LYON, FRANCE
TEL: 33 4 78 37 25 90 FAX: 33 4 78 42 26 02

Lyon is famous for its silks and for its gastronomy, the latter a legacy from the talented chefs who cooked for the famous banking and silk houses. Philippe Chavent has created a Tuscan garden with terraces, waterfalls and ornamental pools as the setting for La Tour Rose. Each of the twelve suites has been named after and decorated by a different Lyon manufacturer, often using the silks quite unexpectedly so that a variety of eras and styles gives individual character to every room. La Tour Rose is, in fact, three Renaissance buildings. Guests walk through their courtyards perhaps to the Jeu de Paume bar and or relax in the sunlit gardens. Silk aficionados move from the restoration rooms to the textile designers' salons where magnificent exhibitions are staged. The restaurant is unique, a former chapel leading onto a terrace. Philippe Chavent's avant-garde talents transform classic dishes into nouvelle cuisine. Close by he has opened Le Comptoir du Bœuf where guests can taste vintage wine selected from the 35,000 bottles in his cellar. Lyon deserves exploring, with its musuems and historical buildings. Guests can attend the cookery school above the hotel kitchen, and enjoy jazz concerts in the evening. **Directions:** Vieux-Lyon. Detailed directions and a map will be sent following reservations. Price guide: Single Ff950–1650; double/twin Ff1200–1650; suites Ff1650–2800.

HÔTEL MONT-BLANC

PLACE DE L'EGLISE, 74120 MEGÈVE, FRANCE
TEL: +33 4 50 21 20 02 FAX: +33 4 50 21 45 28 E-MAIL: mtblanc@internet-montblanc.fr

Situated in the heart of Megève, this well-renowned hotel has been completely refurbished, resulting in a fusion of Austrian, English and Haute-Savoie styles. Surrounded by picturesque mountains and dense forests, the Hôtel Mont-Blanc is a delightful retreat adorned with rich fabrics and wooden furniture creating an elegant and welcoming ambience. The public rooms feature exquisite antiques and period furnishings whilst the charming Reading Lounge has an interesting selections of old books. The 40 bedrooms are individually decorated in a most tasteful manner, each with its own theme such as the arts or hunting. Those wishing to be pampered will be delighted with the heavy quilts, soft chairs and many thoughtful extras. Although there is no restaurant, breakfast and delicious afternoon teas are served and guests are often invited by the pleasant owners to dine at special tables and indulge in the mouth-watering local delicacies. Megève is a lovely ski resort for children, beginners and skiers of all abilities. The health centre includes many facilities such as a sauna, solarium and Jacuzzi. Valet parking is available during the day. **Directions:** Take the A40 towards Chamonix, then exit at Sallanches and follow the signs up to Megève. The hotel is right in the centre, by the church. Price guide: Double/twin FF890–FF1790; suites FF1690–2980.

LODGE PARK HÔTEL

100 RUE D'ARLY, 74120 MEGÈVE, FRANCE
TEL: +33 4 50 93 05 03 FAX: +33 4 50 93 09 52 E-MAIL: ldgepark@internet-montblanc.fr

The Sibuet family's aim of promoting the "art de vivre" is clearly evident in this charming American lodge-style property. Dating back to the early part of this century, Lodge Park Hotel is beautifully located in the heart of Megève, surrounded by striking mountains and trees. A cosy atmosphere pervades the interior, where the enchanting log fires and soft furnishings add character to the public rooms. Much of the furniture is fashioned from wood, from the chairs and tables to the ceiling whilst the hunting and fishing themes are present throughout the rooms. The spacious bedrooms are individually decorated and feature Ralph Lauren fabrics. Most of the 50 rooms have small balconies overlooking Megève. The large restaurant serves traditional French cuisine, specialising in local delicacies including rich cheese recipes. During the summer months, guests may dine alfresco on the terrace. The fitness centre is superb and there is a sports activities desk and ski shop which can organise ski rentals, passes and a ski safari. Fishing, mountain walking, sleigh rides, snow biking and helicopter rides may also be arranged.
Directions: Take the A40 towards Chamonix, leave at the exit marked 'Sallanches' and take the RN212 to Megève. When entering Megève, follow signs to Albertville. The hotel will be on the left. Price guide (per person): Single FF1190–1560; double/twin FF790–1140; suites FF1550–1850.

L'Antarès

LE BELVÉDÈRE, 73550 MÉRIBEL LES ALLUES, FRANCE
TEL: +33 4 79 23 28 23 FAX: +33 4 79 23 28 18

Méribel first became a ski resort in 1939, with just one lift. Today it reigns supreme, having hosted the Winter Olympics in 1992. High up in the Belvédère area the Hotel l'Antarès is a sophisticated dome shaped chalet, encircled by balconies, thus ensuring every room has spectacular views of the Alps. L'Antarès has a dramatic atrium and eclectically furnished salons. The guest rooms have every imaginable modern comfort. Lunch is a joyous occasion, on the sunny terrace. Later, guests meet in the intimate Piano Bar, while deciding whether to feast on brilliant gourmet dishes in the gastronomic restaurant Cassiopée, decorated with amusing murals, or relax over Savoyard specialities in the Altair.

Two state-of-the-art conference rooms are much in demand, as is the excellent fitness centre. Winter sports are for all ages, Les Petits Loups free for skiers under 5 years old. Snowshoe tours, snowbikes and special passes for the gondolier lifts ensure non-skiers enjoy themselves. There is a ski-shop in the hotel. The hotel has a great pool. Méribel has a fabulous golf course, tennis, rafting and fishing can be arranged; it also has a vibrant night-life. Children have their own programmes. **Directions:** From Moutiers follow signs Méribel les Allues, then to Le Belvédère, finding the hotel indicated. Price guide: Single FF1430–2080; double/twin FF1590–2350; suites FF2560–4265.

CHÂTEAU DES VIGIERS

24240 MONESTIER, FRANCE
TEL: +33 5 53 61 50 00 FAX: +33 5 53 61 50 20 E-MAIL: vigiers@calva.net

This beautiful 400 year old château, set on a 425 acre estate with its own vineyards, in the heart of the Bordeaux country, is now a luxurious hotel enjoying many accolades including Johansens European Country Hotel Award 1998. The well-known golf architect and writer Donald Steel has added Château des Vigiers to the list of élite courses which he has designed or improved, including St Andrews and it is now a prestigious golf and country club. Michel Roux created the fantastic kitchen and gourmet restaurant. The bridge and tea salons, the library and billiard room are regal with handsome antiques, rich rugs and fine paintings. The guest rooms are equally impressive, with French country house furniture. Perigordian suites in the adjacent Dépendences have their own terraces. Excellent conference facilities are also available. At night a sophisticated restaurant, Les Fresques, serves Périgord specialities such as home-made foie gras with wines from the estate. Alternatively, the Club House/Brasserie serves simpler food both at lunchtime and in the evening. The estate also offers swimming, tennis, cycling, fishing and fitness centre. The hotel staff are pleased to organise wine tasting excursions to St. Emilion, Pomerol and the Médoc. **Directions:** From Bordeaux N89 to Libourne, D936 towards Bergerac, at Sainte-Foy-la-Grande D18 towards Eymet. Price guide: Single/double/twin FF700–1450; suites FF900–1800.

CHÂTEAU DE LA BOURDAISIÈRE

37270 MONTLOUIS-SUR-LOIRE, FRANCE
TEL: +33 2 47 45 16 31 FAX: +33 2 47 45 09 11 E-MAIL: labourd@club–internet.fr

In the Loire Valley, between the River Cher and the River Loire there is a magnificent Renaissance château, built for a King's mistress. Today it belongs to the de Broglie family whose motto is appropriate for this elite hotel – For the Future Generations. The Château has been modernised with great care, its history evident in the splendid black and white tiled 14th century entrance, the salons with graceful Louis XIV furniture and the formal gardens, resplendent with topiary and terraces. Deer roam in the surrounding parkland. The guest room walls are covered with romantic toiles or fine wallpaper, antiques abound and the fabrics are gorgeous. Some are in the towers or 'annexes' of the Château.

The hotel has an 'honour bar', guests serving themselves to aperitifs, or maybe digestifs after returning from a gourmet expedition to one of the excellent restaurants in the neighbourhood. Private or corporate entertaining can be arranged in the great vaulted XIVth century hall and there are good facilities for seminars. The park has an outdoor pool and tennis court; windsurfing and golf are nearby. There are wines to be tasted at famous vineyards, fascinating museums and the famous Châteaux of the Loire to visit. **Directions:** A10, exit Tours centre towards Amboise (D751), after 10km watching for signs to the Château. Parking. Price guide: Double/twin FF 650–1100.

HOTEL DE MOUGINS

205, AVENUE DU GOLF, 06250 MOUGINS, FRANCE
TEL: +33 4 92 92 17 07 FAX: +33 4 92 92 17 08 E-MAIL: info@hoteldemougins.com

Mougins is an enchanting town, about 5 miles from Cannes, high up above the Côte d'Azur, with intriguing artists' ateliers off its narrow winding streets. A fine hotel has been created by carefully restoring a lovely old farmhouse, adding four delightful villas, and transforming the immediate surroundings into gardens, scented by lavender, mimosa and rosemary. The cool salons are elegant, contemporary Provençal style, opening onto an attractive terrace, and the charmingly decorated bedrooms are mostly in the 'Bastides', all having a balcony or patio. They are air-conditioned and provided with many 'extras'; the bathrooms are well designed. The hotel has two bars, a convivial one by the pool terrace, adjacent to the 'summer grill' where informal meals are prepared, and the other an inviting room next to the superb La Figuière Restaurant, which serves gourmet interpretations of local specialities, either in the delightful dining room or in the shade of an old ash tree, accompanied by good wines. Golf is the dominating sport, with nine excellent clubs nearby. Other activities are tennis, boules and swimming. Expeditions should be made to the perfumeries of Grasse, the Picasso Museum in Antibes, the glass-blowers at Biot and exciting shops in Cannes. **Directions:** Autoroute 8, then Voie Rapide second exit, for Antibes. Price guide: Single/double/twin FF820–1150; suites FF1700.

Paris

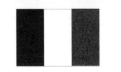

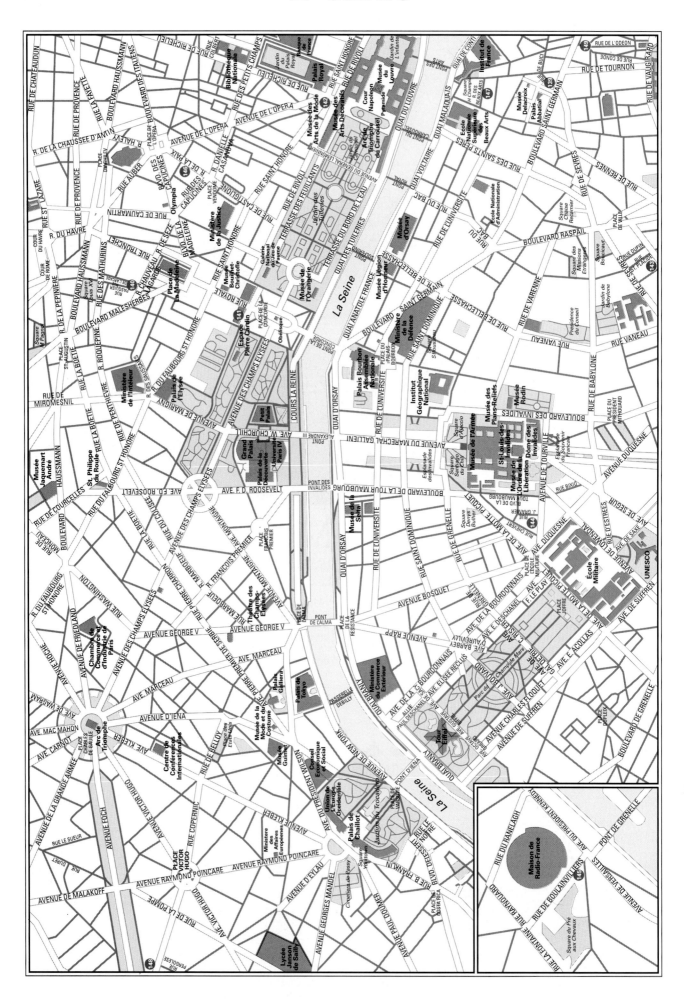

HOTEL BUCI LATIN

34, RUE DE BUCI, 75006 PARIS, FRANCE
TEL: +33 1 43 29 07 20 FAX: +33 1 43 29 67 44

This intriguing small hotel is for francophiles who are determined to find the Latin Quarter as described by the literati. It is close to St. Germain, in a maze of narrow streets where market stalls vie for business with luxurious boutiques. The atmosphere is vibrant. Hotel Buci Latin has no restaurant, but there are many exciting bistros and clubs nearby. It does, however, have an excellent coffee bar, with water cascading into a small plant-filled pond. The interior is unique, 20th century art deco perhaps, with unusual lights, much wrought iron and eclectic furnishings to add to its charm. The doors have all been painted by different artists and graffiti are all along the stairwell. The bedrooms are spotlessly clean and equipped with all modern amenities – and the doorknobs are made from boules! In one of the suites there is a little terrace where drinks can be enjoyed on fine evenings. There is so much to do in Paris – watch the Left Bank artists at work, ascend the Eiffel Tower, explore Notre Dame or cross the Seine to visit the Louvre, drink the traditional onion soup in Les Halles, stroll down the Champs Élysées, go shopping or make an expedition to Versailles. At night take a boat down the river or find good jazz near the hotel. **Directions:** Saint Germain Des Prés is the nearest Metro Station, the hotel has no parking facilities. Price guide: Double/twin FF970–1250; suite FF1650–1750.

HÔTEL DE L'ARCADE

9 RUE DE L'ARCADE, 75008 PARIS, FRANCE
TEL: +33 1 53 30 60 00 FAX: +33 1 40 07 03 07

This graceful 19th century town house, the renovations clearly carried out with love as well as skill, is now a haven in the heart of the business district of Paris, close to the Madeleine, the Opera and the Place de la Concorde. The facade and the interior have been brought back to their original elegance, reflecting the talents of the well known designer, Gerard Gallet. The salons are decorated in muted colours creating an ambience of tranquillity away from the busy world outside. Stone fireplaces, Louis XVI pieces, lovely paintings on the walls, comfortable chairs, discreet lighting and big bowls of flowers add to the pleasure of staying in this elite hotel. The sound-proofed bedrooms are equally delightful, with white bedspreads and softly coloured linen drapes. Thoughtful planning is evident in the furnishings and accessories and the marble bathrooms have amusing windows opening onto the bedroom to catch daylight. Only breakfast is served in the restaurant but the area abounds with bars, cafés and a wide choice of excellent places to dine. Guests enjoy wandering past famous boutiques and couture houses, exploring the Louvre, or heading for the Tuileries Gardens. **Directions:** Rue de l'Arcade is just off the Place de la Madeleine and cars can be parked opposite by prior arrangement. Price guide: Single FF790–890; double/twin FF980; duplex (apartment) FF1170.

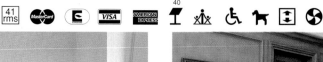

HÔTEL DE CRILLON

10, PLACE DE LA CONCORDE, 75008 PARIS, FRANCE
TEL: +33 1 44 71 15 00 FAX: +33 1 44 71 15 02

Built during the reign of Louis XV, the Hôtel de Crillon was one of two magnificent buildings designed by the famous architect Jacques-Ange Gabriel on the north side of the Place de la Concorde, one of the most beautiful squares in the world. This prestigious hotel enjoys a premier location and has attracted a distinguished list of guests including statesmen, royalty and many of the world's élite dating back to 1909. The interior has remained quintessentially French, elegant and sophisticated. Parquet floors, Aubusson carpets, harmonious grey and gold colour schemes, magnificent tapestries, Louis XV furniture, terraces with Corinthian columns all contribute to the unique ambience of the Crillon. The luxurious bedrooms are sumptuously decorated with exquisite silks and furnished with antiques. All have opulent marble bathrooms. Tea is taken in the delightful Jardin d'Hiver, and the striking bar stocks 80 different whiskies. The original ballroom is now the legendary restaurant Les Ambassadeurs overlooking the square. An inspired chef creates imaginative dishes based on traditional recipes, the sommelier presents an extensive wine list. L'Obélisque serves lighter meals. There is no better place from which to explore Paris, whether to visit the exclusive boutiques nearby or cross the Seine to the Latin Quarter. **Directions:** The Champs-Élysées leads to the hotel. Price guide: Single FF2950; double/twin FF3500–3750; suites from FF4950.

HÔTEL DU LOUVRE

PLACE ANDRÉ MALRAUX, 75001 PARIS, FRANCE
TEL: +33 1 4458 3838 FAX: +33 1 44 58 3801

This deluxe hotel, set in the heart of Paris, facing the Opéra, is renowned for its excellent service and enthusiastic staff. The Hôtel du Louvre has been carefully renovated and the result is a luxurious property which exudes Parisian charm. The building is a fine example of the Belle Epoque architecture and the interior displays elegant décor and rich furnishings. Beautifully appointed, the 195 bedrooms are wonderfully varied, offering a fusion of soft fabrics and modern amenities. Traditional French cuisine comprising delicacies such as pan fried foie gras and filet of cod with chorizo may be savoured in the congenial Brasserie du Louvre. There is also a range of set menus available, to suit all occasions. The extensive wine list has been carefully chosen to accompany the fine cuisine. A conference centre, business centre and the intimate piano-bar are ideal for those organising meetings and seminars. All Johansens readers will be offered a room upgrade, subject to availability. The Musée de Louvre, Ile de la Cité, the Comédie Française and the Tuileries gardens are all located nearby. Paris offers a plethora of exquisite boutiques, many of which are situated in the Place Vendôme and the Faubourg Saint-Honoré. **Directions:** The hotel is situated in the centre of Paris, right next to the Place André Malraux. Price guide: Double/twin FF1850–2500; suites FF3000.

140

 # HÔTEL LE SAINT-GRÉGOIRE

43 RUE DE L'ABBÉ GRÉGOIRE, 75006 PARIS, FRANCE
TEL: +33 1 45 48 23 23 FAX: +33 1 45 48 33 95

This 18th century hotel, set in the heart of the Rive Gauche, offers its guests elegance and refinement in a peaceful environment. Overlooking the interior garden, the intimate lobby is enhanced by the fire which burns during the winter. There are twenty individually decorated bedrooms with period furniture, terrace and private garden. Adorned with paintings and antiques, the rooms offer every modern amenity. Guests are welcome to dine in the vaulted stonewall cellar where an imaginative breakfast menu is served by the enthusiastic staff. Just a few steps away, the hotel's Bistro-style restaurant, La Marlotte, enjoys the convivial atmosphere of the Rive Gauche.

The daily changing menu comprises traditional French cuisine and many of the chef's creations, such as the excellent foie gras terrine, are well-renowned. The area of Saint-Germain offers a plethora of boutiques and department stores. Art enthusiasts will be delighted with the large variety of nearby museums, galleries, antique dealers and bookshops. Underground car parking is available on request. **Directions:** The hotel is very close to La Rue du Bac, next to Rue de Vaugirard and Boulevard Raspail. Price guide: Single FF790; double/twin FF990; suites FF1390. Breakfast FF60.

HÔTEL LE TOURVILLE

16 AVENUE DE TOURVILLE, 75007 PARIS, FRANCE
TEL: +33 1 47 05 62 62 FAX: +33 1 47 05 43 90

Set in the heart of Paris, the Hôtel de Tourville is a magnificent example of neo-classical architecture. The peaceful ambience of the Rive Gauche and its beautiful avenues engulfs the hotel, creating an air of tranquillity. The fusion of soft pastel colours in the lobby evokes a warm atmosphere which is present throughout the house. Old paintings and ancient period features have been carefully selected to complement the furnishings. The thirty rooms, decorated in pale shades of yellow or pink, display antiques bought from flea markets. The marble bathrooms are both delicate and opulent and contain a large range of toiletries. Fine breakfasts are served in the beautiful vaulted cellar room.

Guests may savour the delicious and tempting cuisine served in several highly commended restaurants within the Quartier. This is a good base for those wishing to explore Paris. Many famous attractions are clustered around the hotel such as Les Invalides, the Rodin museum and the Eiffel Tower. Admirers of haute couture will be interested in the well-renowned fashion houses and exclusive boutiques. A paying car park is located close by. **Directions:** Follow the signs to Les Invalides or École Militaire. The hotel is located between the Dôme of Les Invalides and the gardens of the Rodin museum. Price guide: Double/twin FF590–1390; suites FF1990.

HÔTEL SQUARE

3 RUE DE BOULAINVILLIERS, 75016 PARIS, FRANCE
TEL: +33 1 44 14 91 90 FAX: +33 1 44 14 91 99

Situated on the right bank of the river Seine, the Hôtel Square comprises of twenty two stylish bedrooms offering all the latest conveniences. From many of the bedrooms, guests may admire the magnificent view of Paris in all it's splendour and delight in the various amenities, which include cable television, direct line telephone and fax and a mini-bar. The opulent bathrooms, complete with marble décor, are both elegant and spacious. Zebra Square, the café-restaurant renowned for its avant-garde look, serves a host of adventurous dishes alongside some classic French cuisine. The succinct wine list includes the light red Saumar Champigny and the Château de Tigné, a speciality from Anjou.

The downstairs Lounge Bar, with its tranquil atmosphere, is perfect for relaxing and indulging in a quiet drink. The venue is complemented by an art gallery and reading and meeting rooms. Guests are given private access to the nearby fitness centre which has a swimming pool, a sauna, gymnasium and various other health facilities. Nearby attractions include the glorious Eiffel Tower and the Champs Elysées. Guests may stroll in the splendid Jardin des Tuileries or enjoy the numerous art galleries and museums such as the Musée d'Orsay. **Directions:** Rue Boulainvilliers is next to La Maison de la Radio. Price guide: Standard FF1400, superior FF1600–1800; deluxe rooms FF2100; suites FF2300–2600.

HÔTEL WESTMINSTER

13, RUE DE LA PAIX, 75002 PARIS, FRANCE
TEL: +33 1 4261 5746 FAX: +33 1 4260 3066 US TOLL FREE: 1 800 203 3232

Once a convent, this historic building became a coaching house when Baron Haussmann redesigned Paris with its wonderful boulevards in the 1840s. The hotel, celebrating its 150th anniversary, is named after the Duke of Westminster who often stayed there. In a select part of Paris between the Place Vendôme and the Opéra, its architecture is baroque, its style impeccable. The marble lobby is spectacular, with its antiques, massive flower arrangements and glittering chandeliers. It is a popular rendezvous, with thoughtful seating arrangements. The delightful bedrooms, smart suites and sumptuous bathrooms all reflect renovations recommended by an accomplished French interior designer, including double glazing to eliminate street noise. The barman of "Les Chenets" piano bar mixes some exotic cocktails! A Michelin star has been awarded to Le Céladon restaurant, an elegant setting for the chef's magnificent dishes. Superb wines are listed. The Westminster is in walking distance of the Louvre, the Tuileries Gardens, the Champs Élysées and other historic landmarks. Discerning shoppers will enjoy the exclusive boutiques and jewellers in the nearby Rue du Faubourg Saint-Honoré. Owned by Warwick International Hotels. **Directions:** From Place de la Madeleine, drive up Boulevard des Capucines, finding Rue de la Paix on the right. Valet parking. Price guide: Single FF2300; double/twin FF2600; suites FF4300–9000.

L'HÔTEL

13, RUE DES BEAUX ARTS, 75006 PARIS, FRANCE
TEL: +33 1 44 41 99 00 FAX: +33 1 43 25 64 81

This fascinating Parisian hotel, set in the heart of St Germain-des-Prés, is the essence of opulence. A superb tower dominates the interior of this property, with the bedrooms spiralling off on each level. The 27 en suite rooms are delightfully individual and display original antiques and plush furnishings. Rich red fabric and velvet wall prints cover Room 16, the bedroom in which Oscar Wilde died, whilst framed notes and letters by the writer and portraits by artists adorn the walls. Some rooms have a balcony with a patio table for alfresco dining, others overlook the beautiful St Germain-des-Prés church and all offer exquisite marble bathrooms. Downstairs, the intimate reading room, with its beautifully upholstered chairs and antique chandeliers, displays a fine array of books. Although the hotel has no restaurant, an excellent menu is offered for room service including delicious continental breakfasts and traditional soups. The convivial bar, with its interesting "architectural" ceiling, has a vibrant atmosphere. The area is predominantly literary and artistic as the prestigious École des Beaux Arts and many antique dealers are located nearby. The Louvre, Musée d'Orsay and many other attractions are all within easy reach. **Directions:** The nearest metro station is St Germain-des-Prés. The hotel is located on Rue des Beaux Arts, just off the Rue Bonaparte, the road on which the École des Beaux Arts lies. Price guide: Double/twin FF700–2400; suites FF1800–3600.

 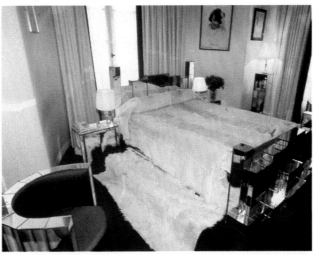

FRANCE (Paris)

L'Hôtel Pergolèse

3 RUE PERGOLÈSE, 75116 PARIS, FRANCE
TEL: +33 1 53 64 04 04 FAX: +33 1 53 64 04 40 E-MAIL: pergolese@wanadoo.fr

The vibrant L'Hôtel Pergolèse is close to the Étoile and the Champs-Élysées. The hotel, a 19th century bourgeois town house, has a subdued exterior but the interior is very chic, for it has been designed throughout by the brilliant futuristic Rena Dumas. Light, warmth and colour make an instant impact on new arrivals: parquet floor, stylish leather chairs, gorgeous rugs and inspired use of the five house colours – blue, golden yellow, apricot, deep red and garden green – create a charismatic ambience. The bedrooms have old fashioned comfort and exciting contemporary furnishings in restful, interesting colour co-ordinations. The television and bar are secreted in a unique mahogany 'tower'. Soundproofing

eliminates street sounds. By contrast the bathrooms are sparkling white: marble, glass and chrome, with amusing stainless steel basins. Breakfast and drinks are served in the foyer, curved glass walls opening onto the plant-filled courtyard. The Pergolèse has no restaurant but all Paris is on the doorstep, offering a choice of informal bistros and smart restaurants. Guests enjoy the proximity of exclusive boutiques and historical buildings, stroll through the Bois de Boulogne and later enjoy the city's fascinating night-life. **Directions:** No 1 line from La Défense, close to the Porte Maillot terminal. Parking nearby. Price guide: Single FF1150–1300; double/twin FF1300–1500; deluxe FF1600–1800.

148

LE RELAIS SAINT-GERMAIN

9 CARREFOUR DE L'ODÉON, 75006 PARIS, FRANCE
TEL: +33 1 43 29 12 05 FAX: +33 1 46 33 45 30

Le Relais Saint-Germain is an attractive small hotel in the heart of the Left Bank area, famous for its culture and association with the arts. Restoration has not detracted from the charm of this 17th century town house, where old and new have been carefully blended – warm tiled floors, handsome oil paintings and beautiful antiques unexpectedly harmonising easily with modern cupboards, mirrors and a fax machine. The character of this hotel is evident in that the bedrooms are named after famous French authors. They also have superb period furniture and enchanting chintz curtains and all still have their original beamed ceilings. They are peaceful and cool, being soundproofed and air-conditioned. The bathrooms are luxurious, all in marble. A delicious breakfast is served and there is an efficient room service available. The hotel wine bar has an excellent selection of French wines. This lively part of Paris offers a choice of restaurants and cafés where guests can mingle with artists, poets, musicians and the cognoscenti. The Relais Saint-Germain is within walking distance of the Louvre, Orsay and Notre-Dame Cathedral, the sophisticated boutiques and the Pompidou Centre. **Directions:** The hotel is just off Boulevard Saint Germain, close to Métro Odéon. Three public car parks are nearby. Price guide: Single FF1290; double/twin FF1550–1750; suites FF2000.

MANOIR DU VAUMADEUC

22130 PLEVEN, FRANCE
TEL: +33 2 96 84 46 17 FAX: +33 2 96 84 40 16

The magnificent Hunaudaye forest encompasses a 15th century manor house, offering a delightful combination of an authentic medieval environment with the very best of modern conveniences. Upon arrival, guests are greeted by the friendly host who has created a warm and homely atmosphere throughout the Manoir du Vaumadeuc. Sculpted beams, ornate fireplaces and wooden floors add character to the public rooms. An imposing granite staircase leads up to the individually decorated bedrooms, each of which is en suite and offers a wide array of amenities. At mealtimes, typically French flavours may be sampled and are complemented by a fine selection of wines. The restaurant is only open during the summer months but an extensive choice of traditional dishes is available on request throughout the year. Enchanting tales of the Manoir are told after dinner and range from the historical visit of Duchess Ann of Brittany to the delightful presence of fairies and elves in the surrounding landscape. Popular excursions include visits to le Château de la Hunaudaye, Mont-Saint-Michel and the interesting towns of St-Malo, Dinan and Moncontour. **Directions:** From St-Malo take the N168 to Plancoët, then Lamballe. Two kilometres after Lamballe, turn left towards Pleven. The hotel is located right at the other end of Pleven. Price guide: Double/twin FF590–1050.

Prima Hotels

GRAND HOTEL VISTA PALACE

ROUTE DE LA GRANDE CORNICHE, 06190 ROQUEBRUNE/CAP MARTIN, FRANCE
TEL: +33 4 92 10 40 00 FAX: +33 4 93 35 18 94

This ultra-modern hotel, having been built into the rocks high above Monaco, commands spectacular views of Monte Carlo, its harbour and Cap Martin. Exotic gardens and terraces are interspersed with blue swimming pools and colourful sunshades. Indoors, contemporary furnishings offer efficient, relaxed modern comfort. The well-equipped bedrooms all have sea views while four of the suites have private swimming pools. Most rooms are in the main building, but a few are in the excellent conference complex which is connected to the hotel. The Presidential Suite is a true paradise, a superb penthouse high up in the sky! Breakfast and lunch are often taken on the terraces. At night guests enjoy cocktails in the spacious Lounge Icare which shares panoramic views of the lights of Monte Carlo and the waterfront with the fabulous Vistaero Restaurant and with La Corniche, famous for its Mediterranean specialities. The wine list is huge and includes a good selection of Provençal rosés. Historical tours of the Eze region can be arranged, while other visitors explore the town, or workout in the hotel's Fitness Centre. After dinner, the Casino of Monte Carlo is the major attraction. **Directions:** Arrivals use the helipad or leave Motorway A8 at Exit 57 to Turbie, following signs to Roquebrune then the Grand Hotel Vista Palace. Price guide: Single IT1050–1800; double/twin FF1700–2700; suites FF3000–7000.

 Prima Hotels

MAS d'ARTIGNY

ROUTE DE LA COLLE, 06570 SAINT-PAUL, FRANCE
TEL: +33 4 93 32 84 54 FAX: +33 4 93 32 95 36 E-MAIL: Mas D'artigny@wanadoo.fr

A unique hotel set in the hills high above Antibes with uninterrupted views of the Côte d'Azur, has 25 individual swimming pools and superb conference facilities. The striking white marble entrance immediately alerts arrivals that their stay at Mas d'Artigny will be memorable. The interior is sophisticated, spacious and uncluttered, with wide archways and graceful furniture, while the magnificent pool is the central focus point. The accommodation offered is superb, the bedrooms, all with luxurious bathrooms, have their own balconies, while the apartments lead onto private patios with their own pool. Additionally there are three villas, ideal for families, with their own pools and gardens. Six meeting rooms have state-of-the-art conference equipment. The fabulous dining room extends onto the Terrace, with a glorious outlook right across to the coastline. Guests linger here while studying the delicious regional and classical dishes. Wines are from the reasonable to the sublime. Mas d'Artigny has its own golf practice ground and tennis courts and the beaches are not far away. **Directions:** Leave A8 at Cagnes-sur-Mer exit taking Route de Grasse, turning left after La Colle sur Loup, before reaching St-Paul-de-Vence on the right. There is a helipad. Price guide: Single FF530–1760; double/twin FF650–1950; suites FF1850–2850.

HÔTEL BYBLOS

AVENUE PAUL SIGNAC, 83990 SAINT-TROPEZ, FRANCE
TEL: +33 4 94 56 68 00 FAX: +33 4 94 56 68 01 E-MAIL: saint-tropez@byblos.com

This unique hotel recently renovated, with its élite clientele, has the ambience of a Provençal village – it is a succession of delightful houses interlinked with flower filled small courtyards, the air scented by the lavender and olive trees. It is just a few minutes from the famous beaches of St. Tropez, close to the fascinating small port. The salons are cool and elegantly decorated. The bedrooms and suites are luxurious, each individually styled with Provençal prints much in evidence. Many of the opulent bathrooms have their own Jacuzzi. Breakfast is served in the proximity of the pool. The gourmet restaurant "Le Byblos" is presided over by the new chef, Georges Pelissier who comes from

the Michelin-starred l'Oasis at La Napoule. His menu is a sophisticated rendition of Mediterranean cuisine with a creative touch. The bistro 'Le Relais des Caves' is open until late at night. The new lounge bar overlooks the pool and Mediterranean with piano player at night. A complete fitness centre with sauna, hammam, massage and body care is available. Golf and tennis are nearby. 'Les Caves du Roy' is the vibrant and famous discotheque of Saint-Tropez. L'Annonciade's Museum exhibiting famous artists' work, the exclusive boutiques and local market should all be visited. **Directions:** A8, then N.98. Price guide: Single FF1150–1860; double/twin FF1500–3260; suites FF2800–9000.

HÔTEL SUBE

15 QUAI SUFFREN, 83990 SAINT-TROPEZ, FRANCE
TEL: +33 4 94 97 30 04 FAX: +33 4 94 54 89 08

Many people are unaware that St Tropez is not just a 20th century beach resort for beautiful people, and they are delighted to discover its fascinating old port, filled with graceful yachts mingling with the fishing fleet. Overlooking the activity of the waterfront there is a small, bright hotel – the Hotel Sube. A warm welcome awaits guests, who instantly appreciate the appropriate nautical ambience – models and paintings of old sailing ships in the reception area – and the small balcony facing the marina is the perfect place to have a cool drink while absorbing the colourful atmosphere. The bedrooms are charming and some have a balcony or terrace – at the back they open out onto a attractive patio, shaded by olive trees, scenting the air. Breakfast is croissants in the sun, watching the multi-national flags on the tall masted boats. In the evening the English bar is a popular rendezvous for both visitors and locals. There is no restaurant but an endless choice of bistros and restaurants to explore nearby. Swim in the sea, go fishing or drive inland to the Provencal wine caves and the perfumeries at Grasse. **Directions:** A8/A7 Le Muy exit, signed St Tropez. Reaching the centre, follow signs to the port, finding the hotel on the quay. Price guide: Single from FF390; double/twin FF590–1200; suites FF990–1500.

HÔTEL VILLA BELROSE

BOULEVARD DES CRÊTES, LA GRANDE BASTIDE, 83580 GASSIN, FRANCE
TEL: +33 4 94 55 97 97 FAX: +33 4 94 55 97 98

An elite hotel standing in a large estate in Gassin, a quiet part of the Cap de St Tropez, where the inspired architect created a Provencal palace with echoes of California, built into the hillside. The Villa has grand sweeping steps leading up to the terrace, from which visitors have spectacular views of the Riviera coastline. The hotel is immaculate and the staff impeccable. The cool salons are the epitome of elegance. Every guest room has a private balcony, and all are exquisite, very light, with classical furnishings and wonderful flowery fabrics. The lavish marble bathrooms have been thoughtfully equipped. The Belrose has been designed for alfresco living, with its many large terraces, one outside the bar, where exotic cocktails and champagne vie with fine old Cognacs and Armagnacs. The sophisticated restaurant also extends outside. The menu is Mediterranean, the cellar holds the best French wines. Residents relax by the enormous pool. Tennis and golf are nearby and the hotel hires out small mopeds or scooters for trips to the beach or into St Tropez, which has good shopping and a colourful nightlife. Other attractions are local vineyards and markets. **Directions:** From A8, exit Le Muy, D25 toward St Maxime then N98 and D98A and 1km before reaching St Tropez enter "le domaine de Sinopolis" on the right and follow the signs Villa Belrose. Excellent parking. Price guide: Single FF1250–2700; double/twin FF1900–3750; suites FF5750–12,000.

FRANCE (Saint-Tropez)

RÉSIDENCE DE LA PINÈDE

PLAGE DE LA BOUILLABAISSE, 83990 SAINT-TROPEZ, FRANCE
TEL: +33 4 94 55 91 00 FAX: +33 4 94 97 73 64

Basking in the glorious Mediterranean sunshine, this de luxe hotel is set on the edge of the waterfront in the glamorous Gulf of Saint-Tropez. Following an extensive renovation by the dedicated owners, the splendour of the hotel is evident in the charming public rooms featuring cosy fires, fine paintings, plush fabrics and other touches of opulence . The spacious bedrooms, most of which afford a panoramic vista across the sea, are beautifully appointed with luxurious furnishings and every modern comfort. Gastronomes will be delighted with the sumptuous dishes created with delicate Provençal flavours, in the elegant restaurant, awarded a Michelin star. Guests frolic in the beautiful outdoor pool, laze on the sunny terraces or on the private beach, hire boats from the hotel and practise water sports. Hours may be passed watching the local village "boulistes" engrossed in their sport and enjoying the relaxed atmosphere which envelopes the South of France. Celebrity-spotting is a keen pastime for many visitors to Saint-Tropez hoping to catch a glimpse of stars such as Brigitte Bardot, Clint Eastwood and Tom Cruise sauntering from their residences on the famed 'Place des Lices'. The majestic Port Grimaud with its fine marina must be discovered. **Directions:** Leave the A8 at the Le Muy exit and then follow the N98. The hotel is situated on the left, 50 metres after the lights at the entrance of Saint-Tropez. Price guide: double/twin FF770–3900; suites FF2520–7300.

CHÂTEAU DES ALPILLES

ROUTE DÉPARTEMENTALE 31, ANCIENNE ROUTE DU GRÈS, 13210 SAINT RÉMY DE PROVENCE, FRANCE
TEL: +33 4 90 92 03 33 FAX: +33 4 90 92 45 17 E-MAIL: chateau.alpilles@wanadoo.fr

This very elegant 19th century château, just a short distance from St. Rémy, is wonderfully secluded. Rare old trees provide avenues, shade and add a touch of the exotic to the verdant surroundings. There are two other buildings, the original 'Mas', now known as 'la ferme', rebuilt to provide modern suites and apartments and the original 'Chapelle', now available to guests as a lovely private villa. The salons in the château reflect its age-old grandeur, with moulded ceilings, mosaic floors, tapestries on the walls, enormous gilded mirrors, antique furniture and rich festooned curtains. Some of the bedrooms repeat this splendour, others are more contemporary with pretty Provençal fabrics. All are air-conditioned. Rooms equipped for seminars are also available. Guests mingle in the intimate bar and those not dining out can enjoy simple regional dishes in the dining area adjoining the reception lounge. Exploring the countryside on foot or on bicycles is a popular pastime, going down the "Old Sandstone Road" to Les Baux. Others stay close to the Château, lazing in the cool gardens, playing tennis or sunbathing by the swimming pool. **Directions:** Leave St. Rémy on the D31 towards Tarascon. Price guide: Single FF900; double/twin FF980–1130; suites FF1320–1690; chapelle FF1490–2000.

DOMAINE DE ROCHEBOIS

ROUTE DU CHATEAU DE MONTFORT, 24200 VITRAC, FRANCE
TEL: +33 5 53 31 52 52 FAX: +33 5 53 29 36 88 E-MAIL: info@rochebois.com

In the heart of the Dordogne and Perigord Noir countryside sits an elegant 19th century residence – Domaine de Rochebois. This is now a superb golfing hotel, offering the highest standards of comfort and luxury throughout. A distinctly English influence can be discerned in the decoration and furnishings of the bedrooms, while those in the adjacent pavilions have a more Italian style. All feature a full range of modern amenities and a private balcony where guests can relax and enjoy the views. A quiet breakfast in the cool of the morning can be enjoyed on the terrace, which is close to the swimming pool. In the evening, a gourmet dinner can be served here – enhanced by spectacular sunsets over the valley – or in the lovely restaurant. Guests are invited to take advantage of the 9-hole golf course or enjoy the beautiful landscape, running along the banks of the Dordogne river and over the hills covered with evergreen oaks. The area offers a host of leisure activities, including walking, hot-air ballooning, canoeing on the Dordogne river or exploring the medieval towns of Sarlat and La Roque Gageac. **Directions**: From Bordeaux take N89 to Libourne. D936 to Bergerac and follow signs to Sarlat. After Beynac follow road to La Roque Gageac and then Vitrac. Price guide: Double/twin FF750–1650; Suite FF1500–1850.

CHÂTEAU DE COUDRÉE

DOMAINE DE COUDRÉE, BONNATRAIT, 74140 SCIEZ-SUR-LÉMAN, FRANCE
TEL: +33 4 50 72 62 33 FAX: +33 4 50 72 57 28

Those seeking an idyllic summer holiday on the edge of Lake Geneva should stay at this enchanting 12th century château, with its fairy-tale turrets and pinnacles, surrounded by a vast private estate. The gardens are immaculate. This is an elite hotel, with just nineteen guest rooms, all furnished with fine antiques, beautifully decorated with the drapes in lovely fabrics. The smart bathrooms are well designed. Some bedrooms are in the oldest parts of the château. Guests to fall asleep lulled by the lapping of the water against the shore. Exquisite salons, an inviting bar and big terrace overlooking the pool and gardens down to the water's edge add to guests' pleasure. Dining is a memorable gastronomic experience – classic dishes presented with great flair, using the best local ingredients, in a superb setting, with immaculate linen, candles, gleaming silver and sparkling crystal. The wines are magnificent. There is also a handsome banqueting hall and the Château has several well-equipped meeting rooms. Residents relax by the pool, enjoy the private beach on Lake Geneva, play tennis in the grounds. Golf and riding are nearby and there is a casino at Evian. **Directions:** From Paris A40, exit Annemasse/Thonon/Evian then follow signs to Sciez Bonnatrait. Price guide: Single from FF680; double/twin from FF780–1480; apartments for families from FF1280–1980.

L'AUBERGE DU CHOUCAS

05220 MONETIER-LES-BAINS, SERRE-CHEVALIER, HAUTES-ALPES, FRANCE
TEL: +33 4 92 24 42 73 FAX: +33 4 92 24 51 60

In the centre of an enchanting Alpine village, next to the XVth century church with its fine steeple, there is a small hotel, L'Auberge du Choucas. This lovely old building is characteristic of the region with a pretty garden in front. The ambience is marvellous, created by the friendly greeting, big log fires in the winter and the aroma of good living – herbs, flowers, wines and cooking. The bedrooms are cosy, many with balconies, light and airy, with attractive oak furniture in alpine style. After a long day's skiing, the dining room is a delight, reflecting the age of the Auberge, with its vaulted archways and walls in the original stone, its tiled floor, candlelight and sparkling crystal. Exquisite creative specialities of the house are served and enjoyed with wines chosen from among the best in France. There is magnificent skiing close by at Serre-Chevalier, a famous winter sports resort (400m from the Auberge). In summer Monêtier-les-Bains is a joy for walkers who appreciate the old stones, the wild flowers and the superb mountain air. Athletic climbers tackle the peaks. A day spent in Briançon (14 km from the Hotel) would be fascinating: a historic old town with 17th century fortifications. **Directions:** Leave Grenoble on the N91 towards Briançon, reaching Monêtier-les-Bains shortly after the Lautaret pass. Hotel is behind the church. Price guide: Single FF500–600; double/twin FF700; suites FF1080–1180 (for 2 people).

HÔTEL REGENT PETITE FRANCE

5, RUE DES MOULINS, 67000 STRASBOURG, FRANCE
TEL: +33 3 88 76 43 43 FAX: +33 3 88 76 43 76

Strasbourg is a fascinating city with its waterways and the Regent has a prime position on the banks of the River Ill in the intriguing Petite France, part of the Old Town. Close to one of the splendid bridges, the façade of this élite hotel is traditional, three centuries old houses joined together, but going through the doors is to step into another era, for the interior is late twentieth century, designed for the Millennium. The brilliantly lit reception hall's seating is a pastiche of colour and vivid contemporary paintings fill the walls. The bedrooms are relaxing, the furnishings extremely modern and comfortable. The views over the canals and Old Town are spectacular. High technology has been discreetly installed and many luxurious extras are provided. The Bar des Glacières is ritzy and amusing. The Coffee Shop is ideal for those wanting light meals and the Pont Tournant Restaurant has a unique elegance. Fabulous regional specialities are on the menu and some wonderful Alsace wines are listed. The hotel also has state-of-the-art conference facilities. Reflecting its industrial past, the Regent has created a Museum of Ice-Making. Boat trips down the canals are entertaining. Sporting guests will find golf and tennis nearby. **Directions:** Leave A35 at Porte Blanche exit, following signs to the town centre. Valet parking. Price guide. Double/twin FF1090–1490; suites FF1850–2300.

Germany

MÖNCHS POSTHOTEL

76328 BAD HERRENALB, GERMANY
TEL: +49 70 83 74 40 FAX: +49 70 83 74 41 22

Bad Herrenalb is an attractive small town in the Black Forest, and the Posthotel, with its traditional half-timbered façade enlivened by green and white shutters, has extensive shady parkland at the back, much appreciated by guests in hot weather. The interior is beautifully decorated in harmony with the wooden beams that remain from the original building, flowers and plants in every corner, fine paintings and lovely antiques completing the picture. The bedrooms and suites have delightful colour schemes, comfortable furniture and opulent bathrooms. The intimate piano bar is an elegant meeting place. The two restaurants are very different – the sophisticated Klosterschänke has fine panelled walls, a reputation for superb cooking and an extensive selection of Bordeaux and Italian wines. The Locanda specialises in Mediterranean dishes, including a variety of pastas. A smart meeting room, with full presentation equipment, is available for seminars. Guests enjoy strolling in the park and relaxing by the heated swimming pool. They can play tennis and golf, walk in the Black Forest and ski in winter. Baden Baden, half an hour away, is full of history. Its casino is a famous inheritance from the 19th century. **Directions:** On the A5 from Basel exit at Rastatt, following signs to Gernsbach or from Frankfurt exit for Bad Herrenalb. Price guide: Single DM180 195; double/twin DM270–360; suites DM470–520.

ROMANTIK HOTEL GOLDENE TRAUBE

AM VIKTORIABRUNNEN 2, 96450 COBURG, GERMANY
TEL: +49 9561 8760 FAX: +49 9561 876222 E-MAIL: romantikhotel.goldenetraube@–online.de

Situated in the very centre of town, the Romantik Hotel is an ideal haven for guests who enjoy strolling through busy, old streets to soak up local atmosphere or wander through the countryside seeking out places of historical interest. Veste Coburg, a castle dating from the Middles Ages, is a favourite with visitors, as is Schloss Rosenau, in Rödental, where Queen Victoria's husband, Prince Albert, was born. Queen Victoria was also a visitor to nearby Schloss Ehrenburgh. The interior of the hotel reflects its past and modernisation does not intrude into its interior. The 70 bedrooms are spread throughout three buildings connected to the main house. Some have been recently renovated. They are all en suite with bright and cheerful lacquered furniture and Laura Ashley-style furnishings. A small, inviting bar opens onto a roadside terrace where guests can relax and watch the street life as it goes by. There is a small, comfortable wine bar in the rear courtyard which also serves light meals. Tasty, traditional dishes are served in the quiet restaurant, where the orange and yellow décor is refreshingly bright. **Directions:** Leave E48 at Bamberg and join B4 to Coburg. Follow the signs to Parkhaus Maure in the centre of the town. The hotel is directly opposite. Price guide: Single DM120–160; double/twin DM170–230.

DESIGN HOTELS

HOTEL CRISTALL

URSULAPLATZ 9–11, 50668 COLOGNE, GERMANY
TEL: +49 221 16300 FAX: +49 221 1630 333

In the centre of Cologne, and very convenient for the convention centre, is the Hotel Cristall, a fin-de-siècle Art Deco building which has moved into the 20th century. The decor of this 'design' hotel is stunning – minimalist geometric lines, strong contrasting colours, unique light patterns. The bedrooms continue the same theme, simplistic and pristine, uncluttered and with surprising touches that add warmth to the austere yet striking furnishings. The bathrooms are contemporary, and very efficient, showers taking preference to baths. Some bedrooms are designated non-smoking. The bar is very trendy, with sculptured green leather chairs, the chrome and marble fittings a curious blend of nostalgia for the Art Nouveau era and moving towards the Millennium. While The Cristall has an excellent coffee shop, it does not have a restaurant – however the concierge will recommend good restaurants in the locality. The hotel exhibits modern art – outside there is the magnificent cathedral, fascinating museums and galleries showing fine collections of paintings. Theatres, opera and river trips to see the Rhine castles will please traditionalists, younger visitors will probably prefer pop art and the city's vibrant night life. **Directions:** On reaching Cologne, follow signs to the Cathedral and city centre. The hotel is adjacent to the railway station. Price guide: Single DM190–270; double/twin DM250–390.

GERMANY (Garmisch Partenkirchen)

REINDL'S PARTENKIRCHNER HOF

BAHNHOFSTRASSE, 15, GARMISCH PARTENKIRCHEN, GERMANY
TEL: +49 88 21 58025 FAX: +49 88 21 73401

Garmisch Partenkirchen, where the Winter Olympics have been held, is a small town standing at the foot of the Zugspitze mountain surrounded by verdant pine forests. The hotel is an attractive building, with flower-bedecked wooden balconies along all sides. Inside there is a feeling of spaciousness, warmth and comfort – the furnishings are traditional. The bedrooms and apartments are delightful, and most have sunny balconies. Not all are in the main building, but close by in the Haus Alpspitz and Haus Wetterstein which are more contemporary without losing their regional charm. The bar is the perfect rendezvous, whether for aperitifs before or for digestifs after a memorable meal in the handsome Reindl's Gourmet-Restaurant accompanied by the finest wines. There are also an elegant banqueting room and conference facilities. There are no shortage of activities – some may prefer to relax in the large pool and sauna while others may exercise in the gym. Outside in winter ski-ing predominates but in summer there is tennis and magnificent countryside to explore – perhaps in the hotel's horse-drawn carriage. At night the casino is a popular venue. Directions: Entering Partenkirchen, turn right at the main crossroads heading towards station. Hotel is 100m down the road on the left. Price guide: Single DM135–160, double/twin DM160– 200; suites DM280–400.

HOTEL KÖNIGSHOF

KARLSPLATZ, 25, 80335 MUNICH, GERMANY
TEL: +49 89 551 360 FAX: +49 89 5513 6113

One of the most prestigious hotels in Munich, in the centre of the city, overlooking the spectacular fountain in the Stachus plaza, the Königshof is ideal for business people or those exploring the metropolis. This is a modern grand hotel, reflecting the talents of skilled interior decorators. The salons are spacious and the piano bar is stylish. Beautiful fabrics have been used throughout, especially in the luxurious bedrooms. All the rooms are soundproofed against the noises of the traffic, air-conditioned and provided with many amenities. The bathrooms are opulent. Shoes are cleaned and laundry returned within 8 hours! The Königshof Restaurant has twice won accolades as the best hotel restaurant in Germany. The tables stand well apart – crisp white cloths set with gleaming silver, sparkling crystal and fine porcelain. The menu offers inspired Bavarian dishes prepared by international chefs. The wine list extends worldwide. There are private dining rooms. Days can be filled exploring art galleries, museums and historic buildings. Evenings may be spent at the theatre, opera and concerts or enjoying the city night-life of clubs, discos and casinos. **Directions:** Exit A9 at Schwabing exit, left into Leopoldstrasse, meeting Altstadt ring, turn right continuing on to Karlsplatz. Private garage. Price guide: Single DM355–400; double/twin DM400–550; suites DM600–1200.

SCHLOSSHOTEL OBERSTOTZINGEN

STETTENER STRASSE 35–37, 89168 NIEDERSTOTZINGEN, GERMANY
TEL: +49 7325 1030 FAX: +49 7325 10370

This elegant small castle built in the 17th century, surrounded by private parkland, has been carefully restored and is now known as the exclusive Schlosshotel Oberstotzingen. Guests mounting the steps to enter the baroque front door appreciate the historic ambience and warm welcome. The reception rooms are charming, in restful colour schemes and extremely comfortable, looking out over the peaceful gardens and leading on to the attractive terrace. The bedrooms are enchanting, with pretty fabrics, gilt mirrors and small chandeliers. Several of these are in an adjacent annex. It should be noted that some of the bathrooms only have showers. The bar is convivial and there is also a small beer garden. The sophisticated restaurant has an unusual vaulted ceiling and residents enjoy substantial regional cooking and good local wines are among those listed. Additionally, there is a galleried dining hall for use on special occasions, where concerts are sometimes held. The superb meeting rooms have topical presentation facilities. There is excellent golf nearby and the hotel offers special packages. It has two tennis courts and riding can be organised. There are castles to explore. **Directions:** Leave A7 at junction with A8 towards Gunzburg, after 5 minutes follow sign to Niederstotzingen. Price guide: Double/twin DM290; maisonette DM390.

BURGHOTEL AUF SCHÖNBURG

55430 OBERWESEL/RHEIN, GERMANY
TEL: +49 67 44 93 930 FAX: +49 67 44 16 13

High up on the Schönburg, a hill overlooking the Rhine, close to where the Lorelei used to lure sailors onto the rocks, there is a romantic castle, built in the 10th century. Behind its ramparts and towers is an intimate and élite hotel. Many of the original features, the stone walls and pillars, archways and old beams have been carefully restored so that history and luxurious comfort are both in evidence. Outside, vineyards slope down to the river and ivy clings to the castle walls. The bedrooms are enchanting with fairy tale drapery over the beds, lovely traditional furniture and big bowls of fruit and flowers. The bathrooms are modern and quite opulent. In the evenings, guests gather for a Bellini in the magnificent salon with stone walls, a handsome fireplace, crossed swords and shelves of leather-bound books before dining on specialities of the Middle Rhine Valley or indulging themselves with the gourmet menu. Dinner is served either in the Knights' Dining Room or on the Rhine terrace with its spectacular view of the river. Prestigious wines are listed. This is a marvellous base for exploring this part of Germany. **Directions:** Take the Oberwesel exit off the A61. Once in the town take a right turn at the Schönberg sign and then follow hotel signs up the hill. Price guide: Single DM110–140; double/twin DM255 355; suites DM355–380.

HOTEL EISENHUT

HERRNGASSE 3-7, 91541, ROTHENBURG OB DER TAUBER, GERMANY
TEL: +49 9861 7050 FAX: +49 9861 70545 E-MAIL: hotel@eisenhut.rothenburg.de

Rothenburg is an unspoilt medieval town standing on the River Tauber. It is surrounded by the original city walls and in the centre stands the Hotel Eisenhut, created from three adjacent 14th century town houses. The hotel has a superb portico entrance and inside, gleaming suits of armour, relics of the imperial armies. Jewel coloured rugs on the stone floors, superb antiques, salons with open fireplaces, tapestries, splendid carved statues and handsome chairs add to the historic ambience. The bedrooms are luxurious and spacious with delightful flowered bedcovers and big gilt mirrors adding to their charm. Modern bathrooms provide those extra comforts that all travellers expect today. Delicious cocktails are sipped to soft music in the inviting bar. The sophisticated international menu offers local specialities. The cellar holds fine German wines in addition to Burgundies and Bordeaux. Guests relax in the beer garden or on the terrace overlooking the garden with its streams and colourful plants. Tennis and golf are accessible. Exploring the town is fascinating. **Directions:** Leave the A7 at the Rothenburg exit and reaching the town centre Marktplatz, watch for signs to the hotel. Price guide: Single DM190–230; double/twin DM200–385; suites DM520–640.

PARKHOTEL SCHLANGENBAD

RHEINGAUER STRASSE 47, 65388 SCHLANGENBAD, GERMANY
TEL: +49 61 29 420 FAX: +49 61 29 41 420

Schlangenbad is a village on the outskirts of the Rhine-Taunus Nature Park and the Park Hotel stands in lovely, peaceful countryside. It is a haven for many guests needing revitalisation, and ideal for conferences. The entrance is spacious and impressive, with archways and marble columns. The elegant salon has a long white terrace and below is a large courtyard for alfresco living. The bedrooms are delightful, the curtains and covers in beautiful materials and many lead onto a balcony. In the sophisticated piano bar wonderful cocktails will be concocted by the barman, non-alcoholic drinks for those guests who prefer them. Menus in the glittering Les Therms restaurant are

hedonistic yet health-conscious. Many German wines are listed and occasionally a wine seminar is held, followed by a feast. Conference facilities are magnificent, with a big theatre for presentation. State-of-the-art equipment is available in all rooms in this complex. The hotel has a big pool, a gymnasium where exercise classes are organised and a beauty salon. The energetic ride mountain bikes or follow the jogging trail. Golf, tennis, horse riding and shooting are other sports in the neighbourhood.
Directions: The B260 from Martinsthal leads to Schlangenbad.
Price guide: Single DM185–220; double/twin DM280–350; suites DM370–500.

RR BINSHOF RESORT

BINSHOF 1, 67346 SPEYER, GERMANY
TEL: +49 6232 6470 FAX: +49 6232 647199

This 250 year-old farm estate has been restored and transformed with tremendous care and commitment into an elegant five-star hotel resort with award-winning spa facilities. Although hailed as the Toskana of the Palatine, its wonderful setting in the centre of a nature reserve, surrounded by fields and lakes, still exceeds expectations. The accommodation is luxurious and exquisite taste is shown in the mixture of antiques and modern designer fittings that can be seen throughout the bedrooms, public rooms and restaurants. Particular attention has been paid to the decorating, using only natural and allergy-friendly products. High-tech communications are integrated into every bedroom, as well as superb modern bathrooms. A host of different tastes are catered for in the five restaurants: the finest is considered to be the gourmet food available in "Fresco di Mare". With direct access from the hotel, guests may experience a unique thermal bath and sauna landscape in RR Binshof Therme covering an area of 4500 square metres with 18 different types of baths and saunas in addition to a fitness studio, physical therapy and beauty farm. **Directions**: Exit autobahn A61 at Speyer/B9. Continue towards Ludwigshafen, turn off right at Binshof. After roundabout, follow village sign for Otterstadt, then turn right at signpost to Binshof Resort. Price guide: Single DM220–280; double DM380–450; suites from DM600.

HOTEL SCHLOSS WALDECK

34513 WALDECK, GERMANY
TEL: +49 5623 5890 FAX: +49 5623 589289 E-MAIL: schlosswa@aol.com

This imposing fortified castle, built in the Middle Ages, perches on a rock soaring 120 metres above the man-made lake of Eder. Inside this memorable hotel, the accommodation reflects the comfort and convenience of modern day life, with single and double bedrooms tastefully decorated and furnished in a contemporary style. The suites have a different design and feature lovely antique beds and fittings. Inviting large leather settees in the bar and lounge are set in front of the fireplace – and this is a perfect meeting point for the evening. Situated in the 1,000 year-old clock tower, the gourmet restaurant – Alte Turmuhr – offers spectacular views down to the lake. One section of the hotel is a museum, where talks of witches, torture and bygone days are brought to life – a torch-lit, night-time tour is a must! There is a cable car connection from the castle entrance down to the lake below, which offers opportunities to enjoy every kind of water sport including sailing, swimming, fishing and boat trips. Good golfing is also available nearby and bicycles and horses can be hired for exploring the area. **Directions**: Exit autobahn A7 at Homberg, follow signs to Wabern, Bad Wildungen and then Waldeck. From autobahn A49 exit at Fritzlar, follow signs to Friztlar, Bad Wildungen and Waldeck. Price guide: Single DM 150–200, double/twin DM270–290; suites DM340–370.

HOTEL BURG WASSENBERG

KIRCHSTRASSE 17, 41849 WASSENBERG
TEL: +49 2432 9490 FAX: +49 2432 949100 E-MAIL: burgwassenberg@at-online.de

This delightful small castle, carefully renovated so that modernisation does not intrude into history, is at the top of a little hill, looking down on to the town of Wassenberg, about 20 miles north of Aachen. The interior reflects its past, with coats of armour, mullioned windows, antiques, wrought-iron candelabra and log fires. A sitting room is over the gateway but now there are no invaders to watch for, only new arrivals! These might be delegates coming to use the excellent conference facilities. The bedrooms are delightful, with rustic furniture and modern amenities. There is efficient room service, and one room has easy access for those with mobility problems. This hotel is ideal for guests who appreciate fine food and drink. Exotic cocktails can be prepared before dinner, perhaps enjoyed by the big open fire, before a feast of beautifully presented dishes accompanied by the best wines. In summer barbecues on the balcony are sumptuous. There is a fitness and health centre, and tennis and golf are a short distance away. Crossing the border into Holland is an interesting excursion. **Directions:** Leave the A46 at the Erkelenz-Sud exit, turning left 3 times and yet again in Wassenberg, take the Burgauffahrt im Kreisverkehr, looking for signs to the hotel. Price guide: Single: DM95–245; double/twin DM200–295; suite DM395.

HOTEL BURG WERNBERG

SCHLOSSBERG 10, 92533 WERNBERG – KÖBLITZ, GERMANY
TEL: +49 9604 9390 FAX: +49 9604 939139

A medieval, moated castle overlooking a picturesque little village has been carefully, tastefully and lovingly restored into today's elegant Hotel Burg Wernberg. Guests stepping over the threshold appreciate the historic ambience and warm welcome. The entrance hall, guarded over by a knight's shining armour, sets the tone for the whole building. There are vast gilded mirrors, beautiful pictures, rich fabrics and furnishings. Each of the 30 enchanting bedrooms has been individually designed to make the most of the unusual lay-outs, guided by the authenticity of the period and at the same time incorporating every modern amenity from hi-fi and television to facsimile and modem connections.

The bathrooms are opulent and the wedding suite, with its hand-painted murals and gold hanging drapes, is truly romantic. Residents enjoy excellent gourmet cuisine in the sophisticated restaurant. More regional dishes are served in the Wintergarten, the Burgkeller and at a rustic bar, situated near the drawbridge of the moat which has been transformed into a colourful garden area. Shooting, riding, fishing and mountain bikes can be arranged and there is excellent golf nearby. **Directions**: Leave the A93 at Werberg-Köblitz and follow the road to the castle. Price guide: Single DM110–200; double DM220–280; suites DM410–490.

SCHWEIZER STUBEN

97877 WERTHEIM – BETTINGEN, GERMANY
TEL: +49 93 42 3070 FAX: +49 93 42 307155 E-MAIL: stuben@relaischateaux.fr

This modern hotel complex, beautifully situated in the Main valley, combines old world charm with contemporary architecture. The bedrooms are in four houses, the hotel itself, the villa and the two landhauses. They are extremely spacious and many have balconies. Pine furniture and floral prints provide a light yet warm ambience. The suites are magnificent. There are two important reasons to visit the Schweizer Stuben and food is one of them. It is the home of Fritz Schilling, one of Europe's leading chefs specialising in Provençal cuisine. He also ensures that fine wines are available to accompany not only his own brilliant cooking, but also that of the chefs in the Italian and Swiss restaurants, found in this gastronomic haven. Sport is the other dominant feature of the hotel, especially tennis as there are six outdoor courts, indoor courts and excellent teaching available. There are golf practice facilities, indoor and outdoor pools and a marvellous beauty salon for total relaxation. Visitors explore the lovely countryside on bicycles or enjoy the flower-filled meadows from the hotel's horse-drawn carriage. The river, castles, lakes and local vineyards are alternative focal points. A member of Relais et Chateaux. **Directions:** From Frankfurt, leave A3 at exit "Wertheim-Lengfurt" turning left onto L2310, then right following signs to the Tennis-Hotel. Price guide (per person): Single DM240–400; double/twin DM145–225; apartment DM260; suite DM315–625.

Greece

THESSALONIKI

SAMOTHRAKI

THASOS

ATHOS

Olympus

LIMNOS

VOLOS

LÉSVOS

VORIAI SPORÁDHES

PSARÁ

SKIROS

KITHIRA

KÍRA

PRÉVEZA

KHIOS

SÁMOS

IKARIA

DELFHI

ANDROS

178

TINOS

KEFALLINIA

ATHENS

KEA

MIKONOS

ZÁKINTHOS

KITHOS

KIKLÁDHES

181

SÉRIFOS

NAXOS

SIFNOS

AMORGÓS KOS

RHODES

MILOS

THIRA

KITHIRA

KÁRPATHOS

KÁSOS

CRETE
IRÁKLION

179 180

HOTEL PENTELIKON

66 DILIGIANNI STREET, 14562 ATHENS, GREECE
TEL: +30 1 62 30 650-6 FAX: +30 1 80 10 314

This impressive, discreet small hotel, in a peaceful residential area of Athens, has attracted many elite visitors since it was built in the 1920s. Following extensive renovations in 1987, its fame spread and today its guest list is prestigious, having welcomed politicians, church leaders and entrepreneurs from all parts of the globe. Fine antiques, gleaming silk curtains and immaculate staff contribute to its select ambience. The bedrooms are luxurious all individually decorated in enchanting French fabrics with harmonising wall coverings. The ornate bathrooms have a marble finish and room service is 24 hours. La Terrasse is a delightful dining room where breakfasts and informal meals are served.

Residents sip cocktails in the bar adjacent to the striking 20th century Vardis Restaurant. On warm evenings diners linger at candle-lit tables under the stars. In summer the garden is often floodlit and apéritifs are enjoyed by the Pool Bar. The Grand Ballroom is an ideal venue for corporate entertaining or special functions. Athens has so much to offer – the Acropolis with the Parthenon and its many temples, home of Socrates, Pluto and Aristotle, while the modern city is fascinating with its shops and the bustling Port of Piraeus. **Directions:** The hotel is located in the exclusive suburb of Kifissia and has private parking. Price guide: Single Dr74,000; double/twin Dr88,000; suite Dr110,000.

ELOUNDA BAY PALACE

72053 ELOUNDA, CRETE, GREECE
TEL: +30 841 41502 FAX: +30 841 41783

Crete is an island of legends, and this splendid hotel, its white buildings close to the sparkling blue waters of Mirabello Bay and set against a background of verdant forests, is fast becoming a legend in itself. Guests either stay in the hotel or in bungalows in the extensive gardens. All bedrooms are air-conditioned, have marble bathrooms and gorgeous views. The design and decorations reflect the region – cool tiled floors, colourful fabrics – very inviting! Guests relax in the stylish lounges or on the colourful terraces, watching the shimmering water. Children have their own supervised activities, games rooms and pool. Thirst-quenching drinks are served at the Poseidon poolside bar or the

Aeolous beach bar, and exotic cocktails are shaken in the Erato Piano Bar far into the night. Brilliant buffet breakfasts and lunches are offered in the traditional Aretousa Restaurant, also five-course dinners. The joyous sea-front Ariadne restaurant serves local specialities, has barbecues, fish evenings and Greek nights with folk dancing. The Palace has a private beach, several pools, a water sports centre and floodlit tennis courts A schooner makes expeditions to other islands; Crete has to be explored. Golf can be arranged. Directions: The hotel is 45 minutes drive from the airport outside Heraklion, signed from Aghios Nikolaos. Price guide: Single Dr31,000; double/twin Dr40,000; suites Dr116,000.

ELOUNDA BEACH

72053 ELOUNDA, CRETE, GREECE
TEL: +30 841 41 412/3 FAX: +30 841 41 375

An idyllic modern hotel complex on the North East coast of this beautiful island which is so steeped in history, Elounda Beach is surrounded by its own verdant estate and clear blue water. It is a sophisticated playground, especially for those who enjoy aquatic sports. Apart from the main hotel building, guests can stay in one of the many private villas on the water's edge or the famous bungalow suites with private swimming pool. A variety of restaurants meets every taste – the splendid Artemis restaurant for gourmet meals, the à la carte Restaurant Dionyssos for dinner, the Argonaut Restaurant for light meals and Italian tastes for dinner while the Kafenion offers Cretan specialities. Guests mingle in the piano bar, relax by the pool bar and enjoy the whole day at the unique Veghera bar in the middle of the sea. For early hours entertainment dance in the Olous nightclub. Children have their own activities while their parents enjoy tennis, a fitness centre, mini-golf and the famed water sport centre for Scuba diving, parasailing, water-skiing and sailing. Others may enjoy a leisurely cruise on the hotel schooner, or exploring nearby Aghios Nikolaos and local fishing villages. For a free video tape kindly fax the number above. **Directions**: Elounda Beach is 45 minutes from Heraklion International Airport. Price guide: Single from Dr51,000; double/twin from Dr63,000; suite from Dr120,000.

BRATSERA HOTEL

HYDRA 180 40, GREECE
TEL: +30 298 53971 FAX: +30 298 53626

In the 19th century, the beautiful harbour of Hydra was covered with sponges waiting to be shipped around the world. Today, on the site of a factory which was founded in 1870 and processed the sponges for 116 years, is the Bratsera Hotel. The original building has undergone a careful and extensive restoration and the result is a most charming and opulent small hotel. The 23 individually-designed bedrooms are fine examples of traditional Hydroit architecture, decorated with a fusion of modern and antique tiles. Awash with natural light, the rooms offer heating, air conditioning and every modern amenity. The relaxed atmosphere of the dining room may be enjoyed at all meal times. Guests are invited to sample the chef's delicious creations and choose from an extensive selection of wines. Alternatively, meals can be taken under the wisteria-covered trellises by the swimming pool. Conferences, exhibitions and special events may be held in the Grand Hall, accommodating 100 people. The garden is a delight for horticulturists with bougainvillaea, jacaranda and other floral displays. There is a variety of activities available in the area such as boat trips around the island, donkey rides, visits to the monasteries and walks in and around Hydra. **Directions**: The hotel is two minutes walking distance from the port of Hydra. Price guide: Double/twin Dr20,000–36,000; suites Dr33,000–53,000.

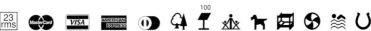

Hungary

DANUBIUS HOTEL GELLÉRT

ST. GELLÉRT TÉR 1, 1111 BUDAPEST, HUNGARY
TEL: +36 1 385 2200 FAX: +36 1 466 6631

Historically this is one of the 'grand' hotels of Europe and with more and more businessmen and travellers coming to Budapest, it is already regaining this accolade. A founder member of Danubius Hotels, The Gellért is in one of the most beautiful parts of the city, the central district in Buda, with the River Danube on one side and a green hill on the other. The style of the interior is art nouveau, with high glass domed ceilings and ornate ironwork. The furnishings are formal, of traditional Central European design. There are many single bedrooms in addition to double rooms and delightful suites, some overlooking the Danube, others Gellért Hill. The hotel has retained its gastronomic reputation, won by the legendary Gundel, offering Hungarian specialities and international dishes, accompanied in the evening by gypsy music. The wines are traditional led by the majestic Tokay, beloved by Louis XIV. The Coffee Shop is famous for its patisseries and ice-creams. Below the hill at the rear of the hotel are the renowned and popular Gellért baths, a variety of warm pools fed by natural springs with age-old healing properties. Budapest prides itself on its architecture, music, night-life, art galleries, its Danube and its beautiful women. **Directions:** Take an expensive taxi or the inexpensive minibus from the airport, or the hydrofoil down the Danube from Vienna. Price guide: Single DM190–250; double/twin DM340–390.

Italy

LE SILVE DI ARMENZANO

06081 LOC. ARMENZANO, ASSISI (PG), ITALY
TEL: +39 075 801 9000 FAX: +39 075 801 9005

This historic small hotel dates back to before the birth of St Francis of Assisi and looking across the beautiful Umbrian countryside, with its deer and horses, one understands how he became the patron saint of animals. Le Silva is 700 metres above sea level, built in local stone on a plateau at the foot of the Subasio mountains. The air is scented by olive groves. The charming bedrooms are pristine with country furniture and there is a choice of bath or shower. The comfortable bar/sitting room looks out over the estate; a pianist plays at weekends. Umbrian cooking is delicious and at Le Silve the bread is baked, traditionally, in the fireplace. Local cheeses are special and wine is from the area. The restaurant is cool and rustic, the ancient beams and walls contributing to its charm. Eating alfresco is encouraged on warm days. The hotel also has four suites in the original farmhouse and the Basaletto, a little further away, has seven interconnecting flats and its own pool. Activities include riding, swimming, tennis, mini-golf and relaxing in the gardens. Excursions can be made to the Basilica of St. Francis in Assisi, Perugia and the wine growers in Orvieto. **Directions:** On reaching Assisi from Perugia, take the S.75, turning right after 12km towards Armenzano. Price guide: Single L140,000–150,000; double/twin L280,000–300,000. Apartment prices on request.

HOTEL BUCANEVE

PIAZZA JUMEAUX 10, 11021 BREUIL-CERVINIA (AO), ITALY
TEL: +39 0166 949119/948386 FAX: +39 0166 948308

Breuil Cervinia is an enchanting village high up in the Alps, at the foot of the awe-inspiring Matterhorn. It is a spectacular setting for this delightful chalet style hotel, be it summer or winter. Hotel Bucaneve has a warm ambience, created by the friendliness of the owners and their staff, open fires and the joyous colourful upholstery of the large, comfortable chairs in the living room. Big bowls of flowers are everywhere. The bedrooms are charming, with traditional furniture, and have gorgeous views over the mountains. Guests usually mingle in the convivial piano bar, but there is a quiet reading room. The rustic dining room is most attractive. Breakfast is a buffet and dinner is fabulous barbecue food, cooked on the open grill followed by luscious homemade puddings. Some superb wines are listed. Cervinia is a sophisticated winter sports resort and the hotel is close to the many ski-lifts and cable cars. After exhilarating days on the pistes, the sauna and Jacuzzi are welcome. In summer guests play golf on the highest 9-hole course in Europe, swim, play tennis and go hiking into the mountains. Afterwards they enjoy the inns, fondues and local night life. **Directions:** Leave A5 motorway at Saint Vincent/Chatillon, It is 25km to Breuil-Cervinia along a winding mountain road. The hotel has a garage and there is also a car-park. Price guide: Double/twin L120,000–180,000; suites L150,000–230,000. Per person half board.

EUROPA PALACE HOTEL

80071 CAPRI (NA), ITALY
TEL: +39 081 8373800 FAX: +39 081 8373191

At the Europa Hotel the art of good living goes hand-in-hand with family tradition and the highest standards of service. Situated in Anacapri, the most exclusive part of the island, the hotel stands at a point 300 metres above sea level. Close by is the chairlift for Capri's highest and most panoramic vantage point, Monte Solaro. The hotel's 78 rooms include 22 junior suites, plus four suites which boast their own gardens and heated swimming pool. Most luxurious of all is the Megaron Suite on the roof garden, which features a hanging garden offering an enchanting view of the Bay of Naples. Guests can enjoy breakfast on the terrace of their rooms or alongside the swimming pool, while lunch is served in the gazebo, surrounded by palms and cluster pines. The lightness of the Mediterranean cuisine provides a perfect foil to the richer flavours of the island's own culinary tradition. Home-made bread, pasta and sweets testify to the tradition of a family business. Housed adjacent to the hotel is the Capri Beauty Farm and Spa, offering a wide range of medical and beauty treatments. Facilities include a fitness centre, sauna, massage, gym, thermal treatments and covered swimming pool. Many of Italy's key attractions are nearby including Ischia, Pompeii, Naples and the Amalfi coast. **Directions:** Take the hydrofoil to the island. The hotel is 10 minutes from the harbour. Price guide: Single L240,000–295,000; double/twin L390,000–680,000; suites L900,000–2,300,000.

ROMANTIK HOTEL TENUTA DI RICAVO

LOCALITA` RICAVO 4, 53011 CASTELLINA IN CHIANTI, ITALY
TEL: +39 0577 740221 FAX: +39 0577 741014 E-MAIL: ricavo@chiantinet.it

This ancient hamlet, part of which dates back to 994, was bought by the owner's family just after the last war and displays many vestiges of its medieval past. Cristina and Alessandro Lobrano have ensured that the Romantik Hotel Tenuta Di Ricavo has retained its original structure and décor. The result is a peaceful and intimate property, ideal for those seeking a relaxing break. Guests are requested to stay for a minimum of three days. A large fireplace dominates the main hall, where soft chairs and sofas nestle in every corner allowing the hotel's guests to recline and converse. The smaller lounges are also designed with the aim of socialising. The bedrooms are refreshingly simple in style yet comfortably furnished and the beds are covered with continental quilts. The restaurant is rustic in style and reservations are necessary. Alessandro Lobrano, the President of Romantik Hotels, is also the chef and his imaginative dishes are a delight to the palate whilst the wines have been carefully chosen to complement the flavours of the cuisine. Pastimes include wine-tastings, perusing the local markets or exploring the Italian countryside and Chianti hill towns on foot or bikes. **Directions:** Leave the A1 at Firenze Certosa and take the Florence Siena highway. Exit at San Donato and then turn left for Castellina in Chianti. Price guide: Double/twin L265,000–395,000; suites L380,000–448,000.

ROMANTIK HOTEL MIRAMONTI

AVENUE CAVAGNET 31, 11012 COGNE (AO), ITALY
TEL: +39 0165 74030 FAX: +39 0165 749378

It is wonderful to visit this enchanting hotel at any time of the year. When snow-capped, it is picturesque and being in the heart of the magnificent Parc National du Grand Paradis, the views are always spectacular. The ambience reflects the loving care given by three generations of the Gilliavod family to this unique hotel, for it is as if they welcome guests into their home. The interior is decorated in grand style and visitors admire the wonderful panelling, hand-painted with traditional designs. Period furniture and handsome family portraits adorn the salon walls. The bedrooms are delightful, light and airy with pretty fabrics, quite compact and equipped with all modern necessities. Every room looks out over the glorious park to the soaring mountains, including the attractive bar where visitors mingle before entering the splendid restaurant where guests indulge themselves with appetising dishes and good wines. The current conference facilities are to be extended to an entire complex, with all the latest technology available. Cross country skiing is the main winter sport and sunbathing in the rooftop solarium or relaxing on the terraces admiring the view is a year-round recreation. Barbecues and tennis are part of the summer programme. **Directions:** Take the Aosta Ouest-St Pierre road in the direction of Aymarilles on SR47 to Cogne.

ALBERGO TERMINUS

LUNGO LARIO TRIESTE, 14–22100 COMO, ITALY
TEL: +39 031 329111 FAX: +39 031 302550

This elegant hotel, a fine example of turn-of-the-century architecture, is close to the Cathedral with a spectacular view across Lake Como. It has an impressive hall with tall pillars and a carved balustrade and all the spacious reception rooms have beautiful ceilings, graceful period furniture, antiques and handsome paintings. The charming, delightfully decorated, bedrooms have soundproof doors and windows and air conditioning. Some are designated non-smoking. The bathrooms are luxurious. The attractive café restaurant "Bar delle Terme" opens on to a lovely garden terrace. The atmosphere is charmingly intimate with places for only 20 guests seated at small tables where they can enjoy dinner, lunch or a snack al fresco while admiring the beautiful lakeside panorama from the very heart of Como. The hotel has its own gymnasium complemented by sauna and massage facilities. Having its own landing stage, boat trips on the Lake can be arranged. Away from the water Como is a fascinating town to explore. **Directions:** From Switzerland on A9 exit at Como Nord, take the Lungo Lario along the lake or from Milan turn off at the Como Sud exit, then Cattaneo Street, joining the Lecco Bergamo road towards the lake. Price guide: Single L180,000–220,000; double/twin L210,000–320,000; suite L420,000–580,000. Breakfast L25,000 per person.

Prima Hotels

HOTEL VILLA FLORI

VIA CERNOBBIO, 22100 COMO, ITALY
TEL: +39 031 573105 FAX: +39 031 570379 E-MAIL: lariovillaflori@galactica.it

Built on the spot where General Garibaldi married his Guiseppina, this traditional hotel is in a superb position on the edge of Lake Como, set against a background of its own verdant park, fragrant from the orange and lemon trees which thrive in the temperate climate. It has its own landing stage for guests arriving by yacht or motor boats! All the spacious bedrooms have period furniture and balconies overlooking the lake where lapping ripples romantically lull guests to sleep. 18th century splendour is reflected in the salons, with their draped windows, decorated ceilings and chandeliers. Outside, the sunny terraces are ideal for enjoying apéritifs. The Raimondi Restaurant has large picture windows so diners can appreciate the lovely gardens and waterfront. Aromatic Italian dishes are served and a wide selection of fine Italian wines is listed. Villa Flori is only a short drive from Milan and its excellent conference facilities and choice of meeting rooms, which transform into elegant private dining rooms, have made it a popular venue for corporate events. Guests enjoy boat trips on Lake Como and exploring the countryside with its ancient villas and museums. **Directions:** Leave A9 exit Como North direction Como. The hotel has good parking arrangements. Price Guide: Single L170,000–250,000; double L200,000–320,000; suite L380,000–500,000.

HOTEL VILLA PARADISO DELL'ETNA

VIA PER VIAGRANDE 37, 95030 SAN GIOVANNI LA PUNTA, ITALY
TEL: +39 095 7512409 FAX: +39 095 7413861

This grand hotel is in a magnificent position at the foot of Mount Etna. It was built in 1927 and immediately had an elite clientele of artists and well-known personalities of the era. Today, having been renovated and discreetly modernised it is a sophisticated and luxurious hotel. The façade is very elegant, with pillars, wrought iron balconies and tall windows. The surrounding grounds are beautifully kept and the sight of the volcano from the Roof Garden is breathtaking. The salons are exquisite with inlaid marble floors, trompe l'oeil and lovely plaster mouldings. Fine antiques, traditional comfortable seating, Art Deco stained glass and cheeky cherubs add to the stylish ambience. The bedrooms are sumptuous,

with lovely drapes in strong colours, Sicilian period furniture; the bathrooms are lavish. Some are designed for those with mobility difficulties. The American Bar is a handsome meeting place, with a pianist playing at night and La Pigna restaurant is famous for its superb interpretation of Sicilian and cosmopolitan dishes, with great wines from many Italian regions in the cellar. The villa has a lovely pool; tennis and the 'Riviera' are nearby and golf 40kms away. Excursions to Catania, Etna and Acireale can be arranged. **Directions:** A18, exit San Gregorio, then head for San Giovanni La Punta and look for signs to the hotel. Price guide: L200,000; double/twin L280,000; suites L400,000.

ALBERGO ANNUNZIATA

PIAZZA REPUBBLICA 5, 44100 FERRARA, ITALY
TEL: +39 0532 201111 FAX: +39 0532 203233 E-MAIL: annunzia@tin.it

Nestling in a quiet location on a central square opposite the splendid Estense Castle, this very modern hotel is renowned for its tranquil atmosphere and excellent and friendly staff. It is believed that Casanova stayed at Albergo Annunziata over two centuries ago and this hotel is now patronised by several artists and musicians as the Visitors Book testifies. Whilst the interior is largely decorated in a contemporary fashion, the building preserves all its 18th century beams, providing a superb contrast with the modern nuances. The bar and hall are intimate yet contain every possible necessity including an extensive collection of art books to consult at one's leisure. Zeno Govoni, the hotelier, is an engineer with artistic talents and the walls of the entrance hall are adorned with his creations. Black and turquoise furnishings predominate the beautifully appointed bedrooms. Each has a unique layout and offers many of the latest facilities. The small lounge and breakfast room feature bright décor and are the essence of comfort. There is a variety of nearby attractions including the Palazzo Dei Diamanti, located on one of the most beautiful streets in Europe. **Directions:** Leave the A13 at Ferrara Sud or Nord and travel towards the centre of town and follow the signs for the hotel. Price guide: Single L220,000; double/twin L320,000; suites L450,000.

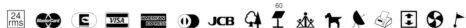

Ripagrande Hotel

VIA RIPAGRANDE 21, 44100 FERRARA, ITALY
TEL: +39 0532 765250 FAX: +39 0532 764377 E-MAIL: ripa@mbox.4net.it

Ferrara is the perfect place to stay or to break a journey between Venice and Florence, for it is a lovely university town and the capital of the Dukes of Este. On the banks of the Po in the old part of the town is this superbly restored XV century palace – the élite Ripagrande Hotel. The Renaissance interior is appropriate to the history of the hotel and the entrance hall is spectacular with its marble staircase and pillars, wrought iron banisters and beamed ceiling. Cool, elegant salons and terraces encourage guests to relax while upstairs, the spacious bedrooms are in excellent contemporary style, some having terraces cut into the slope of the tiled roofs. The furnishings are comfortable, in discreet colours.

The attractive Ripa restaurant serves many traditional Ferrarese specialities. Superb Italian wines are featured. Two enchanting courtyards make wonderful settings for banquets. The breakfast room offers an excellent buffet to start the day, perhaps before a seminar in the well-equipped meeting room. Bicycles are the popular way to explore this fascinating medieval town, with its castle, cathedral and the Diamond Palace. Sophisticated boutiques offer fine leather and high fashion. **Directions:** Ferrara is off the A13, 112 km from Venice and 150 km to Florence. Price guide: Single L250,000; double/twin L320,000; Junior suites L340,000–380,000.

GRAND HOTEL VILLA CORA

VIALE MACHIAVELLI 18, 50125 FLORENCE, ITALY
TEL: +39 055 2298451 FAX: +39 055 229086 E-MAIL: villacora@explorer.it

Villa Cora, as it is called today, was originally "Villa Oppenheim". It was built in the mid-to-late 1860s by Baron Oppenheim in honour of his beautiful wife. In its great halls, the élite of Florentine and foreign society were received and entertained with lavish parties. Eventually abandoned by the Baron and his wife, it became home to a succession of famous and fascinating people. In time it fell into a state of disrepair and it was only 25 years ago, when it became a hotel, that the Villa was renovated and refurbished to its current superb standard. The furnishings have mostly been specially constructed following original drawings, but many are authentic period and antique pieces. Columns, frescoes, high ceilings, marble bathrooms and silk wall hangings and curtains abound. The restaurant, which reflects the luxury and elegance of the neoclassic style, enjoys an excellent reputation for its cuisine and excellent standard of service. The villa stands just outside Florence, with its many famous attractions, but guests will also doubtless be tempted to stay within its walls and take advantage of the stunning outdoor swimming pool. **Directions:** Leave A1 at Firenze Certosa or A11 at Firenze and follow the road for Roma, exit Certosa. Follow signs for Florence and then Michelangelo and hotel. Price guide: Single L335,000–440,000; double L470,000–820,000, suite L820,000–1,900,000.

160

195

HOTEL J&J

VIA MEZZO 20, 50121 FLORENCE, ITALY
TEL: +39 055 234 5005 FAX: +39 055 240 282 E-MAIL: jandji@dada.it

This is a veritable retreat for travellers, a charming transformation from a convent to a delightful small hotel. There is a wonderful tranquillity about Hotel J & J, far from the bustle of the commercial world, despite its location in the very heart of Florence. The bedrooms vary, each one having its individuality; some look out over the rooftops, others look down on to concealed courtyards. They are furnished with antiques and hand-woven fabrics, extremely comfortable and the white bathrooms are well-equipped. The lounge is very elegant and a small bar leads into a courtyard which is a pleasant spot for drinks in fine weather. There is no restaurant but the hotel staff will direct guests to interesting restaurants nearby. This is an ideal base for exploring old Florence, the Renaissance Palace with its fine frescoes, graceful cloister and Doric columns being not far away and the Duomo only a short distance from there. The Baptistry, the Uffizi Gallery, the Medici chapels, the Opera House, many museums and art galleries all make the days and evenings so busy. When seeking a break from culture, the shops are truly magnificent. **Directions:** The hotel is located near Borgo Pinti close to the city centre. Car parking is provided. Price guide: Double L400,000–450,000; suite L500,000–650,000.

HOTEL IL NEGRESCO

LUNGOMARE ITALICO 82, 55042 FORTE DEI MARMI (LU), ITALY
TEL: +39 0584 78 7133 FAX: +39 0584 78 7535 E-MAIL: hnegresco@sole.it

Those seeking the delightful atmosphere of a seaside establishment will be impressed with the conviviality of the Hotel Il Negresco. A friendly ambience is evident in all the rooms of this small, modern hotel which enjoys glorious views over the splendid Versilia beaches and the rose-tinted Apuan Alps. The interior is largely decorated in pale hues of yellow, orange and blue with brilliant white colour emanating from the striking Aorcan lilies, scattered throughout the hotel. The bedrooms, all with pastel furnishings, are simple yet charming. Comfort is an important criterion in the bar and lounge areas, where guests recline and enjoy an afternoon or pre-dinner drink.

A refined ambience is evoked in the restaurant as excellent recipes, using seasonal produce, created by the imaginative chef are served in the evenings. Fitness enthusiasts will be pleased with the outdoor swimming pool with children's area, the 18-hole golf course and yachting clubs close by. Daily excursions include visits to the historic cities of Lucca, Pisa and Le Cinq Terre, the famous Carrara marble quarries and seaside activities whilst at night-time, the local bars and nightclubs are well animated. **Directions:** Leave the A12 at Versilia and follow the signs to Forte dei Marmi, situated along the seafront. Price guide: Single L160,000–240,000, double/twin L230,000–380,000.

70

HELLENIA YACHTING HOTEL

VIA JANNUZZO 41, 90835 GIARDINI NAXOS (ME) ITALY
TEL: +39 0942 51737 FAX: +39 0942 54310

The Hellenia Yachting Hotel is ideal for a seaside holiday and new arrivals relax as soon as they see the soft pink, typically Sicilian, building so close to the beach – it has a happy ambience, definitely a place for enjoyment. Many of the cool, white bedrooms open onto a balcony or terrace, curtains and covers are in vibrant colours and some of the bathrooms are in black marble. Children are very welcome and there is a baby-sitting service available. The reception rooms are spacious, well-lit and comfortable; the hotel is particularly proud of its new conference rooms, also available for private celebrations. While much of the eating and drinking is alfresco on the terraces, the piano bar has its own aficianados. It is decorated in 'sea colours' and has friendly, efficient staff. The smart restaurant is spacious, with soft golden overtones. Local fish, wonderful salads and Sicilian specialities feature on the menu and many of the wines listed are Italian. There is also a poolside bar and the private beach has its bar and restaurant, umbrellas and deck chairs. Windsurfing, pedal boats and tennis are available. Taormina is fascinating to explore and has an antiques market on the last weekend of each month. **Directions:** A18, Giardini Naxos exit, left following signs to Recanati, then hotel is signed. Price guide: Single L140,000–180,000; double/twin L210,000–250,000; suites L280,000–340,000.

HOTEL MIRAMARE E CASTELLO

VIA PONTANO 9, 80070 ISCHIA (NAPLES), ITALY
TEL: +39 081 991333 FAX: +39 081 984572 E-MAIL: mircastl@metis.it

New arrivals relax as soon as they see the sparkling white and soft pink exterior of this seafront hotel, situated in the attractive village of Ischia Ponte. It is one of the most beautiful parts of the island and is an ideal venue for a sunny seaside holiday. Fronting onto its own private beach, the Miramare E Castello has a welcoming ambience and is ideal for those seeking enjoyment and relaxation. Many of the comfortably furnished bedrooms and suites open onto a balcony and have splendid views over the deep blue waters of the Mediterranean towards ancient Aragones Castle and the islands of Vivara, Procida and Capri. All are en suite, have air-conditioning and every facility from satellite television and minibar to a hairdryer and safe. The reception rooms are spacious and well lit. An elegant restaurant, overlooking the sea, serves excellent international cuisine while another on the rooftop features Mediterranean dishes. There are long, shaded terraces to sit or lie back on, a tearoom and a colourful roof-garden with a bar and 2 Jacuzzi pools. Inside, the convivial bar is a favourite with guests who enjoy pre or post dinner drinks accompanied by melodious piano playing. The hotel has two indoor pools, a sauna and a gymnasium. Every seaside activity is available, together with excursions to nearby islands. **Directions:** Ferry to the island and then take a taxi. Price guide: Single L190,000–280,000; double/twin L320,000–500,000; suites L580,000–760,000.

LA VILLAROSA ALBERGO E TERME

VIA GIACINTO GIGANTE, 5, 80077 PORTO D'ISCHIA (NAPLES), ITALY
TEL: +39 081 99 13 16 FAX: +39 081 99 24 25

Ischia, 'The Green Island', is where the Phoenicians traded metals in an earlier millennium and mythology transformed volcanic activity into monsters. La Villarosa, an exquisite old farmhouse was converted in the 1950s into an elite and idyllic hotel, surrounded by a luxuriant garden. An ambience of country house living has been created by simple furnishings, lovely antiques and discreet decorations, all in impeccable taste. The salons are dedicated to pleasure. The cosy sitting-rooms are perfect for reading or letter-writing and the Piano-bar, where the barman creates exotic cocktails, leads onto the colourful thermal swimming pool area. The entrancing bedrooms, each uniquely designed, look out to the sea or over the botanical garden, a few having small balconies. Exclusive chalets are hidden among the foliage. The attractive dining rooms lead onto a romantic roof garden, and guests feast on Ischian dishes, fresh fish, pastas and delicious local wines. The thermal pool in the grounds, spa waters and supervised treatments in the clinic are highly recommended. The hotel boat visits the various bays and beaches. Excursions can be made to Pompeii, Capri and the Amalfi coast. **Directions:** Ferry (75 mins) or hydrofoil (20 mins) from Naples. Price guide (per person per day): Single L110,000–190,000; double/twin L90,000–120,000.

GRAND HOTEL FASANO

VIA ZANARDELLI 160, 25083 GARDONE RIVIERA (LAKE GARDA), ITALY
TEL: +39 0365 290220 FAX: +39 0365 290221

This truly aristocratic hotel on the shores of Lake Garda has an art nouveau façade, flanked by palm trees. It stands in an extensive park filled with exotic foliage and beautiful, flowering plants. The reception area and salons are regal, with elegant period seating vying with fine antiques. Staff with the courtesy of yesteryear enhance the hotel's imperial heritage. All the bedrooms have a balcony overlooking the lake with its spectacular sunrises and sunsets. They are luxuriously furnished and decorated and the well-appointed bathrooms have either shower or bath. The cocktail bar is full of rich colour with dramatic wall hangings and plush chairs. An extravagant breakfast buffet is provided in the soft morning air overlooking the water and later in the day Italian specialities, tempting antipasto, salads and gourmet dishes are served either outside or in the grand restaurant. Romantic evenings under the stars, listening to soft music watching the lights on the waterfront are idyllic. Steamboat and hydrofoil trips, sailing, water-skiing, windsurfing and golf are close at hand. The hotel has its own pool and tennis court and strolling through its park is very relaxing. **Directions:** Densenzano/Brescia – follow signs for Salò, then Gardona Riviera. Price guide (per person): Single L125,000–280,000; double/twin L95,000–255,000; suites L250,000–350,000.

ITALY (Madonna Di Campiglio)

HOTEL LORENZETTI

VIA DOLOMITI DI BRENTA, 119, 38084 MADONNA DI CAMPIGLIO (TN) ITALY
TEL: +39 0465 44 14 04 FAX: +39 0465 44 06 44 E-MAIL: hotlorenzetti@well.it

This enchanting chalet-style hotel, with its flower-bedecked balconies, looking across the Brenta Chain, stands apart from the main ski-lifts and village centre, enabling guests to relax in peace! The interior is very elegant. The views over the mountains are spectacular. Three of the pleasant bedrooms have been designed for those with mobility problems. The suites are special, some having hydro-massage. All have their own balconies. On sunny days, guests enjoy a drink on the terrace and in the evening they congregate in the splendid bar before dining in style in the handsome restaurant which offers both international and delicious local dishes. The reading room is a quiet place to end the day. The hotel can host small conferences, having an ideal meeting room and modern presentation equipment. Winter sports enthusiasts appreciate the fine skiing and the ice rink. In summer, residents stroll in the lovely gardens, walk in the mountains, play golf, tennis or fish close by while all year the fitness centre and games room are very popular. **Directions:** From Milan after 3 hours leave the motorway at Brescia Est, following signs for Madonna di Campiglio. The hotel has a heated garage for 20 and outside parking for a further 40 cars. Price guide per person (half board): Single L100,000–255,000; double/twin L85,000–230,000; suites L115,000–305,000.

202

ALBERGO SAN LORENZO

PIAZZA CONCORDIA 14, 46100 MANTOVA, ITALY
TEL: +39 0376 220500 FAX: +39 0376 327194

The Albergo San Lorenzo is a city hotel, widely reputed to be the best in Mantova. A pastel green colour scheme dominates the interior, with antique furniture and interesting period pieces adorning the spacious and comfortable lounge. Gilded mirrors and hand-crafted wooden furnishings feature in the intimate hall, creating a warm and welcoming atmosphere. The bedrooms are simple yet stylish and the nine suites are decorated in shades of pink or deep turquoise and display every imaginable comfort including professional hairdryers. Overlooking the magnificent San Lorenzo rotunda and the fine dome of St Andrew's cathedral, the terrace of the hotel is often frequented by guests wishing to indulge in an afternoon drink and enjoy the glorious panoramic vista. The meeting rooms are well-equipped and provide an ideal venue for conferences, seminars and other events. The city museums, the Palazzo Ducale and the Palazzo Te, the summer residence of the Gonzaga family, are all popular destinations for day trips. Places of interest nearby include the historic towns of Verona, San Benedetto Pó, Padua and Sabbioneta. **Directions:** Exit A22 at Mantova Nord and follow the central roundabout and then follow the signs for the hotel. Price guide: Single L180,000–250,000; double/twin L216,000–300,000; suites L252,000–350,000.

ROMANTIK HOTEL VILLA CHETA ELITE

LOC. ACQUAFREDDA, 85041 MARATEA (PZ), ITALY
TEL: +39 0973 878 134 FAX: +39 0973 878 135

Many travellers never explore the beautiful southern tip of Italy, but those that do return again, especially if they are fortunate enough to stay at this lovely Liberty-style villa. It has been meticulously restored, and is a glorious sight, painted sienna and cream, with graceful balconies, black shutters and elegant mouldings. Acquafredda di Maratea is a fascinating small village on the coast, and just above it, the hotel looks out to the Mediterrean. The surrounding gardens are exquisite, filled with statues and urns, brilliant flowers, exotic trees and foliage, the air redolent with their perfume. The interior of this romantic villa reflects the Art Nouveau era, with its stained glass panels and

Tiffany lamps. The bedrooms are pristine, and most have superb views. The traditional dining room has immaculate white lace tablecloths – but most days the climate is so balmy that guests prefer to take breakfast and dinner on the terrace, sipping good southern Italian wine under the stars and relishing the aromatic home-cooking. Communication may be a slight problem but big smiles say it all. Visitors enjoy the beach, just minutes away, go out in fishermen's boats and explore the port, the Pollino National Park, grottos, and historical edifices. **Directions:** Leave A3 exit Lagonegro Nord – Maratea, and follow signs to Sapri – Maratea. Price guide: Double/twin L195,000–220,000.

ROMANTIK HOTEL OBERWIRT

ST FELIXWEG 2, 39020 MARLING-MERAN, ITALY
TEL: +39 0473 22 20 20 FAX: +39 0473 44 71 30

An inn offering hospitality since the 15th century, this hotel has been owned by the Waldner family since 1749. Part of it has an even longer history, the outdoor pool being built on an original Roman design. The traditional architecture has not been marred by modernisation. Window-boxes and shutters enhance the original tower and white walls, set against a background of the majestic Dolomites. There are now 44 bedrooms, luxuriously appointed, with views across the valley to the mountains. The Tyrolean bar is very convivial, although on fine days guests may prefer to sip their apéritif on the flower-bedecked terrace, which is floodlit at night. The Waldners are proud of their elegant restaurant. The meals are exquisite and the carefully selected wines reasonably priced. When sunbathing by the Roman pool is not possible, guests appreciate the fitness centre, with its indoor heated pool, sauna, Jacuzzi and massage facilities. The hotel has a relationship with two golf clubs reducing green fees for guests, also with the Riding Club of Meran. Seven tennis courts, two indoor, with a coach available are 1km away. **Directions:** Leave the Innsbruck Verona road at Bozen Sud for Meran, then follow signs to Marling (3km). Price guide: Single L126,000–148,000; double/twin L126,000–148,000 per person; suites L148,000–192,000 per person.

MUSEO ALBERGO ATELIER SUL MARE

VIA CESARE BATTISTI, 98070 CASTEL DI TUSA (ME), SICILY
TEL: +39 0921 334 295 FAX: +39 0921 334 283 E-MAIL: apresti@eniware.it

The coastline between Palermo and Messina is magnificent and in one of the many beautiful bays is the small holiday resort of Castel di Tusa. Contrasting with the traditional homes of its fishermen is a dazzling white unique hotel, the Museo Albergo Atelier sul Mare. The interior is exciting, truly avant garde. The reception area is filled with 20th century objets d'art and unusual sculptures and the bar-hall, where guests enjoy exotic cocktails, has videos playing work by the Fiumara d'Arte group. This merges into a relaxing drawing room. Each bedroom has been designed by different contemporary artists, contributing their own interpretation of serenity, some being simplistic, others reflecting imaginative philosophies. The walls of the big, light restaurant are covered in paintings, and here guests can enjoy the finest Sicilian food – marvellous fish, colourful vegetables and fragrant herbs. Delicious local wines are suggested. This is a place for living and breathing contemporary art – imbuing a philosophy that enriches the soul – taking a course in pottery, relaxing in the sun, learning from the artisans of Santo Stephano di Camastra, going out in the fishing boats. **Directions:** Leave Palermo, driving east, on A20 to Cefalu, then follow the coast road towards Messina. Price guide: Single L80,000–140,000; double/twin L60,000–100,000.

HOTEL AURIGA

VIA PIRELLI 7, 20124 MILAN, ITALY
TEL: +39 02 66 98 58 51 FAX: +39 02 66 98 06 98 E-MAIL: hotelauriga@virtualia.it

Built in the 1950's, the recent addition of a new marble façade has brought the Hotel Auriga into the 1990's. Set in the centre of Milan, the property is a fine hotel for both the business and leisure traveller featuring every contemporary convenience whilst affording many luxurious nuances. The interior has been decorated in beautiful bold colours creating a warm ambience. A yellow Venetian stucco in the public rooms reflects Milan's sunny climate and retains the calm and elegant style which is evident throughout the hotel. The comfortable bedrooms are well-appointed with delicate fabrics and attractive furnishings. Colour satellite television and controllable air conditioning are thoughtful extras. The spacious bathrooms are decorated in marble and feature radio and telephone. Special events, seminars and business meetings for up to 30 people may be held in the conference room. The hotel is in an ideal location and guests may experience everything Milan has to offer from museums and theatres to shopping arcades, art galleries and the beautiful Duomo cathedral. The interesting quarter of Brera with its bistros, street artists and lively bars is nearby. **Directions:** The hotel is situated close to the Milano Centrale railway station and Linate airport. Those travelling by road must exit any motorway and head towards Milano Centro or the railway station. Price guide: Single L180,000–270,000; double/twin L240,000–370,000; suites L400,000.

THE REGENCY

VIA ARIMONDI 112, 20155 MILAN, ITALY
TEL: +39 02 39 21 60 21   FAX: +39 02 39 21 77 34

This 18th century residence has been transformed recently into an elegant hotel, ideal for those attending the Milan Fair and Exhibition Grounds, being just a few minutes' walk away. It is also only a few minutes by taxi from the city centre. The bedrooms – some designated non-smoking – have been very well designed and clever use of colour plays an important part in their attraction. The marble bathrooms are contemporary, mostly having power showers rather than baths. Vibrant, beautiful fabrics add to the charm of the reception rooms, where the stylish furniture reflects the talents of Italian designers and the bar has a warm ambience – enhanced by a big fire in the winter months.

The hotel has good conference facilities, with well-equipped meeting rooms. Buffet breakfasts are served but other meals are not available, although there is room service. The management will direct guests to excellent restaurants close by. Milan has many historic buildings – its wonderful Opera House, the Duomo, the Brera Art Gallery to name but a few. For those touring Europe, Milan has good motorway access to Venice, Turin, the Italian Lakes and Switzerland. **Directions:** Leave the A4 at Certosa. Via Arimondi is just off the Piazza Firenze, close to Garibaldi Station. Parking is nearby. Price guide: Single L260,000, double/twin L340,000, suites L410,000.

POSTHOTEL WEISSES RÖSSL

VIA CAREZZA 30, 39056 NOVA LEVANTE (BZ), DOLOMITES, ITALY
TEL: +39 0471 613113 FAX: +39 0471 613390

Situated at the end of the impressive Val d'Ega, in the heart of the magnificent Dolomites, lies this former staging post with its frescoed façade and flower-bedecked balconies. Since 1865, the Wiedenhofer Family has been welcoming guests, in winter for skiing, in summer for walking, climbing and golf in this alpine wonderland. The lounge, with its marble floor and traditional wooden ceiling, radiates a peaceful atmosphere overlooking meadows and forests. Guests gather for drinks in the cosy ambience of the bar with its rustic, local-style furniture, adorned with hunting trophies. Lunches are informal, in summertime on the sunny terraces, dinners are fine and delicately elaborate, a delicious range of Tyrolean and Mediterranean dishes, accompanied by selected wines from South-Tyrol and Italy. The sympathetically restored bedrooms are cheerful, all with a balcony and a wonderful view of the near mountains. Countless pleasures to choose from, such as outdoor and indoor swimming pool, tennis, whirlpool, sauna, steam bath, massage, beauty salon, solarium and billiards. Playroom and outside playground for children with childminder in charge. **Directions:** Autostrada A22, exit Bolzano North, driving south following signs for Val d'Ega – Lago di Carezza, reaching Nova Levante after 18km Price guide (per person, half-board): Double/twin L120,000–200,000.

RELAIS VILLA POMELA

VIA SERRAVALLE 69, 15067 NOVI LIGURE (AL), ITALY
TEL: +39 0143 329910 FAX: +39 0143 329912

Set on a hill in the verdant countryside of Northern Italy, the Villa Pomela with its elegant façade and high roof resembles an ancient medieval castle. The attractive villa is surrounded by beautifully tended gardens resulting in a tranquil haven, ideal for alfresco entertainment during the summer months. The public rooms are well-appointed with classical overtones and colours, stucco and antiques and mixed with comfortable sofas and armchairs. Furnished in a stylish manner, the bedrooms are cosy and smart whilst the bathrooms are spacious and contain many modern amenities. Guests may dine in the two interlocking rooms of the Al Cortese restaurant which leads on to the fine jardin d'hiver. The impressive menu comprises a fusion of local Mediterranean delicacies with some international flavours. The estate produces its own wines which are served with a comprehensive range of other vintages. The distractions are wonderfully diverse, ranging from golf at the nearby course to visiting the Roman ruins and castles. The hotel is close to the historic cities of Alessandria and Arquata Scrivia. **Directions:** Leave the A7 at Serravalle Scrivia and head towards Novi Ligure. The hotel is 3 kilometres from the exit of the highway. Price guide: Single L200,000; double/twin L320,000; suites L400,000.

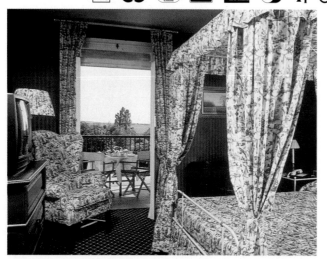

ALBERGO PIETRASANTA – PALAZZO BARSANTI BONETTI

VIA GARIBALDI 35, 55045 PIETRASANTA (LU), ITALY
TEL: +39 0584 793727 FAX: +39 0584 793728

The Albergo Pietrasanta is an authentic 17th century palace in true Renaissance style, restored and maintained in a most unusual fashion. In the main hall, abstract paintings blend well with antique furniture, marble chip floors and beautiful moulded stucco and fresco ceilings. Covered in glass, the courtyard has been transformed into a superb bar with a deep green colour scheme and excellent garden-style furniture. The enchanting waterfall in one corner completes the evocative charm of the room. The individually appointed bedrooms are spacious and feature attractive fabrics and antique décor. Each room has satellite television, a minibar and many of the latest amenities. The large bathrooms are marble and have been decorated in various shades of colour. Although the hotel does not have a restaurant, one of the most prestigious and renowned restaurants in Versilia is just in front of the hotel and there are several bistros and brasseries within easy reach. The hotel has its own garage and valet parking is also offered. The towns of Tuscany, Lucca, Pisa and Florence are a delight to explore whilst sports enthusiasts will be pleased with the nearby opportunities for golf and horse-riding. The famous Forte dei Marmi beach is only 4km away and the many seaside activities are a must for sun-worshippers. **Directions:** Leave the A12 at Versilia and follow the white signs to the hotel. Price guide: Single L200,000–250,000; double/twin L300,000–500,000; suites L400,000–630,000.

HOTEL RELAIS LA SUVERA

53030 PIEVESCOLA – SIENA, ITALY
TEL: +39 0577 960300 FAX: +39 0577 960220

The Relais La Suvera has a fascinating history, first in 1197 a castle, then a gift in 1507 to the reigning Pope who had it transformed into a Renaissance villa. In 1989 the Marchese Ricci and his wife Principessa Eleonora Massimo created this elite and luxurious hotel – composed of four beautifully restored houses surrounding the courtyard. To have an opportunity to stay in the Marchese's Tuscan home is a unique experience – the elegant Reception has a welcoming ambience, enhanced by a display of wines from their own vineyard. The exquisite salons are filled with the finest antiques and the family art collection, a connoisseur's paradise. The heavenly guest rooms and magnificent suites are scattered between the four main houses, the Papal Villa, the Stables, the Olive Oil House and the Farm. Decorated in rich colours, furnished with lovely antiques, the rooms also have modern amenities. The bathrooms are opulent. The traditional Bar is in the Olive Oil House, as is the classical Oliviera Restaurant. Gorgeous Tuscan dishes accompanied by superb wines from the estate combine to make a feast each night. The residence has tennis and a swimming pool, guests can visit the vineyard, play golf or fish nearby. **Directions:** From Superstrada Siena-Florence, exit Colle Val d'Elsa, head towards Grosseto, following signs to Relais La Suvera. Price guide: Double/twin L370,000–970,000; suites L700,000–1,170,000.

IL PELLICANO

58018 PORTO ERCOLE (GR), ITALY
TEL: +39 0564 858111 FAX: +39 0564 833418 E-MAIL: info@pellicanohotel.com

What hotel in Italy can compare with the spectacular setting of Il Pellicano? 'One of the most delightful, intimately-sited hotels in the world' (Sunday Telegraph). A cluster of cottages are centred around the main ivy-clad villa, with traditional tiled roofs, ochre walls and flower patios interspersed with tall pine, cypress and olive trees overlooking the breathtaking Argentario Peninsula. 'The atmosphere of Il Pellicano is like a very private club' (Harpers & Queen). The bedrooms and suites are individually furnished and enjoy spectacular views. Guests can choose between the mouth-watering barbecue buffets or romantic candlelit dinners in the beautiful restaurant, providing the best in national and international food and wines. Enjoy sports such as water-skiing, tennis and cycling or just relax in the heated swimming pool, on the terraced private beach or in the beauty centre. For those who crave more activity, there's plenty going on in the nearby marina and waterfront. Play a game of golf or explore the Roman and Etruscan ruins, within driving distance in the hotel limousine if preferred. On a verdant hillside, overlooking a shimmering sea, Il Pellicano is a veritable delight!
Directions: Take the A12 from Rome towards Civitavecchia, then the Orbetello exit towards Porto Ercole. Double L350,000–990,000; suites L730,000–1,950,000.

ROMANTIK HOTEL VILLA GIUSTINIAN

VIA GIUSTINIANI 11, 31019 PORTOBUFFOLÉ TREVISO, ITALY
TEL: +39 0422 850244 FAX: +39 0422 850260

Set in the medieval town of Portobuffolè in the province of Treviso, the Romantik Hotel Villa Giustinian is a 17th century Venetian villa with Renaissance overtones. This extremely elegant property, situated on a wime route, features stuccos and frescoes whilst the marriage of the colours is an aesthetic delight. The public rooms are spacious and boast attractive period and antique furniture. Excellent taste abounds in the bedrooms, adorned with stylish Venetian painted furniture and offering an array of thoughtful extras such as the chilled bottle of Prosecco which awaits each new arrival. Guests may savour the local specialities and inventive cuisine in the exquisite restaurant. The extensive wine list includes regional vintages. The meeting rooms are furnished to the highest of standards and offer all of the latest facilities. This is a fine venue for the business traveller and the rooms are suitable for conferences, small meetings and seminars. Interesting exhibitions are frequently organised in Portobuffolè and the monthly antique market is a delight to explore. Venice with its fine villas is within easy reach. **Directions:** At the A4, exit at San Donà or Lessalto exit. Leave the motorway here and continue in the direction of Oderzo. Price guide: Single L140,000–160,000; double/twin L220,000–250,000; suites L450,000–550,000.

ROMANTIK HOTEL POSEIDON

VIA PASITEA, 148, 84017 POSITANO (SALERNO), ITALY
TEL: +39 089 811111 FAX: +39 089 875833 E-MAIL: poseidon@starnet.it

Positano, the 'jewel of the Mediterranean' is situated on the spectacular Amalfi coast, a combination of sea and mountains, with pastel shaded houses clinging to the cliffs. The four star Romantik Hotel Poseidon, owned and run by the Aonzo family, was once their private summer residence and is located in the heart of town. The charming, pristine bedrooms, decorated with rustic furniture, have balconies overlooking the village. The spacious, comfortable living room and bar, are nearby to the sunbathing terrace and swimming pool. The decor and atmosphere of the indoor dining area are in total harmony with the rest of the hotel. In the warmer months the restaurant service takes place on a vast terrace covered with vines. There is a wide varied menu, including fresh fish specialities and the best Italian wines are available. The Laura Elos Beauty Centre offers a full range of body treatments, facials, massages, Turkish bath and complete Fitness programme. There is a conference room for up to 50 people. Sea-fishing trips in the Gulf can be arranged. **Directions:** Driving South from Naples on A3, take the exit Castellammare di Stabia, turning off at Meta di Sorrento and follow the signs to Positano. Garage: L35,000 per day. Price guide: Single L270,000–390,000; double/twin L290,000–410,000; suites L550,000–750,000.

ITALY (Rimini)

IL GRAND HOTEL DI RIMINI

PARCO FEDERICO FELLINI, 47900 RIMINI, ITALY
TEL: +39 0541 56000 FAX: +39 0541 56866

The Il Grand is everything a five star hotel should be. The tall, majestic and stately façade with ornate plasterwork and delicate wrought-iron framed balconies complements the opulence and elegance of the interior. It personifies luxury, from its rich furnishings and décor to its excellent facilities, cuisine and impeccable service. 18th century French and Venetian antiques, exquisite paintings, chandeliers and magnificent floral displays abound. Built in the early part of this century the hotel stands in large, tree-shaded grounds just 100 yards from its own private beach which is clustered with sunbeds and umbrellas surrounding a circular bar-restaurant and children's pool. There are beach cabins, each with hot and cold showers.

Instructors are at hand for sailing, windsurfing, water skiing and swimming. The 121 bedrooms and suites, many with sea views, are luxurious and have every modern amenity. Diners in the sumptuous Veranda Room restaurant are spoiled for choice. Extensive menus feature international specialities whilst traditional dishes are served at the beach restaurant. The open-air terrace is renowned for its evening entertainment and dances. There is a large heated pool, two tennis courts, a fitness room, a children's playground, beauty centre and a nightclub. **Directions**: Exit from A14 towards the seafront. Turn left and the hotel is at the roundabout. Price guide: Single L230,000–350,000; double/twin L380,000–580,000; suites L590,000–960,000.

HOTEL FARNESE

**VIA ALESSANDRO FARNESE, 30 (ANGOLO VIALE GIULIO CESARE), 00192 ROME, ITALY
TEL: +39 06 321 25 53 FAX: +39 06 321 51 29**

An aristocratic 19th century villa, set in a quiet tree-lined residential area of Rome. You enter through a small, lovely fronted garden, up an impressive stone stairway to the reception desk. Graceful archways and elegant classical Italian furniture, chandeliers from Murano and decorative frescos, antiques and fine colourful rugs together enhance the charming reception areas of the ground floor of the original villa. Downstairs, a buffet breakfast is the only meal served in the subterranean dining room – but drinks will be brought to the roof garden overlooking St. Peter's Square or the terrace off the reception lounge. Several interesting restaurants are to be found locally. Raphaël murals, parquet floors and period furniture make the bedrooms very attractive and they have delightful marble bathrooms, equipped to meet the needs of modern travellers. Most conveniently situated among all the historical buildings to explore in this city, it is particularly close to the Castel St. Angelo, St. Peter's and the Vatican. Those visiting Rome on business appreciate the easy accessibility to the commercial districts. **Directions:** There is private parking space for residents' cars, alternatively the Lepanto Metro station is only 50 metres from the hotel. Price guide: Single L260,000–L320,000; double/twin L380,000–470,000; junior suite L500,000.

ITALY (Rome)

HOTEL GIULIO CESARE

VIA DEGLI SCIPIONI 287, 00192 ROME, ITALY
TEL: +39 06 321 0751 FAX: +39 06 321 1736 E-MAIL: giulioce@uni.net

The Giulio Cesare, situated close to some of the most glorious streets in Rome, is the essence of comfort. Offering its guests a unique blend of hospitality, relaxation and excellent service, this 18th century neo-classical hotel is ideal for either business or pleasure. The fine entrance is enhanced by the two imposing columns. Featuring Persian carpets, antique mirrors, comfortable furnishings and wall tapestries, the public rooms are classically lofty. Currently undergoing a complete refurbishment, the bedrooms are attractively decorated in shades of blue and pale yellow with modern furniture fashioned from a warm, natural wood. Some of the rooms feature authentic antiques dating back to the early 800s. The intimate bar is delightful, very well-stocked and offering an excellent standard of service. It leads on to the attractive courtyard, adorned with tables for either drinks or food. Whilst there is no restaurant, tasty pasta dishes and other sumptuous main courses are served, at all times of the day, in the bar and garden. Breakfast comprises a very rich buffet and British or American dishes are prepared by the talented chef at no extra cost. Many exquisite shops and boutiques are nestled around the area. The hotel is situated close to the centre and is within easy reach of the Piazza del Popolo. Everything Rome has to offer is on its doorstep. **Directions:** The hotel is 100 yards away from the nearest tube station, Lepanto. Price guide: Single L370,000; double/twin L475,000.

218

ROMANTIK HOTEL BAROCCO

PIAZZA BARBERINI, 9, 00187 ROME, ITALY
TEL: +39 06 48 72 001 FAX: +39 06 48 59 94

This delightful intimate hotel, its architecture indicating that it was built during the 19th century art deco era, is in the centre of Rome. Local landmarks are the famous Trevi Fountain and the Spanish Steps, yet it is also convenient for the business sector. Lovely warm cherrywood dominates the interior décor – in the fin de siècle entrance hall and in the bedrooms. These are delightful and thoughtfully designed to ensure guests have all possible modern amenities, including insulation from the noise of the city below. The Junior Suite which has its own terrace, overlooks the Piazza and can be reserved. The bathrooms are contemporary and luxurious, furnished in marble. The hotel has a small bar. There is a breakfast room on the ground floor. Breakfast is also served in bedrooms. There is no hotel restaurant but the staff will always suggest good restaurants that are nearby. Rome is an exciting city to explore, with St Peter's and the Vatican, the Colosseum and Pantheon in the ancient city, world famous museums and art galleries, the exclusive boutiques and luxurious shops. It also offers a sophisticated night life. **Directions:** Piazza Barberini is where Via Barberini meets the Via del Tritone and Via Veneto. Parking is 300 metres from the hotel. Price guide: Single I 350,000; double/twin L450,000. Weekend rates available.

LA POSTA VECCHIA

PALO LAZIALE – 00055 LADISPOLI, (ROME), ITALY
TEL: +39 6 9949501 FAX: +39 6 9949507

At the beginning of this decade, this superb 17th century villa was converted into a luxurious hotel and has since provided accommodation to many illustrious and famous figures. Overlooking the sea and six hectares of lovely parkland, it is built on 2,000 year-old foundations. Much of its original structure, including some stone doorways and fireplaces, has been carefully preserved and some of the ancient mosaics can be viewed in the small Roman museum on the ground floor of the hotel. The result of a painstaking and sensitive conversion is a charming marriage of the old and new. All the bedrooms are spacious and airy, furnished with enormous beds and decorated with marvellous antiques. In some of the generous bathrooms there are sculpted marble sinks, antique taps and in one, even a staircase! Guests have the use of a private beach and there is an excellent range of leisure facilities available either on-site or nearby. These include swimming, horse-riding, golf, tennis and many seaside activities. There are also various excursions to a number of Etruscan sites. The hotel is conveniently placed just 40 minutes drive from Rome and 20 minutes from the airport. **Directions**: Leave A12 at Tozze in Pietra, follow SS1 North to 37th Kir. Turn left after bridge and follow signs. Price guide: Double/twin L775,000–990,000; suite L1,550,000–2,380,000.

HOTEL VILLA SIRIO

VIA LUNGOMARE DE SIMONE, 15, 84072 SANTA MARIA DI CASTELLABATE, ITALY
TEL: +39 0974 960162 FAX: +39 0974 961099

The Villa Sirio is located on the seafront in the heart of the historic centre of Santa Maria di Castellabate. Once the summer house of a patrician family, it first opened its doors to guests in 1997. The present owners have taken great care to maintain the charming characteristics of the original house, while teaming old and new to create maximum comfort. In the romantically-furnished and air-conditioned bedrooms there are a range of amenities, including shower, telephone, satellite television, minibar and safe. Located on the upper floors, some of them look on to the green hills of Castellabate, which are surrounded by the walls of its 12th century castle. Others offer heavenly views of the sparkling blue sea. A similar vista greets those eating in the dining room, where simple food and delicacies are served. The sun terrace, which almost hangs over into the sea, is the perfect place to watch the lovely sunsets and to gaze over to Capri. Hotel Sirio has its own private sunbathing platform and there are opportunities to enjoy a number of water sports. This is an excellent base from which to explore the many places of interest within easy reach, including Pompeii and the Vesuvius volcano. **Directions**: Leave the A3 at Battipaglia drive through Paestum and Agropoli to Sante Maria di Castellabate. The hotel is on the seafront. Price guide: L110,000–220,000.

PARKHOTEL SOLE PARADISO

VIA SESTO 13, SAN CANDIDO (BZ), 39038 DOLOMITES, ITALY
TEL: +39 0474 913120 FAX: +39 0474 913193

San Candido is an enchanting village surrounded by the majestic Dolomites. The Parkhotel Sole Paradiso is well named, for it is a glorious large chalet, the balconies filled with flowers in summer and with spectacular views across the snowfields in winter. Steeped in history, previous guests include the curator of the St Petersburg museum, Field Marshal Badoglio and the Italian Prime Minister, De Gasperi. The Ortner family greet guests in the pine reception area before showing them to their rooms, the beds draped in local lace, the furniture from the region, some leading onto balconies. The bathrooms are modern and efficient. The lounge is cosy and relaxing, with panelled walls, bright upholstery and an amusing old figurehead swinging from the ceiling. The bar is another fascinating room and the elegant dining room, part Viennese, part Tyrolean, with a 1930's influence and natural light, is in the talented hands of Chef Hubert Leitgeb and his team. His inspired interpretations of regional dishes will delight the most discerning guest. This is a wonderful centre for langlauf and downhill skiing, curling and sled excursions, a bus taking visitors to the pistes. Summer sports include tennis, golf and climbing. The hotel has a superb pool with spa facilities. **Directions:** A22, exit Brixen-Bressanone, driving 60km along S49, the Val Pusteria, to Innichen San Candido, where the hotel is signed. Parking. Price guide: Single L120,000–190,000; double L300,000–380,000.

ROMANTIK GOLF HOTEL – CASTELLO FORMENTINI

VIA OSLAVIA 2, 34070 SAN FLORIANO DEL COLLIO (GORIZIA), ITALY
TEL: +39 0481 884051 FAX: +39 0481 884052

High in the hills above Gorizia nestles the charming village of San Floriano del Collio, famous for its wines. There are few places that could provide more temptations for wine lovers and gastronomes! Amid this haven of peace and quiet, lies Romantik Golf Hotel – Castello Formentini. This hotel comprises two completely restored 16th century houses, situated next to the 14th century castle of Count Formentini. The interior is fitted with furniture and prints from the 17th and 18th century and antiques abound. All the bedrooms are named after a prestigious wine of the region and it is always possible to sample these! Three of the hotel's bedrooms are actually in the old castle, most of which was badly damaged in the First World War. The ground floor is also the setting for an excellent restaurant, where there is an accent on wild boar, game and local specialities. On Saturdays from late October to early May, wonderful medieval banquets are reconstructed. As well as a lovely outdoor swimming pool, guests are invited to take advantage of the on site tennis courts and golf course. The hotel is next to a museum of wine, which displays the actual utensils used in the traditional wine-making methods of Collio. **Directions:** Exit Superastrada (S5351) at Gorizia and follow signs for Castello Formentini. Price guide: Single L160,000–195,000; double/twin L260,000–325,000; suites L380,000–485,000.

TERME DI SATURNIA

58050 SATURNIA, GROSSETO, ITALY
TEL: +39 05 64 601 061 FAX: +39 05 64 601 266 E-MAIL: info@termedisaturnia.it

The Terme di Saturnia is the panacea for those wishing to return from their vacation fitter in mind and body as well as having had an enjoyable holiday with interesting people and diverse activities amid beautiful surroundings. The complex combines a spa with modern hospitality. The turn of the century building surrounds a 37C natural thermal spring where it is possible to bathe all year round . The elegant bedrooms are comfortable and the prestigious Villa Montepaldi restaurant has one part reserved for those on special diet regimes. The cellar holds fine wines. Away from the main building is the charming country house Albergo La Stellata, with 14 bedrooms, its own Tuscan restaurant leading on to a pretty terrace and the Saturnia Country Club with additional bedrooms, and the Madre Maremma restaurant featuring typical cusine. Visitors staying at both these houses enjoy the hotel amenities. A medical team advises guests on appropriate treatments at the spa, many based on the properties of the sulphurous waters. With a splendid pool, golf driving range and wonderful countryside to explore on bicycles, there is so much to do or the opportunity to relax and do nothing. **Directions:** Saturnia is an ancient village in Southern Tuscany between Grosseto and Rome, 1¹/2 hours by car from Rome Airport. Price guide: Single L275,000–345,000; double/twin L470,000–710,000; suites L1,000,000.

GRAND HOTEL VILLA BALBI

VIALE RIMEMBRANZA 1, 16039 SESTRI LEVANTE (GE), ITALY
TEL: +39 0185 42941 FAX: +39 0185 482459

Sestri Levante is on the Italian Riviera, south of Portofino and the Villa Balbi was built as a summer palace in the 17th century. The hotel of today stands in a secluded private park that contains magnificent old trees, overlooking the spectacular Gulf of Tigullio. The Villa has a graceful façade, flanked by tall palm trees and the interior rooms are very elegant – tall pillars and soaring arches reaching up to enchanting frescoed ceilings, brilliant chandeliers, marble floors, antique pieces and comfortable chairs. The charming bedrooms are peaceful, traditionally furnished and decorated in tranquil colours, all having lovely views over the water or the park. Some are designated non-smoking. There is a pleasant bar, but guests often prefer their apéritifs on the splendid terrace overlooking the Mediterranean. Breakfast is also served here. The Il Parco Restaurant specialises in Ligurian dishes and fish straight from the sea. Fine Italian wines are listed. With such peaceful surroundings, marvellous views, the pool and private beach, many residents seldom leave the hotel but golf and tennis are nearby. Boat trips can be organised and excursions made to Portofino and Baia del Silenzio. **Directions:** Leave A12 motorway at Sestri Levante exit, following signs for Centro Citta. Price guide: Single L90,000–210,000; double/twin L190,000–320,000; suites L350,000–460,000.

GRAND HOTEL COCUMELLA

VIA COCUMELLA, 7, 80065 SANT'AGNELLO, SORRENTO, ITALY
TEL: +39 081 878 2933 FAX: +39 081 878 3712 E-MAIL: hcocum@tin.it

La Cocumella, the only 5 star hotel in Sorrento, has a long tradition of hospitality, its origins dating back to the 16th century, when it was a Jesuit Monastery. It was transformed into a hotel in 1822 when Sorrento became an important stop on the Grand Tour. The hotel is surrounded by parkland stretching down to the coast, culminating in a splendid terrace with spectacular views over the Gulf of Naples to Vesuvius. Traces of the monastery still remain, the elegant hall having been the cloisters and the chapel is still used for weddings and concerts. Many charming guest rooms have magnificent antique furniture and the bridal suite has an exquisite painted ceiling. The Scintilla restaurant is enchanting with art deco lampshades and a romantic terrace overlooking the garden. Guests feast on aromatic Mediterranean dishes and local wines, while in summer light buffet lunches are enjoyed in the Orange Grove by the pool. The hotels' historical tall ship, Vera, is perfect for excursions to Capri and the Amalfi Coast. Pompeii is a fascinating expedition. Staying within the hotel grounds, guests can enjoy tennis, go down by lift to the private solarium or relax in the beauty farm. **Directions:** Motorway from Naples to Castellammare di Staba then follow the coast road to Sorrento. Price guide: Single L290,000–410,000; double/twin L460,000–650,000; suites L650,000–1,500,000.

GRAND HOTEL EXCELSIOR VITTORIA

PIAZZA TASSO 34, 80067 SORRENTO (NAPLES), ITALY
TEL: +39 081 807 1044 FAX: +39 081 877 1206 E-MAIL:exvitt@exvitt.it

The Grand Hotel Excelsior Vittoria was built at the turn of the century, and stands on the Sorrento waterfront, with its own moorings. The architecture is graceful fin de siècle, and the grounds are wondrous, filled with exotic subtropical plants and scented from the orange groves and olive trees. This legendary establishment has been in the hands of the same family for four generations, and is immaculately furnished and decorated. The salons are elegant and cool, with Bergère chairs, fine antiques, beautiful rugs on the tiled floors, gilt mirrors, delicate plaster mouldings and palm trees. The meeting rooms are Art Nouveau, with glorious murals and vaulted ceilings (modern technology is available!). The guest rooms, most having balconies or terraces with views over the Bay or gardens, and the suites are magnificent. All have luxurious bathrooms. Eating is "La Cucina Italiana", accompanied by superb wines. The Sala Vittoria Restaurant is very grand, with marble pillars; guests can enjoy al fresco dining in the delightful Restaurant Panoramico; lighter meals are served in the pretty Piscina snack bar. Relaxing by the pool, shopping in Sorrento or expeditions to Capri, Pompeii and Amalfi fill the day. **Directions:** A3, exit Castellamare di Stabia, follow signs to Sorrento. Price guide: Single L347,000; double/twin L431,000–619,000; suites L789,000–1,300,000.

ROMANTIK HOTEL STAFLER

MAULS, 10, 39040 FREIENFELD NR STERTING (BZ), ITALY
TEL: +39 0 472 77 11 36 FAX: +39 0 472 77 10 94

This romantic hotel has been offering hospitality to travellers for some 500 years, being one of the oldest inns in the Eisack Valley, just south of the Brenner Pass between Austria and Italy. It is built in the local style, against an impressive background of pine-clad mountains, the perfect place to stop on a leisurely European tour. The reception area is very handsome and the salon, with its fine panelled ceiling, is a charming place to relax. Stone walls, low archways and lovely antiques are reminders of the inn's history. The bedrooms are light and roomy, comfortably furnished, having soft, harmonious colour schemes and good bathrooms. Some are suitable for those with mobility problems. The intimate bar is very convivial. Eating here is a feast, succulent regional dishes based on local produce are prepared by the talented chef and wines from the area are recommended. This is a marvellous place for families, the big well-kept gardens having room for children to play while their parents relax in the sun. The hotel also has an indoor pool. Skiing is good in this area; in warmer months tennis is close by, the driving range is only 9km away and mountain bikes can be hired to explore the countryside and local villages. **Directions:** Autostrade A22, exit for Brixen Bressanone, driving North following signs for Brenner, reaching Mauls after 20 km. Price guide: Single L105,000–130,000; double/twin L170,000 –220,000; suites L170,000–220,000.

ROMANTIK HOTEL TURM

KIRCHPLATZ 9, 39050 VÖLS AM SCHLERN, SÜD TIROL (BZ), ITALY
TEL: +39 0471 72 5014 FAX: +39 0471 725474

Parts of this fine tower date back to the 13th century and at one time it was a dungeon. However, all traces of such inhospitality have disappeared, as today it is a splendid hotel offering a warm welcome to its guests. It stands quite high up, in the centre of a wildlife park. The family are collectors of art and have about 2000 works, including Picasso and De Chirico. The bedrooms, some in the Kraiterhaus, are charming, comfortable and pretty, with local fabrics and old carved pine furniture. The hall is delightful with a big open stove and fascinating prints on the walls. The lounge is a typical Tyrolean Stube, with pine walls and rustic chairs. The convivial bar is similar. The handsome restaurant, one of the five best hotel restaurants in Italy, is supervised by Othmar, the maitre, whilst Stephan, the award-winning chef and owner, demonstrates his skills in the kitchen. Aromatic variations of local specialities are accompanied by fine wines. The Turm is close to good skiing and other winter sports. In summer, activities include hiking, riding, tennis, boating on the lakes and exploring the nature reserve. Special mountain-trekking weeks are organised, twice a year, in June. The hotel also has a sybaritic indoor pool and spa area. **Directions:** A22, exit Bolzano North, towards Brennero, take left hand tunnel for Altipiani. The hotel is near the village church. Price guide (per person): Single/double/twin L96,000–145,000; suite L126,000–175,000.

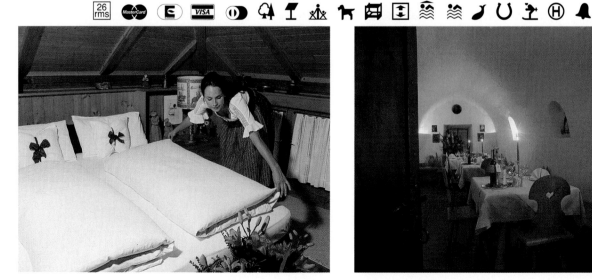

HOTEL VILLA DIODORO

VIA BAGNOLI CROCI 75, 98039 TAORMINA (ME), ITALY
TEL: +39 0942 23312 FAX: +39 0942 23391

The Hotel Villa Diodoro, within easy walking distance of the historical centre and the Greek theatre, is surrounded by magnificent gardens and affords fine views across the bay of Naxos and Mount Etna. Following a careful and extensive renovation during the winter of 1996, the hotel is now one of the most desirable four-star hotels in Taormina. The 102 rooms are well-appointed and feature every modern convenience including individually controlled air conditioning, satellite television and a minibar. Dominating the entire coastline, the view from the hotel is unrivalled in Taormina, particularly in the spacious bar. A local artist's colourful work fuses with the Mediterranean shades reflected from the outside creating a convivial ambience. Guests dine in the large restaurant which serves an à la carte menu specialising in Sicilian dishes. There are ample facilities for conferences and seminars including the well-equipped convention room. Sun worshippers will be pleased with the private beach. Places of interest nearby include the towns of Taormina, Etna, Messina and Castelmola. **Directions:** Leave the A18 at Taormina and follow for Centro. Follow the hotel signs for Villa Diodoro; the hotel is down a long winding road, about 500 yards after the town hall on the right. Price guide: Single L180,000–250,000; double/twin L260,000–350,000.

 # ROMANTIK HOTEL VILLA DUCALE

VIA LEONARDO DA VINCI, 60, 98039 TAORMINA, SICILY
TEL: +39 0942 28153 FAX: +39 0942 28710 E-MAIL: villaducale@tao.it

Once a coaching inn, then the summer villa of a nobleman – an ancestor of the present owner – on the edge of Taormina, this delightful small hotel with spectacular views of Naxos Bay and Mount Etna is in rural surroundings. The interior is charming, with a déjà-vu ambience, and guests can relax in the small lounge decorated with fine pieces of Sicilian pottery. The bedrooms, all different shapes and sizes, have individual colour schemes, fresh flowers, tiled floors and elegant period furniture. There is no formal restaurant but a leisurely breakfast, with a wide range of sweet and savoury dishes, is served until 11.30am on the terrace,

where delicious hot snacks and wines are available all day. From the terrace on clear days you can see across to Catania. There is a good choice of restaurants, pizzerias and cafés in the village round the corner. A cable car descends to a sandy beach at Mazzaro, and buses go to Etna and Agrigento. Golfers will enjoy the superb Il Picciolo Golf Course, some 30 minutes' drive away. **Directions:** Take highway A18 from Catania to Taormina, then take the road to Castelmola. The hotel has a small car park. Price guide: Single L200,000–260,000; double/twin L280,000–400,000; suites L380,000–600,000.

HOTEL VILLA SANT' ANDREA

VIA NAZIONALE 137, 98030 TAORMINA MARE (ME), ITALY
TEL: +39 0942 23125 FAX: +39 0942 24838

This unique and gorgeous hotel was a private villa built in the 1830s and it has retained its dignified ambience whilst being transformed into a small part of paradise on the bay of Mazzaro. Set right on the water's edge, the Sant' Andrea is protected by exotic tropical gardens. New arrivals are delighted with the interior, with its graceful archways, cool tiled floors and marvellous collection of fine antiques, handsome paintings and views across the water. The bedrooms are light and airy, many with balconies facing the sea. Some are in the 'dependence' just metres away – all are pretty and comfortable. The elegant salon is peaceful and watching the lights of the fishing fleet from the well stocked piano bar is a pleasant way to spend an evening, perhaps later dancing the night away under the stars. The Olivero Restaurant also extends under the floodlit trees on the terrace, a brilliant scenario at night. Gorgeous Mediterranean food and good Italian wines enhance the ambience. The hotel has its own beach, with sunbeds, windsurfing and other water sports on request. A nearby cable car will take guests to Taormina, the Roman and Greek theatre and tennis courts. Between Mount Etna and Taormina lies the "Picciolo Golf Club". **Directions:** Leave Route 18 at Taormina exit, then follow signs to the hotel. Price guide (per person): Single L205,000–370,000; double/twin L310,000– 540,000 ; suites L105,000 supplement.

HOTEL VICTORIA

VIA N. COSTA 4, 10123 TORINO, ITALY
TEL: +39 011 5611909 FAX: +39 011 5611806

This charming family-run town house hotel is spacious, airy and – despite its central location – quiet and peaceful. All the rooms are well-furnished, with those in the new wing of the house being of a particularly high standard. Throughout the interior, a light shade of green is the predominant colour and an abundance of plants and flowers adds an extra personal touch to the surroundings. The public rooms are airy and spacious, with the lounge and bar divided into areas on different levels and scattered with lovely antiques which the hotel's owners have acquired during their travels throughout the world. In the bedrooms, great attention to detail is evident in the carefully chosen fabrics, which are mixed and matched to attractive colour schemes to create maximum effect. All the rooms are very individual, with their design and décor achieving a sense of lightness and space. Constant improvement is a philosophy much in evidence. In the newer part of the hotel, the bathrooms are marble and all are supplied with monogrammed bathrobes. There is no restaurant, but the breakfast room is very pleasant and overlooks a colourful internal courtyard garden. **Directions**: From A4 exit at Turin/Torino and head towards "Centrio citta". Parking is in Piazza Valdo Fusi. Porto Nuova station is a five minute taxi ride away. Price guide: Single L170,000–200,000; double/twin L230,000–260,000; suites L300,000.

GRAND HOTEL TREMEZZO

VIA REGINA 8, 22019 TREMEZZO (CO), ITALY
TEL: +39 0344 40446 FAX: +39 0344 40201 E-MAIL: tremezzograndhotel@traveleurope.it

Built in 1910, this comfortable and welcoming liberty villa features many period ornaments and is enhanced by some fine Art Nouveau pieces. Striking columns and deep colours dominate the interior of Grand Hotel Tremezzo and the exquisite salons, which are ideal for relaxing or conversing with friends. The 100 bedrooms are beautifully appointed with rich fabrics and elegant décor whilst the marble bathrooms are spacious and well-equipped and display attractive extras such as original art deco mirror vanity units. An imaginative à la carte menu is served in the terraced restaurant 'Limonaia' and in the Sala Contessa whilst in the main restaurant Regina a four-course daily changing menu is offered. Light snacks and drinks may be savoured in the convivial Escale bar and the gazebo by the pool. Pastimes include swimming, playing tennis in the superb grounds, enjoying the sauna and gymnasium, walking, visiting the nearby villas and shopping in Como. The prestigious 18-hole golf course, Menaggio Cadenabbia, is only 5km away. Baby-sitting is available upon request. The local towns of Bellagio and Campione are fascinating to explore whilst nature enthusiasts will enjoy the Villa Carlotta botanic gardens and museum, adjacent to the hotel. **Directions:** Leave A9 at Como Nord and follow signs for Menaggio (5km from Tremezzo). The hotel is on the lake road. Price guide: Single L240,000–310,000; double/twin L360,000–520,000; suites L510,000–900,000.

ROMANTIK HOTEL LOCANDA DEI MAI INTEES

VIA NOBILE CLAUDIO RIVA 2, 21022 AZZATE (VA), ITALY
TEL: +39 0332 457223 FAX: +39 0332 459339 E-MAIL: maiintees@tin.it

The Romantik Hotel Locanda Dei Mai Intees has been imaginatively converted from an old country villa and now offers guests the highest standards of comfort in lovely surroundings. Many of the charming features from earlier days have been retained, including the original frescoes which can be admired in the restaurant. Wooden beamed ceilings abound and add character. The beautifully-appointed and spacious bedrooms, which are all individually named to create a personal touch, are well-equipped, warm and welcoming. Equally inviting are the public rooms, which include a bar – the perfect place to relax and sample a small grappa! The restaurant offers an extensive menu of delicious cuisine, complemented by a good range of wines. Two rooms are available for private diners. In the hot summer months, the walls of the Piano bar open onto the pretty garden. It is here that guests can soak up the wonderful atmosphere created by lively events such as jazz evenings. Within easy reach of the hotel are many factory shops, selling shoes and leather goods, as well as a selection of places that are worth visiting. **Directions**: Exit A8 at Buguggiate and follow brown signs for Lagi di Varese and then Azzate. From then on follow hotel signs – the hotel is very close to the castle. Price guide: L220,000–320,000; double/twin L260,000–350,000; suites L850,000.

METROPOLE HOTEL

SAN MARCO, RIVA DEGLI SCHIAVONI 4149, 30122 VENICE, ITALY
TEL: +39 041 520 5044 FAX: +39 041 522 3679

Do try and arrive at this excellent hotel on a Friday – when the usual doorman's welcome is given by characters from the Commedia dell'Arte – including Harlequin and Brighella. This will confirm that the Metropole is rather special. The architecture is 18th century and its position is superb, overlooking the canal and the lagoon, just three minutes walk from St Mark's Square. The talented Beggiato family have had great pleasure in restoring this lovely building to its former splendour. Exquisite painted ceilings, lovely panelling, over 2000 antiques – including a beautiful clock embraced by cherubs – rich colourful décor and a friendly angel beckoning guests into the Zodiac Bar, which has a special cocktail for each of the twelve signs, combine to make it a fine place to stay. The air-conditioned bedrooms, overlooking the waterfront or the gardens, are charming. The Buffet Trattoria, a popular rendezvous for Venetians as well as hotel guests, serves an extensive menu of exotic and traditional dishes and often hosts special dinners with romantic musical themes. During the summer, guests may dine alfresco in the gardens Live music is played every night, throughout the seasons. There is Venice to explore by day, the casino to enjoy at night, boat trips to Murano to watch glass blowers at work, Lido beach and a good golf course. **Directions:** Vaporetto to St Marks. Price guide: Single L230,000–450,000; double/twin L330,000–650,000; suites L600,000–800,000.

VILLA CONDULMER

31020 ZERMAN DI MOGLIANO VENETO, TREVISO, ITALY
TEL: +39 041 457100 FAX: +39 041 457134

The Villa Condulmer – an immaculate and magnificent 18th century mansion just 18 kilometres from Venice – has an illustrious past. It has been home to a pope, cardinal, famous soldiers, diplomats, men of law and even a saint. Today this patrician house, with its graceful façade, is a prestigious, secluded hotel, surrounded by extensive parkland. A warm greeting awaits arrivals at this grand house, with its glorious hall, fine antiques and Moretti Laresi frescoes. The bedrooms are classically furnished in the Venetian style. Guests enjoy apéritifs in the elegant piano bar while selecting appetizing and aromatic dishes from the menu of the traditional restaurant, the tables are set with gleaming crystal and silver. Superb Italian wines are proffered. A meeting room able to seat 100 delegates is available for corporate events. The Villa has its own 27-hole golf course, swimming pool, tennis court and stables. The undulating park provides delightful walks with its lake, bridges and shady trees. Venice must be explored – St Mark's Square, The Doge's Palace, the sophisticated Lido, superb shops and little boats take visitors to the islands to see glass-blowing and lace-making. **Directions:** Leave A/4 for Mogliano, then follow signs to the Villa. Price guide: Single L180,000–260,000; double/twin L300,000–400,000; suites L400,000–600,000.

ALBERGO QUATTRO FONTANE

30126 LIDO DI VENEZIA, ITALY

TEL: +39 041 526 0227 FAX: +39 041 526 0726 E-MAIL: quafonve@tin.it

A distinctive country house set in an idyllic garden on the Lido amongst orchards and productive vineyards on this long island, away from the hustle and bustle of Venice, the Albergo is only ten minutes by water-bus from San Marco square. The outside is more reminiscent of a Swiss chalet, while the interior is more traditional, with tiled floors and big stone fireplaces. Signore Bevilacqua, whose family has owned Albergo Quattro Fontane for over forty years, has collected some very unusual antique furniture, art and artefacts from all over the world. A unique ambience greets you when you enter the Barchessa, the attractive annexe adjacent to the Albergo, where the bedrooms maintain the simplistic charm of individually chosen antique furniture. Large windows look out over the extensive terraces, where there is an outdoor dining area for summer meals. The menu is based on Venetian specialities, with the emphasis on traditional country cooking. The wines are from local vineyards. Regular water-buses to Venice. The Lido has its own famous beach and a golf course by day and the casino at night. **Directions:** Either a private water-taxi from the airport straight to the Albergo with its own canal or a public water-bus every hour from the airport to the Lido via San Marco, then five minutes taxi ride to the Albergo. Price guide: Single L290,000–380,000; double/twin L380,000–500,000.

HOTEL VILLA MICHELANGELO

VIA SACCO 19, 36057 ARCUGNANO (VICENZA), ITALY
TEL: +39 0444 550300 FAX: +39 0444 550490

Built during the end of the 18th century, this Venetian villa is an exquisite fusion of past and modern styles, retaining its period building and featuring some contemporary interiors. The Hotel Villa Michelangelo is surrounded by superb gardens, overlooking the Berici hills and displaying original 18th century parapets which have been restored to their former lustre. A welcoming ambience is evident throughout the public rooms where the wooden ceilings and marble floors blend harmoniously with the modern armchairs and works of art. The bedrooms are individually appointed with an amalgam of antique and current styles and offer many of the latest amenities including satellite television, minibar and air conditioning. The suites are glorious with their glass walls, fine fabrics and Venini lamps creating a magnificent visual display of colour. The elegant restaurant, with its subtle play on light and space, serves an exciting menu incorporating the delicate flavours of the local herbs and leaves. The splendid pool, which opens its roof and glass walls during the summer months, is ideal for both fitness enthusiasts and those wishing to relax by the poolside and enjoy an exotic cocktail from the piano bar. **Directions:** Leave the A4 at Vicenza Ovest and follow the signs for Arcugnano. Then turn into the hills, following the large white signs for Villa Michelangelo. Price guide: Single L200,000–220,000; double/twin L285,000–330,000; suites L400,000–430,000.

Latvia

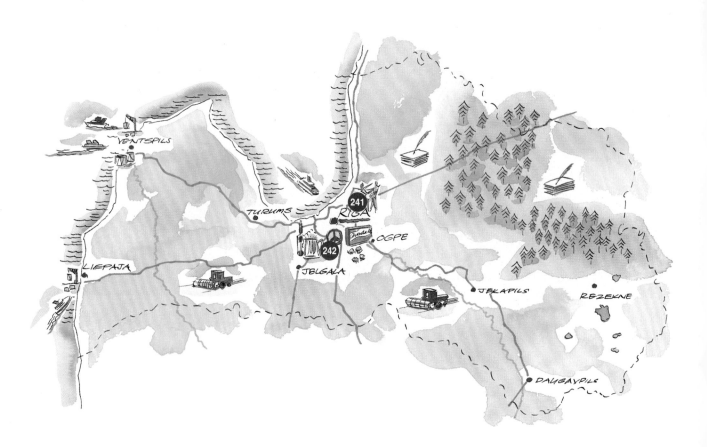

HOTEL DE ROME

KALKU IELA 28, 1050 RIGA, LATVIA
TEL: +371 7087600 FAX: +371 7087606

Latvia became independent in 1990 and this delightful hotel, one of the grand establishments in the 1920s and 1930s, reopened in 1991. In an excellent position, ideal for business people, being close to the commercial section of Riga, it overlooks the city gardens and the Freedom Monument. The new Hotel de Rome has a splendid façade, influenced by the Latvian Art Deco era, but the interior is contemporary. The bedrooms are spacious, decorated in harmonious colours and have comfortable modern furniture. Each floor has a lounge overlooking the Atrium, exhibiting exciting paintings. The smart Aspazijas Bar is a popular rendezvous. The Piano Bar is adjacent to the elegant Restaurant Otto Schwarz, renowned for delicious food and superb wines. Opera music is played daily and nightly in the Café "Romas Operas Galerija", famous for its cosy and relaxing atmosphere and used by opera lovers and business people alike. The well-equipped conference rooms have a 'no alcohol' regime. Interpreters and secretarial services available. The hotel is five minutes from the River Daugava, the markets, theatres and Latvian National Opera. The Art Nouveau street and Old Town are fascinating. To the west is Jurmala, a summer resort on the Baltic Sea and the countryside is glorious. **Directions:** Riga can be reached by ship, plane, train or car. Parking. Price guide: Single LS91; double/twin LS100; suites LS125.

HOTEL "KONVENTA SETA"

KALEJU STREET 9/11, 1050 RIGA, LATVIA
TEL: +371 708 7501 FAX: +371 708 7515

The Konventa Seta is situated in the Latvian capital of Riga, an 800 year-old Hanseatic city on the banks of the Daugava. It comprises a unique hotel complex, with apartments and small shops housed in an ensemble of buildings dating back to the Middle Ages. Behind the historical façade lie 80 rooms and 60 apartments, pleasantly furnished with every contemporary comfort. Evident in each bedroom are charming elements of the old construction, blending in effortlessly with the modern day amenities, but nevertheless creating a sense of bygone days. The ruins of a 13th century castle is now a part of the hotel's interior. Many rooms offer fantastic views of the old town, now in the midst of a revival and attracting thousands of business people and tourists to it. In the cosy bar "Melnais balodis", where guests can enjoy a selection of drinks, wines, spirits and snacks, the walls are graced with original Latvian paintings. This is an ideal place to relax before moving on to the restaurant, with its delicious cuisine, intimate atmosphere and excellent service. The complex offers good facilities for business meetings, supported by state-of-the-art equipment. Riga is steeped in history and has many varied attractions to offer visitors. **Directions:** The hotel is situated in the heart of the Old Town, 200m from Hotel de Rome. Price guide: Single LS44; double/twin LS55; suites LS60–70.

The romantic side of life!

Being a guest at a Romantik Hotel or Restaurant is special and goes far beyond just eating, drinking and sleeping well. As a guest here, you can enjoy a perfect individual hospitality in an environment of historical ambience.

EVERYTHING YOUR HEART DESIRES ...

we cannot anticipate, however we "Romantiks" would like to extend the special attention you deserve. We take this very seriously and guarantee this special service through the personal and warm attention only the proprietor of the individual hotels can give our guests.

A PART OF HISTORICAL AND CULTURAL EUROPE ...

you will discover with each visit to a Romantik Hotel or Restaurant. You will find a well-tended architectural personality because each Romantik Hotel is unique, displaying its own biography and personal charm.

A CULINARY TICKLE TO THE PALATE ...

will be one exciting experience of your stay. The complete harmony of stylish ambience combined with specialities from the kitchen and wine cellars help to create an atmosphere of festivity while dining in a Romantik Hotel or Restaurant.

Experience a distinct and individual hospitality with historical ambience
in 180 Romantik Hotels in 16 countries.

Pick up your FREE copy of the Romantik Guide in any Romantik Hotel or order it by fax or eMail (please reference Johansens).

ROMANTIK HOTELS & RESTAURANTS
INTERNATIONAL

ROMANTIK HOTELS & RESTAURANTS INTERNATIONAL
P.O.BOX 11 44 • D-63786 KARLSTEIN • GERMANY
TELEFAX: +49 (0) 6188/6007 • eMail: Romantik@t-online.de • Internet: http://www.romantikhotels.com/

Diem, Maskallis & Partner 103.808

Liechtenstein

PARKHOTEL SONNENHOF

MAREESTRASSE 29, 9490 VADUZ, PRINCIPALITY OF LIECHTENSTEIN
TEL: +41 75 232 1192 FAX: +41 75 232 0053 E-MAIL: real@sonnerhof.LOL.li

The microstate of Liechtenstein, just 61 square miles, on the east bank of the Upper Rhine, dating back to 1342, is delightful and easily accessible from the Swiss motorways or international trains heading for Austria. On the fringes of Vaduz, this enchanting hotel is surrounded by verdant countryside and has uninterrupted views across to the mountains. The house is resplendent with ivy, colourful window boxes and bright sun blinds shading the individual balconies and patios. The inviting gardens are well tended and filled with flowers – although this is also a winter sports haven. After a peaceful night's sleep in the enchanting bedrooms, guests enjoy a fabulous breakfast buffet. The reception hall has a rustic charm; the library is a handsome, relaxing room with a chess table set out by the winter fire and the bar is convivial. Big picture windows add to the attractions of the spacious, elegant restaurant; beautifully presented, original dishes accompanied by good wine ensure every meal is a special occasion. Convenient for businessmen meeting in Vaduz, the hotel is also popular with skiers, the slopes just 15 minutes away. Tennis, cycling, golf and walking fill summer days. The hotel has an indoor pool, other water sports are on Lake Constance. Hotel closed 20/12–6/1. Restaurant closed 20/12–28/2. **Directions:** A12 Feldkirch exit, watch for hotel signs on left before reaching Vaduz. Price guide: Single Sfr190–Sfr370; double/twin Sfr270–Sfr400; suites Sfr390–Sfr450.

Luxembourg

PARC HOTEL

16 RUE DE GRUNDHOF, 6550 BERDORF, LUXEMBOURG
TEL: +352 790 195 FAX: +352 790 223 E-MAIL: parcber@pt.lu

This charming hotel on the outskirts of the village of Berdorf, built on the forest edge, was founded some sixty years ago. It is a peaceful retreat away from the commercial activity of Luxembourg, standing in its own parkland, the well-tended gardens having romantic pools with bulrushes and waterlilies as well as rare, exotic trees. The bedrooms retain their original charm, but have been modernised to suit today's traveller. Many have balconies looking across the verdant countryside. The panelled salon is handsome, the ideal spot for a digestif after enjoying dinner in the spacious restaurant, with its unusual circular serving area in the centre of the room. The chefs are very creative, the menu cosmopolitan and the dishes beautifully presented. The wine list is extensive and reasonably priced. On fine days guests take their apéritifs and eat alfresco on the cool terrace, with green vines winding up the pillars and across the ceiling. Relaxing on comfortable garden chairs in the park is a popular pastime while more energetic guests walk in 'Little Switzerland' or use the hotel open-air pool. Tennis and mini-golf are nearby. **Directions:** Leave the E44 from Luxembourg City, taking the E29 to Echternach, following signs to Berdorf. There is parking at the hotel. Price guide: Single BF2200–3800; double/twin BF3000–4900.

HOTEL SAINT NICOLAS

31 ESPLANADE, 5533 REMICH, LUXEMBOURG
TEL: +352 69 8888 FAX: +352 69 8869 E-MAIL: hotel@pt.lu

Set in the picturesque town of Remich, the family run hotel affords fantastic views across the esplanade and lush vineyards as it lies on the banks of the river Moselle. Renowned for its excellent service and fine cuisine, Hotel Saint Nicolas boasts an unusual interior, decorated in a most eclectic style. In the public rooms, interesting paintings abound whilst blue glass lights add a touch of modernism to the corridors. The 40 bedrooms are furnished in a simple style with very contemporary fabrics and en suite facilities. Named after the Knight of the Holy Grail, the Lohengrin Restaurant is a gastromonic delight comprising traditional French cuisine. Moselle wines complement the inspired menu. Alfresco dining may be enjoyed during the summer months in the attractive garden. Guests may indulge in wine-tasting with vintages from the hotel's own cellar. Fitness facilities such as a sauna, solarium, Hammam and shiatsu are offered whilst the more energetic may enjoy canoeing and golf. Other pastimes include boat rides on the Moselle and exploring Trior, the oldest German town nearby. **Directions:** From Luxembourg, take the E29 to Remich, finding the hotel on the main esplanade opposite the Moselle river. Price guide: Single BF2500; double/twin BF3300; suites BF3900. Gastronomic offer (include 2 nights) BF5900.

The Netherlands

AMBASSADE HOTEL

HERENGRACHT 341, 1016 AZ AMSTERDAM, THE NETHERLANDS
TEL: +31 20 62 62 333 FAX: +31 20 62 45 321

The Ambassade is a most attractive hotel in the heart of Amsterdam. Originally ten separate houses, each the home of a wealthy merchant on the Herengracht (The Gentlemen's Canal), the hotel has been converted into one building which retains all the erstwhile interior architecture and the external façades. No two bedrooms are alike and each has its own colour scheme in accordance with its style. The graceful furniture complements the history of the building. The five suites are superb and the apartment luxurious. Overlooking the canal are two elegant and spacious lounges, with tall windows, splendid oil paintings on the walls and fine Amsterdam grandfather clocks. Breakfast is served in the traditional dining room, or guests can take advantage of the efficient room service available. There is no restaurant in the Ambassade, but there is a wide choice of places to eat in the city such as the historic Vijff Vlieghen and many small bistros along the canal sides. The luxurious float and massage centre, "Koan Float" owned by the hotel is situated on the Herengracht Canal. Those seeking the ultimate form of mind and body relaxation will enjoy the float cabins, filled with warm saline water. The famous Rijksmuseum, Van Gogh Museum and Anne Franks' House are nearby. Guests must sample Amsterdam's lively nightlife. **Directions:** Parking is not easy. 20 mins by taxi from Schiphol Airport. Price guide: Single FL260–270; double/twin FL325–335; suites FL425–525.

HOTEL DE ARENDSHOEVE

MOLENLAAN 14, 2861 LB, BERGAMBACHT, THE NETHERLANDS
TEL: +31 182 35 1000 FAX: +31 182 35 1155 E-MAIL: juwo@euronet.nl

This élite hotel, just a pleasant drive from Rotterdam, has achieved a timeless ambience with its graceful lines, ornamental garden and a traditional windmill as its landmark. Under this windmill is "Onder de Molen", one of the hotel's two restaurants, which serves more regional cuisine. The hotel is a long, low building and the interior is entrancing – all Europe is reflected in the decorations and furnishings, each fireplace, piece of carved panelling or fine antique having its own history, be it from a castle or private mansion. The bedrooms have a character of their own – a mélange of the past and present, with many hospitable extras. The lounge is a perfect rendezvous and the sociable Scarlatti Bar

is ideal for drinks at the end of the day. The pièce de résistance is Restaurant Puccini, with its exquisite South European renaissance décor, in the octagonal pavilion overlooking the gardens. Guests feast on imaginative, appetising dishes and superb wines. There is a dramatic Roman-style indoor pool with adjacent spa facilities and the Vithalgo Health Spa Centre, or tennis and a putting green for those needing fresh air. Ample meeting facilities. Cycling through the countryside is another diversion. **Directions:** From Rotterdam head for Capelle, then follow N210 to Bergambacht finding the hotel close to the windmill. Price guide: Single FL235–285; double/twin FL315–365; suites FL395–475.

HOTEL DE DUINRAND

STEEGERF 2, 5151 RB DRUNEN, THE NETHERLANDS
TEL: +31 416 372498 FAX: +31 416 374919

The top twelve restaurants in Holland belong to an exclusive club, "Les Patrons Cuisiniers" and Restaurant "De Duinrand" is one of these elite dozen, while also having superb residential facilities. It stands in woodlands, yet is easily accessible from the motorway. Peace and privacy are ensured as the hotel is surrounded by extensive well-kept gardens. The suites and bedrooms are very stylish, with exciting contemporary furniture and every imaginable extra, including double basins and bathrobes. The suites have Jacuzzis and patios, while the VIP-Suite is on two floors with its own champagne bar! Disabled guests have been remembered. Before dining, guests can order cocktails in the lounge or on the terrace, while deciding which exquisite dishes to order from the menus, with wine suggestions for each course. The handsome restaurant is sophisticated, with pristine linen, sparkling crystal and intriguing flower arrangements. Breakfast is alfresco on fine mornings. There are also excellent meeting rooms. Smoking is discouraged. Those needing exercise cycle through the countryside or play tennis nearby. Golf is further away. Others relax in the gardens, take a boat down the canal or explore Heusden and 's-Hertogenbosch, historic cities in the region. **Directions:** From A2 take A59, on reaching Drunen follow signs to the restaurant. Price guide: Single FL195; double/twin FL225; suites FL325–600.

MANOIR RESTAURANT INTER SCALDES

ZANDWEG 2, 4461 NA KRUININGEN, THE NETHERLANDS
TEL: +31 113 38 1753 FAX: +31 113 38 1763 E-MAIL: inter.scaldes@alliance.nl.

Known for its oyster cultivation, Kruiningen lies on the South Boulevard peninsula, almost equidistant from the Eastern and Western Scheldt. The Manoir Restaurant Inter Scaldes, situated in this small town, is furnished in a stylish manner with luxurious décor and fine ornaments. The restaurant and hotel are in separate buildings, surrounded by the beautiful English garden. With different fabrics and their own garden and balcony, the 12 suites are both spacious and individual, some with wonderful stone floors and others with a whirlpool or Jacuzzi. The restaurant is a very large conservatory with wickerwork furniture and country-style fabrics and has been awarded two Michelin stars for the superb cuisine made with fresh regional fish and other local products. Outdoor pursuits such as golf, tennis, renting bicycles and boats, walks by the sea or boat trips on the river may be enjoyed nearby. There are many historical cities within the area and the theme village of Vaete is worth a visit. Fishing enthusiasts will be pleased with the opportunities at Yerseke. **Directions:** From Antwerp, take the A4 Marerd Breda/Bergen op Zoom. Turn onto the A58 marked Vlissingen and take exit 33 Hansweert–Yerseke. There are several maps displayed throughout the town and visitors must look for the signs to Zandweg. Price guide: Single FL280; double/twin FL335; suites FL405–460.

HOTEL RESTAURANT DE SWAEN

DE LIND 47, 5061 HT OISTERWIJK, THE NETHERLANDS
TEL: +31 135 23 3233 FAX: +31 135 28 5860 E-MAIL: swaen@swaen.nl

To stay at De Swaen is an epicurean experience, for this enchanting hotel, overlooking the town square and English Garden, has a proprietor who is an enthusiastic chef and sets himself the highest standards of hospitality. De Swaen dates back to 1628; then a brewing house. Today, having maintained its historic charm, it is an elegant building with a decorative balcony along its façade and attractive terraces for alfresco refreshments. The richly decorated lounge, full of colour and comfort, is an ideal meeting place. The guest rooms, each unique, are luxurious and air-conditioned and gorgeous antiques blend happily with fax machines and other contemporary needs. Disabled visitors have been remembered.

Delicious appetizers in the intimate bar titillate the palate; the most exacting bon viveur will appreciate the fabulous dishes exquisitely presented in the magnificent restaurant – bergère chairs, big gilt mirrors, gleaming silver and immaculate napery. The wines are sublime. Less formal is the attractive Ammussery De Jonge Swaen, a sophisticated bistro serving tasty, reasonably priced dishes. Hosting corporate events, seminars and banquets is effortless at this exclusive hotel. Golf, cycling, tennis and riding are all within easy reach. **Directions:** From Einhoven E38, then A58, Moergestel exit, finding De Swaen in centre of Oisterwijk. Valet parking. Price guide: Single FL285; double/twin FL325–395; suites FL495–795.

HOTEL DE WIEMSEL

WINHOFFLAAN 2, 7631 HX OOTMARSUM, NETHERLANDS
TEL: +31 541 292 155 FAX: +31 541 293 295

An enchanting medieval village and a thriving farm form the background of this excellent and attractive hotel located some 80 miles east of Amsterdam. The architecture is typical of the region and the surroundings are rural. There is a marvellous feeling of space, with wide arches dividing the reception rooms and big windows overlooking the terrace or verdant countryside. The furnishings are contemporary and colourful. There are also smart, well-equipped meeting rooms. There are more suites than bedrooms, all are spacious and have been decorated in relaxing colour schemes, while the bathrooms are luxurious, marble with gold taps. Outdoor living is encouraged, with bright garden furniture set out on the terrace round the outdoor pool – perfect for al fresco breakfast or apéritifs. Both the Restaurant de Wanne as well as the Restaurant de Gouden Korenaar are very elegant, an appropriate setting for superb cosmopolitan dishes accompanied by fine wines. Marvellous picnic hampers can be arranged for those borrowing bicycles to explore the countryside. The hotel offers tennis and a superb health/beauty complex with a pool. Hot-air balloon trips start from the garden. **Directions:** A1 towards Hengelo, exit Oldenzaal/Ootmarsum, after 12 km, in Ootmarsum, take the road to Denekamp. Price guide: Single FL285; double/twin FL335; suites FL300–425.

 # RESTAURANT HOTEL SAVELBERG

OOSTEINDE 14, 2271 EH VOORBURG, THE NETHERLANDS
TEL: +31 70 3872081 FAX: +31 70 3877715

This enchanting hotel with its second name, 'Vreugd & Rust', which means 'Pleasure and Peace', the name of the lovely 17th mansion and its park, can be found in the old village of Voorburg, not far from The Hague. It has been restored with great care and is now a listed historical building. Guests are immediately aware of the grace evocative of its past combined with the luxury of today. The bedrooms and suites are spacious and light, overlooking the estate, and have every modern comfort. The elegant lounge is a quiet rendezvous, alternatively the big terrace is ideal for an apéritif in the sun. The excellent meeting rooms, with full office support and presentation equipment available, quickly transform into impressive private dining rooms suitable for corporate entertaining or special celebrations. The handsome restaurant is a very important part of this hotel, having won many accolades for its inspired use of seasonal fare and absolutely superb wine list. It offers both gourmet, à la carte and delicious set menus. Strolling round the lake enjoying the country air is a peaceful way to end a busy day.
Directions: From Amsterdam A4 towards Rotterdam/Delft, the A12 to Voorburg, finding the entrance to the hotel in Oosteinde 14. Price guide: Double/twin FL250,00–300,00; suites FL450,00–495,00.

Norway

TRONDHIEM

262

264

266

258

267

259

BERGEN

261

OSLO

263

260

STAVANGER

265

KRISTIANSAND

NORWAY (Balestrand)

KVIKNE'S HOTEL

5850 BALESTRAND, NORWAY
TEL: +47 57 69 11 01 FAX: +47 57 69 15 02 E-MAIL: booking@kviknes.no

Hospitality at Balholm, the site of this impressive residence, has been a tradition since 1752. The Kvikne family, who own the hotel, made this imaginative purchase in 1877 and now, over a century later, it is one of Norway's largest prestigious hotels. Its situation is magnificent, on the shores of the fjord at Balestrand and the register records many eminent names over the decades. The interior of Kvikne's is an antique collector's dream, so many beautiful pieces, together with fine objets d'art and handsome paintings. The Hoiviksalen is a magnificent example of hand-carving in the Dragon style: the chairs, tables, ornaments are all unique – and comfortable! The bedrooms are charming and such is the popularity of this hotel that a new wing has been added to accommodate the influx of guests. Most have balconies overlooking the fjord and all have modern amenities. Drinks are enjoyed in the bars or on the terraces and enjoying superb Norwegian specialities, including a fabulous Smorgasbord, in the spacious, restaurant is a great pleasure. Boat trips down the fjord, helicopter rides over the mountains, are exciting; fishing and exploring the region are more leisurely occupations. **Directions:** From the airport, take the main road for Balestrand, finding Kvikne's Hotel in the centre. Parking for residents. Price guide (per person): Single NOK610–945; double/twin NOK410–745; suites NOK760–895.

GRAND HOTEL TERMINUS

ZANDER KAAESGT 6, PO BOX 1100, 5001 BERGEN, NORWAY
TEL: +47 55 31 16 55 FAX: +47 55 31 85 76

Set in the heart of the second biggest city in Norway, the Grand Hotel Terminus is a fine example of 1920s high style architecture. It's excellent standard of accommodation and hospitality has attracted the rich and the famous since its opening in 1928 and it enjoys an unrivalled reputation throughout Norway and beyond. The décor is largely original – especially noteworthy is the reception area, which is a fine example of traditional Bergen craftsmanship. The hotel has exceptional dining facilities. Not only does it boast an impressive banqueting hall, but it also has a restaurant and cafeteria, as well as a number of private dining rooms of varying size. The larger rooms are ideally suited to business functions, while the smaller chambers create the perfect atmosphere in which to enjoy to an intimate candlelit dinner. All serve exquisite international cuisine and local specialities, complemented by an excellent selection of fine wines. Those of a literary bias can relax with a good book in the "litteraer salong", while there is a small gym for the more active and as expected in a Scandanavian hotel, full sauna and solarium facilities. The large conference hall can accommodate 400 people theatre-style. **Directions**: The hotel is in the centre of Bergen, next to the railway station. Price guide: Single NOK940–1190; double/twin NOK1190–1360.

NORWAY (Dalen)

DALEN HOTEL

PO BOKS 123, 3880 DALEN, NORWAY
TEL: +47 35 07 70 00 FAX: +47 35 07 70 11 E-MAIL: dhh@atm.no

Once a favourite retreat for the crowned heads and aristocracy of Europe, Dalen Hotel offers today's guests the opportunity to relax and enjoy life in beautiful surroundings steeped in history and tradition. The hotel was built in 1894, its architecture inspired by Norway's historic stave churches. The imposing structure was created in the dragon style – the Norwegian version of the 'Swiss chalet' architecture popular throughout Europe at the time – with its dragon heads, turrets and cornices. In renovating and restoring the hotel, its owners have been painstaking in their efforts to ensure that the spirit of the original building is retained and enhanced. The main hall, featuring medieval-inspired carving, is mainly unchanged. The entire ceiling is a large glass painting with the Norwegian coat of arms as the central motif. To guarantee the highest standard of comfort, the cosy bedrooms offer every modern facility. In the elegant dining room, Norwegian specialities and international cuisine are featured on the excellent à la carte menu. The hotel is set at the end of The Telemark Canal, one of the recommended sights of cultural heritage in the 'Europa Nostra' and still frequented by old passenger boats which travel over 100km from the sea. **Directions**: The hotel is on rd.45, between Stavanger/Oslo (20km south of E134) and can be reached by Norway bus-express Price guide: (per person) Single NOK695; double/twin NOK535; suites NOK645. An extra NOK50 for a balcony and garden view.

GRAND HOTEL HONEFOSS

STABELLSGT 8, 3500 HONEFOSS, NORWAY
TEL: +47 32 12 27 22 FAX: +47 32 12 27 88 E-MAIL: dhh@atm.no

The Grand Hotel Honefoss was built in 1809 and originally opened as a small inn. Over the years it has had various additions including the classical façade of the main section, which contributes much to its distinctive character. There are 37 bedrooms, each individually designed and furnished with elegant simplicity and good taste. The small bar and lounge are both cosy and intimate places in which to relax and unwind before moving on to dinner. In the elegant dining room, an excellent range of cuisine is served. Among the starters, soups, meat and fish dishes, a number of Norwegian specialities are included. With a capacity for 80 guests, it is an ideal venue for many different occasions and celebrations. The Winter Garden, resplendent in wood panelling, is suitable for meetings and conferences for up to 20 people, while the Grand Hall can cater for up to 50 participants. Honefoss offers excellent opportunities for shopping and there are also a great variety of restaurants providing a range of entertainment. There is plenty to explore within easy reach. Toverud Power Station, now a museum, is located on the western shore of Lake Randsfjorden, while Blaafarveverket at Modum features fascinating cobalt mines. The "Sister Churches" at Gran are also worth a visit. **Directions:** From Oslo take the E16 to Honefoss. The hotel is situated in the centre and there are ample parking facilities. Price guide: Single NOK900; double/twin NOK1100.

NORWAY (Norangsfjorden)

HOTEL UNION ØYE

6196 NORANGSFJORDEN, NORWAY
TEL: +47 70 06 21 00 FAX: +47 70 06 21 16

Emperor Wilhelm II of Germany, Queen Willemina of the Netherlands, Henrik Ibsen and Karen Blixen are some of the many names to be found in Hotel Union Øye's guest book. It is not surprising that this hotel is often frequented by royalty as it offers a superb standard of accommodation and excellent service. The Union was opened as a hotel in 1891 and restored to its original style in 1989, giving its visitors the chance to experience the refined atmosphere of past ages. The 25 bedrooms, most of which offer four-poster beds and en suite bathrooms, are individually appointed. In order to retain a more elevated ambience, facilities such as televisions, telephones, newspapers and radios have deliberately been excluded. After dinner,

guests are told the poignant tale of the hotel's resident ghost, Linda. As the owner chronicles her tragic life, guests are treated to the unusual combination of garlic and cognac. Fine salmon and trout fishing may be enjoyed in the Øje River. Hikers and climbers will be pleased with the hotel's location as Slogjen, the most renowned mountain in the Sunnmøre Alps, lies at the foot of the garden. The hotel provides its own mountain guide for groups (min 15 pers.); guests must experience the stunning view afforded from its peak . **Directions:** From Oslo, travel towards Lillehammer, through Otta, Lom and Stryn. Continue to Hornindal, then Øye. Price guide per person: Double/twin NOK454–845 (NOK200 extra for single room supplement).

FIRST HOTEL BASTION

SKIPPERGATEN 7, 0152 OSLO, NORWAY
TEL: +47 22 47 77 00 FAX: +47 22 33 11 80

Old Oslo is fascinating – dating back to the Middle Ages and now re-emerging with fine old buildings being renovated and the vibrant Stock Exchange located there. In the midst of this stimulating ambience, at the foot of the Akershus Fortress, there is a new hotel, The First Bastion. It is a modern hotel with contemporary fabrics, fireplace and lighting in the Library/Bar, yet it has lovely polished old wooden floors enhancing the ambience. The bedrooms, decorated in warm colours and with comfort an important criterion, meet various needs – non-smoking, smoking, adapted for those with mobility problems or suitable for guests with special business needs such as fax or cordless telephones so they can be accessed throughout the hotel. The hotel does not have a restaurant, however there is a marvellous 'Oslo Breakfast' served in the attractive dining room. A lunch buffet is served Monday to Friday and at night the concierge will recommend good places to dine. The Bastion has a small fitness centre and spa, popular with delegates participating in seminars in the self-contained conference area at the top of the hotel. The hotel is ideally situated for the ferries, trains and buses. It is close to shops, restaurants, museums and the commercial centre. **Directions:** In the centre of old Oslo. There is parking. Price guide: Single NOK545–1245; double/twin NOK690–1495.

NORWAY (Sandane)

GLOPPEN HOTELL

6860 SANDANE, NORWAY
TEL: +47 57 86 53 33 FAX: +47 57 86 60 02 E-MAIL: glopphot@vestdata.no

Steeped in tradition and history, this charming hotel nestles at the head of Gloppenfjord, in the rural area of Sandane. The wild and captivating landscape encompasses the Gloppen Hotell, which is often frequented by angling enthusiasts. Dating back to 1866, the oldest part of the hotel is Swiss-style and is a fine example of historic architecture. A warm and friendly atmosphere envelopes the property and is present throughout the cosy public rooms. All of the 30 bedrooms feature comfortable furnishings and the double room in the old building has been renovated in the style of the 1890s with nuances of the art nouveau period. Guests may recline in front of the open fireplaces in the sitting rooms and

enjoy a preprandial drink. In bygone times, the salmon fishermen indulged in hearty meals and this tradition has been retained as guests feast upon four-course dinners in one of the enchanting dining rooms. The Gloppenelva river provides excellent salmon fishing whilst those interested in other outdoor pursuits will be pleased with the nearby opportunities for canoeing, mountain-climbing, angling and coastal walks. The beautiful Norwegian landscape with its glaciers, plateaux, mountains and valleys must be explored. **Directions:** The hotel is situated in the centre of Sandane, only 10 minutes away from the airport. Price guide: Single NOK845; double/twin NOK1090.

KRONEN GAARD HOTEL

VATNE, 4300 SANDNES, NORWAY
TEL: +47 51 62 14 00 FAX: +47 51 62 20 23

Set amid beautiful scenery and surroundings, the Kronen Gaard Hotel is an intimate and friendly hotel offering the highest standards of service. It was originally built at the turn of the century by timber merchant, Gunner Block Watne. Designed as a summer residence and lying in 60 acres of land, it was – by the standards of that time – a very big and impressive house. The older buildings that, in part, make up today's hotel, have been carefully blended with tasteful modern additions. There are 34 charming bedrooms, including three suites and all are nicely decorated and furnished. Every possible amenity has been included to guarantee guests' comfort. A magnificent weeping beech, thought to be around 100 years old, can be seen from the windows of some of the rooms on the southern side. In the intimate candlelit restaurant, excellent international cuisine is served, with a selection of Norwegian specialities included on the menu. Kronen Gaard has a variety of course and conference rooms, catering for a maximum of 60 participants. Also suitable for private occasions such as weddings and parties, all banquet sections feature a fully licensed bar. The building that was formerly the stable now houses the small, English-style Gaardshuset Pub. From April through to September barbecues are held on the terraces. **Directions**: From the airport follow signs to Sandnes and then to hotel. Price guide: Single NOK995, double/twin NOK1290, suites NOK1495.

WALAKER HOTELL

5815 SOLVORN, SOGN, NORWAY

TEL: +47 576 84 207 FAX: +47 576 84 544 E-MAIL: walaker.hotel@sf.telia.no

This historic hotel started life as a farm with an inn and coach station and its original buildings date from about 1650. The property has belonged to the Nitter Walaker family for over 300 years and the excellent, personal service provided reflects the best traditions of a family-run hotel. The main building was built in 1934 and has eight guest rooms, reception, sitting room and dining room, where traditional meals are served. The oldest house is still called the Court house because it was used as such for centuries. The bedrooms in this building are furnished in a simple style and retain an appeal for guests wishing to experience the atmosphere of bygone times and sleep under an old roof. The barn, built in 1883, has been restored and turned in an art gallery – where exhibitions of contemporary art are held every summer – and conference facilities comprise four meeting rooms. There are a host of fascinating places to visit within easy reach of the hotel including the Urnes Stave church, an item on UNESCO's World heritage list, the wooden renaissance church in Gaupne and the Sogn folkemuseum. Guided ice walks are available at the glacial centre in Jostedal, while trout fishing is an option in the fjords near the airport. **Directions:** By the Sognefjord, 3km off road 55(Lom–Sogndal). Distance from Oslo 350km. From Sogndal airport 35km. Price guide: Single NOK550–980; double/twin NOK880–1180.

FLEISCHER'S HOTEL

5700 VOSS, NORWAY
TEL: +47 56 51 11 55 FAX: +47 56 51 22 89

This grand and favourite hotel is in a superb position, overlooking the lake and not far from the station, one hour from Bergen. The façade, with its towers and pointed dormer windows, is reminiscent of Switzerland. The surrounding countryside is spectacular, Voss being between two large fjords. Built in 1889 and still run by the same family, Fleischer's has been discreetly modernised, without losing its original charm. There is a warm ambience in the foyer with its convivial coffee shop and the elegant salons lead onto the attractive terrace which, with its magnificent views over the water, is popular for alfresco refreshments. The pretty bedrooms are light and comfortable, some having balconies. All have modern amenities and the bathrooms are efficient. The panelled and well-stocked bar has a pianist in the evenings. Delicious food, including local fish and Norwegian specialities, is served in the restaurant – with its big windows and warm colour scheme. Leisure facilities include a pool with spa, tennis, riding, fishing, bikes to explore the fascinating countryside, canoeing and white water rafting on the river. Boats and bikes can be hired. It is a good base for winter sports too. **Directions:** From Bergen take E16 towards Voss, finding the hotel on the lakeside. Price guide: Single NOK925; double/twin from NOK1190.

Portugal

CASA DOMILU

ESTRADA DE BENAGIL, APARTADO 1250, PRAIA DO CARVOEIRO, 8400 LAGOA, PORTUGAL
TEL: +351 82 358 409 FAX: +351 82 358 410 E-MAIL: casa.domilu@mail.telepac.pt

Designed and built by Mr D'Almeida, the owner, the hotel was originally a private villa, set in subtropical gardens. Now a family-run residence, the Casa Domilu is set in a secluded location, ideal for those seeking privacy or a peaceful break. The interior is furnished in an elegant style with warm rugs, fresh flowers and fine paintings. The eclectic bedrooms are a fusion of the past and present – filled with antiques whilst offering every modern amenity. The comfortable lounge featuring meeting facilities and the attractive private bar are available for small functions, accommodating 12 people. Specialising in traditional Portugese dishes and complemented by a selection of international cuisine, the restaurant, overlooking the swimming pool, offers a light luncheon menu à la carte. Tuesday evenings are particularly convivial with live music and barbecues. Daily activities include mountain biking, golf, swimming, tennis and a variety of water sports. Glorious sunsets may be admired on the sandy beaches nearby, whilst the villages of the Algarve are a delight to explore. **Directions:** From Faro, take IP1 in the direction of Portimao. At Lagoa turn left towards Carvoeiro. After 2km, turn left towards Benagil and follow the signs to Casa Domilu. Price guide: Standard Esc4,500–7,500; studio Esc5,000–8,000; junior suites Esc6,000–10,000; suites Esc9,000–18,000 (All prices are per person).

HOTEL QUINTA DAS LAGRIMAS

SANTA CLARA, 3040 COIMBRA, PORTUGAL
TEL: +351 39 44 1615 FAX: +351 39 44 1695

Quinta das Lagrimas was the country Estate of the Tears – but the only sadness staying in this exquisite hotel will be leaving it. Here, centuries ago, Dona Ines de Castro, beloved by the Prince Dom Pedro, wept as she died. Coimbra is the home of the Fado, tragic poems sung by the students of Portugal's oldest university in the medieval quarter of the town. The hotel is quintessentially Portuguese, a palatial 18th century villa with terraces, a graceful façade, balustrades and ornate mouldings, surrounded by extensive, immaculate gardens. The salons have graceful chairs and stylish terracotta colour schemes. The bedrooms are prettily designed and have cool wooden floors and modern amenities.

The suites have four-poster beds. Guests relax in the bar over canapés and apéritifs, then enter the lovely restaurant, with its romantic terrace, to linger over superb Portuguese dishes and fine wines. Residents wander among the exotic trees and fountains in the grounds, swim (pool bar) or play tennis. There are endless treasures and ancient buildings to explore while in Coimbra and opportunities to sample port in cellar restaurants. **Directions:** From Lisbon Motorway A1-IP1 towards Porto, take Coimbra exit, following signs to Santa Clara Convent, finding hotel signed on the right. Price guide: Single Esc15,000–22,000; double/twin Esc18,500–27,000; suites Esc50,000–60,000.

LA RÉSERVE

SANTA BARBARA DE NEXE, 8000 FARO, ALGARVE, PORTUGAL
TEL: +351 89 9994 74 FAX: +351 89 9994 02

An élite small hotel that is a magnificent example of the best of modern Portuguese architecture which stands in its own well-tended estate in air scented by the eucalyptus, with almond and olive trees on the surrounding hills. The interior comprises imaginative traditional furniture in sophisticated surroundings. The suites are superb, each with its own terrace looking out to the distant sea and luxurious bathrooms with big robes and designer toiletries. The spacious, marble-floored foyer with decorative wrought-iron work, bowls of flowers and colourful seating is a pleasant meeting place en route to the bar before entering the brilliant La Réserve restaurant for a gourmet meal prepared by the chef-patron who will also suggest which of the fine local wines would be appropriate. For lunch informal meals are served at the poolside snack bar. Apart from swimming, guests play tennis or wander through the lovely gardens. Several good courses in the vicinity will challenge golfers. Those seeking a change of scenery can enjoy the coast with its golden beaches or drive through the countryside exploring the old towns and villages. The hotel is conveniently located 10 km from Faro airport and Faro centre. **Directions:** From Faro N125 to Patacão, then follow signs to Santa Bárbara de Nexe. Price guide: Single Esc18,000–30,000, double/twin Esc28,000–40,000, suites Esc30,000–44,000.

271

MONTE DO CASAL

CERRO DO LOBO ESTOI, 8000 FARO, ALGARVE, PORTUGAL
TEL: +351 89 990140 FAX: +351 89 991341

This elegant Algarve country house, built in the 18th century, is wonderfully peaceful, surrounded by almond, olive and fruit trees, with Bougainvillaea climbing up the terraces and a view across the countryside to the coast. Several of the cool, spacious bedrooms are on the ground floor with direct access to the pool and sun terraces, while the rooms higher up have their own terraces and lounge areas. Breakfasts of squeezed orange juice and fresh bread from the village bakery are the perfect start to the day! The bar and restaurant are in the converted coach house. The bar is inviting, with doors leading onto the terrace. While light lunches are available, dining is an important part of the programme – magnificent International dishes, superb Portuguese specialities, including the regional smoked swordfish and fine wines from the extensive cellar. Strolling in the gardens and swimming in the floodlit pool are evening diversions. Unspoilt beaches, famous golf courses, Loule market on Saturdays, boat trips to the islands of Olhao and exploring Faro add to guests' enjoyment. **Directions:** Follow the blue signs marked IP1 to the motorway, then take exit 5 for Faro, turn left into Estoi and follow the yellow signs for 3km towards Moncarapacho. Price guide: Single £44.25–£83.25; double/twin £59–£128; Suite £78–£154.

ROMANTIK HOTEL VIVENDA MIRANDA

PORTO DE MOS, 8600 LAGOS, ALGARVE, PORTUGAL
TEL: +351 82 763 222 FAX: +351 82 760 342 E-MAIL: romantik-hotel-viv.miranda@ip.pt

Vivenda Miranda is a delightful small hotel, with Moorish influence evident in its architecture, built high up on the cliffs of Western Algarve. Its secluded position is enhanced by the exotic gardens around the terraces – which have spectacular views across to the Atlantic Ocean as well as looking down on the Porto de Mos beach. The cool bedrooms are pleasantly furnished and extremely comfortable, guests should enjoy many a peaceful night's sleep. A few rooms, equally charming, are in the nearby annexe. Some bathrooms have showers only. Both the lounge and dining room – drinks are served in the former from a most attractive bar – have spectacular views over the water at night.

Breakfast is on the terrace and the lunch menu is brief but good. Dinner at night is more of an occasion – gourmet dishes with organic ingredients accompanied by the best of Portuguese wines. There are restaurants on the beach and tennis nearby, mountain bikes available, sailing and wind surfing at the Marina. Local golf courses offer hotel guests discounted green fees. Weekly inclusive packages for golfers are a feature of Vivenda Miranda – which has its own pool and spa offering therapeutic treatments and massages. **Directions:** From Faro follow the EN 125 to Lagos, then watch for signs to Praia de Porto de Mos. Price guide: Single £52 £75; double/twin £47 £75; suites £52 £80.

PORTUGAL (Lisbon)

AS JANELAS VERDES
RUA DAS JANELAS VERDES 47, 1200 LISBON
TEL: +351 1 396 81 43 FAX: +351 1 396 81 44 E-MAIL: jverdes@heritage.pt

Once the home of the famous Portuguese writer, Eca de Queiros, this classical 18th century town house in the old part of Lisbon, close to the River Tagus, is now an exquisite small hotel. Graceful archways, a wide staircase with ornate banisters, mahogany woodwork, alcoves filled with pedestals of flowers and warm yellow walls are an appropriate setting for the elegant period furniture, antiques and paintings in the charming salons. The bedrooms are peaceful, all double-glazed and air-conditioned, traditionally furnished and very comfortable. The back of the house is clad in ivy, and there is a delightful patio where guests enjoy breakfast in the summer, and refreshments are served later in the day. In cooler months they retreat to the reading room. The hotel staff will suggest restaurants with national and cosmopolitan menus for dinner at night. Lisbon is a fascinating city to explore, starting at the Museum of Ancient Art right next to the hotel, and there are so many beautiful buildings – cathedrals and palaces – botanical gardens and the castle to visit. Tramcars are in walking distance, and golfers have a choice of 10 good golf courses within 20km of Lisbon. **Directions:** Rua das Janelas Verdes is just off the Avenida Vinte de Quatro de Julho. Price guide: Single Esc20,200–32,000; double/twin Esc21,500–35,200. American buffet breakfast and taxes included.

HOTEL TIVOLI LISBOA

AV DA LIBERDADE 185, 1250 LISBON, PORTUGAL
TEL: +351 1 319 8900 FAX: +351 1 319 8950

This is one of Lisbon's oldest hotels, renowned both for business and leisure. Established in 1933, it offers unparalleled comfort, complemented by the highest standards of hospitality and a very personalised service. There are 327 bedrooms, which include 15 suites and 15 junior suites. These have been recently refurbished using a variety of different styles to create a sense of individuality. All combine an excellent standard of luxury with every modern facility – air conditioning, direct dial telephone, radio, satellite television and a minibar. Panoramic views over Lisbon can be enjoyed from most windows. A relaxing drink can be enjoyed in any of the three bars, all totally different in character. During the day, the bar by the side of the hotel swimming pool is particularly popular. For an unforgettable dining experience, guests can choose from two excellent restaurants. Testimony to the unrivalled reputation of The Terrace Grill is the number of prominent members of Portuguese society who frequent it. In an atmosphere of luxury and grandeur, guests can choose from an extensive selection of dishes on the à la carte menu. The Zodiac restaurant is another prestigious attraction. The hotel is perfectly placed to explore the multifarious attractions of this historic city. Parking facilities are available. **Directions**: Located in the heart of Lisbon, on the city's main thoroughfare. Price guide: Single Esc39,000; double/twin Esc43,000; suites Esc58,000–70,000

QUINTA DA BELA VISTA

CAMINHO DO AVISTA NAVIOS, 4, 9000 FUNCHAL, MADEIRA, PORTUGAL
TEL: +351 91 764144 FAX: +351 91 765090

This is the perfect hotel for those seeking country house living in peaceful surroundings – it is a joy to stay in this traditional house, with its tall windows and green shutters, overlooking Funchal Bay and surrounded by exotic gardens. The interiors are a blend of sophistication and rich, classical furnishings – lovely antiques, fine paintings and great comfort. The suites are all in the original building, having period furniture and luxurious bathrooms, while the bedrooms are in the new, adjacent annex and therefore, rather more contemporary. Most have twin beds and many have balconies overlooking the Bay. Guests enjoy their apéritifs in the cheerful bar or on the sunny terraces before choosing between the elegant restaurant serving fine food and the best wines or the more informal dining room with its à la carte menu, which is also open at lunchtime. Afterwards they probably relax over a glass of Madeira wine in the charming salon or the library. Leisure facilities abound, there is a freshwater heated pool with its own snack bar, tennis, billiards, a gymnasium with a sauna and Jacuzzi. A regular minibus service is available for those wishing to visit the shops or explore the town. Excellent golf is nearby. **Directions:** Take main road west from Funchal. Turn right along Rua do Dr Pita. At the end of the road, turn left. After 30 yards turn left again. Car parking available. Price guide: Single Esc17,700–30,000; double/twin Esc23,600–38,000; suite Esc49,800– 56,000.

VINTAGE HOUSE HOTEL

LUGAR DA PONTE, 5085, PINHAO, PORTUGAL
TEL: +351 54 730 230 FAX: +351 54 730 238

Set on the edge of the river Douro, The Vintage House Hotel is a peaceful hotel comprising an old house, lodges and gardens which have been lovingly and sensitively refurbished in the local style. Great care has been taken to preserve the buildings' unique history, while providing the most up-to-date facilities for guests. The hotel derives its name from the surrounding Port vineyards, considered to be the oldest demarcated wine region in the world. Steeped in history, the site of the hotel is an old "Quinta" or wine estate, dating back to the 18th century. The 43 bedrooms are tastefully decorated with interesting antiques and feature either balconies or private terraces. Traditional Portugese glazed tiles,

Azulejos, adorn the walls of the large bathrooms. The pleasant bar, situated in the restored port wine lodge around which the rest of the hotel was built, is often frequented by those wishing to indulge in a quiet drink. The elegant vaulted dining room serves delicious cuisine and offers an extensive wine list. The Vintage House Hotel is an ideal base from which to explore the surrounding countryside or the local sites of historic and cultural interest. For those interested in port wine, guided tours and tastings can be arranged. **Directions:** From Porto, take the A4-IP4 to Pinthao by car, train or river boat. Price guide: Single Esc12,500–15,000; double/twin Esc15,000–17,500, suites Esc20,000–22,500.

HOTEL PÁLACIO DE SETEAIS

RUA BARBOSA DE BOCAGE, 10, SETEAIS, 2710 SINTRA, PORTUGAL
TEL: +351 1 923 32 00 FAX: +351 1 923 42 77

This magnificent eighteenth century neoclassical palace, with its dramatic triumphal arch, added in 1802 in honour of visiting royalty, was transformed into a hotel during the 1950's – great care being taken to preserve its aristocratic elegance. Its location is spectacular, on the Sintra mountain and the hotel has extensive grounds filled with fragrant flowers, exotic shrubs and shady trees. The interior is exemplary – very light, with attractive rugs on polished floors, an ornate staircase and balustrades in pale wood. The salons are flawless, one having exquisite mythological frescoes, The chairs are graceful, the chandeliers brilliant and the drapes are in soft harmony with the paintings. The guest rooms match the era of the Palace; lovely antiques and pieces of local furniture, muted colours, blissfully cool and quiet – television sets can be installed on request! The stylish bar has amusing murals; the attractive terrace is ideal for sipping cocktails. The enchanting Oval Dining Room and grand Restaurant offer a sophisticated menu and great wines. A traditional meeting room is available. The Palace has its own attractive pool, tennis courts and riding school; golf is nearby. Lord Byron praised the Old Town and the Serra de Sintra is paradisiacal. The beaches are good and local vineyards must be visited. **Directions:** Sintra Mountain and Seteais are signed from Sintra. Price guide: Single Esc42,000; double/twin Esc46,000.

Quinta De São Thiago

2710 SINTRA, PORTUGAL
TEL: +351 1 923 29 23 FAX: +351 1 923 43 29

Sintra is fascinating – it has been the summer home of Portuguese royalty, celebrated by Lord Byron in his poem "Childe Harold" and has two palaces and a Moorish castle. With spectacular views across the forest and countryside, the Quinta de São Thiago – a monastery in the 16th century – is now the enchanting home of Mrs Bradell, who welcomes guests as friends. This immaculate house, with its pink tiled roof, is surrounded by beautifully kept gardens and steps leading down to an attractive pool. The charming bedrooms are furnished with classic period furniture. The Drawing Room, where residents gather for pre-dinner drinks, white port perhaps, has the original tiled floor, beamed, arched ceiling and fine Portuguese antiques; the Library shelves are full and the Music Room abounds with records. On special evenings, delicious candlelit dinners in Mrs Bradell's Dining Room or barbecues on the patio end the day. House pursuits are swimming, tennis and sunbathing. Golf, riding and the beach are nearby, Sintra and the hills deserve exploring and the casino at Estoril is an evening diversion. **Directions:** Leave Lisbon on Sintra road, take S. Pedro road at Mobil garage, head for Seteais, one mile after palace find sign on right to the Quinta, drive 900 metres – green wooden gate. Price guide: Single Esc18,000; double/twin Esc21,000; suites Esc26,000–30,000.

Slovenia

GRAZ

281

LJUBLJANA

TRIESTE

POSTOJNA

ZAGREB

VENEZIA

HOTEL VILA BLED

CESTA SVOBODE 26, 4260 BLED, SLOVENIA
TEL: +386 64 79 15 FAX: +386 64 74 13 20

This villa has an illustrious past, having been the summer home of the Yugoslavian royal family between the two World Wars. In the late 1940s Tito played host to many world leaders here, including the present Emperor of Japan. Bled is in the Southern Alps and this lovely predominantly 1950s style hotel stands in secluded flower-filled parkland overlooking Lake Bled with awe-inspiring mountains on the horizon. The region is famous for its long warm summer, pure air and exhilarating spa waters. Many of the delightful bedrooms and suites have balconies with magical views over the lake at night. The salons reflect the 50s era. Marble and glass are much in evidence in the reception hall and stylish bar where guests gather while deciding which of the exquisite dishes to eat, either on the romantic terrace watching the lights on the water, or in the traditional restaurant. The wines are Slovenian, the whites from Styria while the reds include the famous 'black' varieties. Relaxation includes rowing, visiting the old castle, enjoying the private beach and strolling in the lovely grounds. Energetic visitors use the hotel tennis court, indulge in water sports or play golf 2km away. After dark Bled offers discotheques, clubs and its Casino. **Directions:** E55 from Salzburg and at the Karawankentunnel on the Austrian border follow E61/A1. Price guide: Single £66–£90; double/twin £91–£114; suites £100–£251.

Spain

HACIENDA EL SANTISCAL

AVDA. EL SANTISCAL, 129 (LAGO DE ARCOS), 11630 ARCOS DE LA FRONTERA, SPAIN
TEL: +34 956 70 83 13 FAX: +34 956 70 82 68

Surrounded by fields of sunflowers, this 15th century manor house, exquisitely restored, offers glorious views of the historic town of Arcos. A welcoming atmosphere envelopes the property as Mrs Gallardo invites guests into her home to enjoy the atmosphere of a traditional Andalusian Hacienda. The impressive entrance hall, with its oak staircase, leads on to the covered terrace and gardens and affords a fine vista of the lake. The Hacienda el Santiscal is a private house and guests may stay in the 12 spacious bedrooms. All are en suite and offer every modern amenity. The addition of an intimate conservatory complements the beamed dining room. Dining by candlelight, overlooking the breathtaking countryside, is a romantic experience. The daily set menu comprises traditional home-cooked dishes and much of the fresh produce including vegetables, olives and oranges are grown in the Hacienda's own groves and gardens. Guests must savour the home-made delights at breakfast and enjoy the variety of spreads such as sweet pepper butter. Pastimes include water sports, biking, bird-watching at the nature reserve or excursions to the sherry caves of Jerez. **Directions:** Take the N342 in the direction of Antequera. After the signs to Arcos de la Frontera, take the first right to 'El Bosque'. After the bridge, turn left and follow the signs to the Hacienda. Price guide: Single Pts9,600–13,200; double/twin Pts13,000–16,000; suites Pts18,000–20,000.

DESIGN HOTELS

HOTEL CLARIS

PAU CLARIS 150, 08009 BARCELONA, SPAIN
TEL: +34 93 487 62 62 FAX: +34 93 215 79 70

This unique hotel introduces new arrivals to the lovely architecture of the 19th century, still retaining its graceful Renaissance façade from the era when it was the Palace of the Vedruna family. The interiors are extravagant examples of avant garde design – metres of marble, glass, rare timbers and cast stone. The spacious foyer is dramatic while the lounge beyond is softened by colourful rugs, 5th century Roman mosaics and the gentle sound of a waterfall. The bedrooms are exciting, eclectic in style with antique objets d'art and modern furnishings cleverly blended and opulent bathrooms, some with Jacuzzis. They are soundproofed against the noise of the city. The cocktail bar and the rooftop terrace, with its pool, are perfect places to relax before indulging in the luxuries offered in the Caviar Caspio. Ampurdan cuisine can be sampled in the gourmet restaurant, matched by local wines. Informal meals are in the Restaurant Barbecoe. The state-of-the-art conference and meeting rooms transform into elegant banqueting and private dining rooms. The hotel's Museum demands attention before exploring the City and Cathedral. **Directions:** The hotel is in centre of city in a narrow road, Pau Claris, on north-east side of Paseo de Gracia, where it crosses Calle de Valencia. Parking available. Price guide: Single Pts32,700; double/twin Pts40,900; suite Pts50,000–125,000.

TRASIERRA

CAZALLA DE LA SIERRA, 41370 SEVILLE, SPAIN
TEL: +34 954 88 43 24 FAX: +34 954 88 33 05

Trasierra is a 1000 acre private estate surrounded by glorious Andalusian landscape. The buildings are decorated in a mixture of English, Spanish and Moorish styles and are set in aromatic gardens and terraces dominated by vast ancient terracotta olive jars. The property falls somewhere between a guest-house and a hotel with Charlotte Scott and her family living in the main house whilst guests occupy cottages or suites within the converted wings. The eight beautifully appointed bedrooms are simple yet charming, mixing modern design with traditional Andalusian patterns. Rooms may be rented individually or collectively on a weekly or daily basis. There is also a large, elegant drawing room with a piano and a magnificent open fireplace for cooler evenings. Breakfast comprises marmalade and juice from Trasiera's own orange groves. Lunch and dinner are available by prior arrangement and are served on either the shaded terraces or by the large swimming pool. The menus consist of simple and delicious Mediterranean dishes accompanied by the impressive local wines. Trasierra offers facilities for painting and writing groups and has a sunny and well-equipped studio. Andalusia's historical cities are within easy reach. **Directions:** Trasierra is one hour north of Seville which is only 2½ hours by hourly fast train from Madrid. Detailed directions are available. Price guide: Spring and Autumn Pts12,000; Summer Pts15,000 per person.

PIKES

SAN ANTONIO DE PORTMANY, 07820 ISLA DE IBIZA, BALEARIC ISLANDS, SPAIN
TEL: +34 971 34 22 22 FAX: +34 971 34 23 12

Hotel Pikes is an old 15th century finca beautifully converted into an idyllic hotel. Built in natural stone, it blends easily into the countryside and the surrounding olive groves. Beautiful gardens and flower-filled terraces add colour to this lovely hotel, situated within easy reach of beaches and Ibiza Town, just some 10 minutes away by car. The rooms and suites are of different shapes and sizes, tastefully furnished with a mix of antiques and modern sculptures. The ambience is relaxing – breakfast is served until noon, no need to get up early. The intimate restaurant is renowned throughout the island for its fine cooking and wines. The hotel's special atmosphere is maintained by the friendly and discreet staff. There are numerous sun terraces for relaxing around the swimming pool, a floodlit tennis court, sauna, Jacuzzi and a gymnasium. Hotel staff will organize horse riding, sailing, scuba diving and other activities. Golfers can use the practice nets before playing on Ibiza's championship course. The hotel's Privilege Card gives guests VIP treatment at most disco clubs and the popular Casino as well as food discounts in many first class restaurants. In the summertime special events such as Barbecue nights, Flamenco evenings etc are arranged by the pool side. **Directions:** Pikes is signed off the Camino de Sa Vorera. Price guide: double/twin Pts20,000–27,000; suites Pts24,000–150,000.

HOTEL RIGAT PARK

PLAYA DE FENALS, 17310 LLORET DE MAR, COSTA BRAVA, SPAIN
TEL: +34 972 36 52 00 FAX: +34 972 37 04 11

A huge park of pines, exuding the distinctive aroma common to these trees, surrounds the Rigat Park Hotel. Situated close to the centre of lively Lloret de Mar and only 70km from Barcelona, this is an ideal base for exploring the beaches of Costa Brava and the many small Catalan towns which lie within easy reach. The hotel's bedrooms, which vary in size and style, are decorated and furnished in Mediterranean style. All have tiled floors and marble bathrooms whilst some rooms benefit from impressive sea views. An extensive range of modern amenities ensures maximum convenience and comfort for guests. The sun and fresh air can be enjoyed on the wonderful terraces, while other opportunities for relaxation include billiards or a swim in the swimming pool with its underwater music! Two of the hotel's three restaurants are open-air and overlook the sea, creating a relaxing setting in which to enjoy a wide selection of both regional and international dishes. There are five golf courses within close proximity of the hotel, the closest of which offers special prices to the hotel's guests. Every nautical sport imaginable is available in Fenals, as well as bowling, table tennis, mini-golf and volleyball. **Directions:** From France, take the A7, leaving at exit 9 to Lloret de Mar. Then head towards Fenals beach. From Barcelona, take the A7 or A19 to Palafolls and then to Lloret de Mar. Price guide: Double Pts15,000–26,000; suites Pts28,000 –40,000.

VILLA REAL

PLAZA DE LAS CORTES, 10, MADRID 28014, SPAIN
TEL: +34 9 1 420 37 67 FAX: +34 9 1 420 25 47

A stay at this elite and prestigious hotel in the heart of Madrid is a most memorable experience. The position is superb, the service impeccable and the interior is palatial – spacious salons with wonderful antiques and mirrors, handsome rugs on marble floors, period furniture, fine panelling hung with tapestries and inspired lighting. Recent addtions include an excellent collection of roman mosaics, sculptures and Greek jars dating from the II to IV centuries. All the luxurious bedrooms are suites, with elegant sitting areas, soundproofed from the noises of the city, opulent bathrooms, some with terraces for alfresco breakfasts looking out over Madrid, others with Jacuzzis and sauna. The sophisticated bar is a popular meeting place and the charming Principe de Asturias restaurant offers a choice of quick, light meals or full gourmet meals, accompanied by Spanish wines. The elegant Salón Principe de Asturias is also marvellous for banquets and can be transformed into a superb conference room together with the Salón Cibeles, popular for presentations. The hotel is located nearby the commercial centre, the Prado Museum, the National theatres Le Comedia and La Zarzuela, the Teatro Real, art galleries, antique shops and restaurants. **Directions:** Private parking available. The hotel is in the centre of Madrid near the Puerta del Sol, Gran Via and Retiro Park, just 10 mins from the airport. Price guide: Single Pts31,700; double/twin Pts39,600; suite from Pts55,000.

LA POSADA DEL TORCAL

29230 VILLANUEVA DE LA CONCEPCION, MALAGA, SPAIN
TEL: +34 95 203 11 77 FAX: +34 95 203 10 06

This fine Andalusian hotel enjoys a panoramic vista across 11 acres of almond groves and the breathtaking El Torcal National Park. Recreating the charm and elegance of a bygone era, La Posada del Torcal is peaceful and intimate; ideal for a quiet break. Each of the eight en suite bedrooms is named after a great Spanish artist and this theme is complemented by the replicas of famous paintings which adorn the rooms. The décor comprises a fusion of both antique and modern furnishings, with handmade ceramics by Andalusian craftsmen and brass four-poster beds. The dining room retains a traditional ambience with its enchanting open fireplace and ornate plates. Dried flowers and spices hang from the ceiling, made using 300 year old beams. Guests may savour authentic Spanish recipes such as El Porra, a typical Gazpacho-style dish from Antequera. During the summer months, alfresco dining takes place on the spacious terrace. For recreation, guests can enjoy the mountain bikes, Jacuzzi and sauna. Nearby attractions include the spa town of Carratraca with its Roman baths, the lakes of El Chorro and the historic town of Antequera. **Directions:** The hotel is 40 minutes drive from Malaga airport. Take the N331 in the direction of Antequera. Take exit 148 at Casabermeja. Follow the signs to Villanueva de la Concepción. Price guide: Single Pts12,840; double/twin Pts19,260.

HOTEL VISTAMAR DE VALLDEMOSA

CTRA VALLDEMOSA, ANDRATX, KM. 2, 07170 VALLDEMOSA, MALLORCA, SPAIN
TEL: +34 971 61 23 00 FAX: +34 971 61 25 83 E-MAIL: Info@vistamarhotel.es

This lovely house, recently transformed into an elite and peaceful hotel, is at the top of a beautiful valley, surrounded by pine and olive trees which scent the air and overlooking a fascinating small fishing port on the edge of the Mediterranean. Guests relax immediately on entering the cool pebbled courtyard and are enchanted with the elegant reception rooms, filled with Majorcan antiques and traditional fabrics woven by craftsmen on the island. A picture gallery of fine 19th century Spanish paintings overflows on to walls throughout the house. The bedrooms are delightful, some in the main building and others in the adjacent annex. All are beautifully furnished with local period pieces and many have balconies. The new bathrooms are well designed and equipped. Guests appreciate delicious cocktails in the bar before entering the excellent restaurant with its big terrace for alfresco dining. Mediterranean cooking at its best and good Spanish wines from the extensive cellar make meals here memorable. Vistamar has its own pool. The beach of Port Valldemosa, with clear water, is perfect for swimming and sunbathing. Boat trips can be arranged. Valldemosa has a fine art centre where artists gather. **Directions:** 2km outside of Valldemosa in the direction of Banyalbufar. Price guide: Single Pts17,000–18,000; double/twin Pts25,000 –31,000. Breakfast Pts1800/person. VAT 7% not included.

LA RESERVA ROTANA

CAMI DE S'AVALL, KM.3, 07500 MANACOR, MALLORCA, SPAIN
TEL: +34 971 84 56 85 FAX: +34 971 55 52 58

The untouched beauty of the Mediterranean envelopes this 17th century Mallorcan style Manor House, set in the middle of a 500 acre working farm. The house and its adjacent buildings have undergone careful and extensive conversion, resulting in an elegant yet traditional hotel. Beamed ceilings, fine antiques and works of art and frescoes adorn the interior. The spacious Lounge is the essence of comfort and displays a hunting theme. The 21 bedrooms are en suite, offering a fusion of both modern décor with classical Mallorcan antiques whilst the opulent bathrooms are beautifully marbled and stuccoed. The creative chef and his team of enthusiastic and multilingual staff offer a fresh and imaginative menu comprising sumptuous mediterranean cuisine, using fresh local produce from the nearby market, the sea or the kitchen gardens on the farm itself. The hotel's own 9-hole golf course, the only private course in Mallorca, is both enjoyable and challenging. Swimming, tennis and cycling may be practiced either on site or nearby. Green fees, tennis and bicycle hire are included in the price. Those seeking a more leisurely break will be delighted with the clean beaches and fine marina; both within a 20 minute drive. **Directions:** From Palma, travel in the direction of Manacor. Take the left turn immediately after the Repsol petrol station in Manacor and follow signs to the hotel. Price guide: Single Pts30,450; double/twin Pts33,000–39,400; suites Pts50,400–53,000.

READ'S

CA'N MORAGUES, 07320 SANTA MARIA, MALLORCA, SPAIN
TEL: +34 971 140 262 FAX: +34 971 140 762 E-MAIL: readshotel@mail.todoesp.es

This idyllic 16th century mansion, surrounded by verdant gardens, is now a unique country hotel. Built in local stone, it is set against a backdrop of mountains and breathtaking scenery, yet is only 15 minutes from Palma. Once inside, guests find they are in an exotic treasure trove, the pastel walls making a perfect setting for fine antiques, delicate porcelain and paintings. A grand piano stands at the foot of the sweeping staircase leading to the bedrooms, each of which is spacious and individually designed. One of the salons is an elegant drawing room, another the olive pressing room with its original fittings and the third a wonderful, grand, plant-filled conservatory. The bar is unique, the walls a mural of the sky – visitors sense they are in a magical place. The restaurant, one of the finest on the island, with its 10 metre high arches and exquisitely executed murals, is a perfect setting for the excellent cuisine. In summer, the raised terrace overlooking the mountains offers a delightful alternative. The hotel has a large pool surrounded by lawns and a tennis court. Several golf courses are within a 20 minute drive. Read's is perfectly situated for exploring the beauty that is Mallorca. **Directions:** Take motorway north towards Inca, then exit to Santa Maria. Hotel is signposted between Santa Maria and Alaró. Price guide: Double/twin Pts21,500–41,000; suites Pts34,500–52,000.

The Leading Hotels of the World®

HOTEL PUENTE ROMANO

P.O. BOX 204, 29600 MARBELLA, SPAIN
TEL: +34 95 282 09 00 FAX: +34 95 277 57 66

Located in the heart of the Golden Mile, between Marbella and Puerto Banus, the Hotel Puente Romano lies along the Mediterranean Coast, at the foot of the Sierra Blanca mountains. The hotel comprises low-rise horizontal buildings constructed in traditional Andalusian style and offering secluded and spacious demi-suite rooms with terraces or balconies overlooking waterfalls, fountains and acres of lush subtropical gardens. The enthusiastic staff achieve the balance between privacy and impeccable service. The hotel's restaurants: El Puente, Roberto Italian and the Beach Club, each different in style, offer a wealth of gastronomic delights including spectacular buffets and a range of traditional dishes featuring local fish and seafood. The nightclub is open during the summer months when themed nights are also featured at la Plaza Restaurant. This hotel is a paradise for sporting guests – three swimming pools, two of which are heated, the beach, a championship tennis club/school, with facilities including 10 tennis courts, four paddle tennis tables and a fitness centre. There is a wide selection of golf courses, polo, riding and water sports nearby. **Directions:** Between Marbella and Puerto Banús on the Golden Mile. Price guide: Single Pts23,000–36,300; double/twin Pts26,000–49,500; suites Pts33,000–150,000.

HOTEL RINCON ANDALUZ

CRTA. DE CADIZ, K.M. 173, 29600 MARBELLA, SPAIN
TEL: +34 95 281 1517 FAX: +34 95 281 41 80

This smart hotel complex, built in the style of an Andalusian village, is surrounded by its own extensive parkland yet only 1 kilometre from the high life of Puerto Banus, favoured by the rich and famous. It is a mecca for top sportsmen, close to famous golf courses and other facilities, yet offering some privacy. The air-conditioned bedrooms are in villas and small houses off the 'streets, squares and gardens' of the village – which even has its own chapel. There are large suites especially suitable for families, accommodating up to six people. No building is more than three storeys high. Guests are offered a choice of bars and restaurants – Sir Francis Drake with its large lounge, by the first pool, the Tropical Restaurant in the exotic gardens and the Crocodile Bar & Restaurant by the second pool. Additionally there is the sophisticated Beach Club, with further pools, children's area and beauty salon. Meals are usually buffet-style. Marbella is famous for its magnificent golf courses, all offering special arrangements for the hotel's guests and the tennis club has 11 courts. The Golden Mile has splendid beaches, with windsurfing and water skiing off shore and a jet-set nightlife, with discos and casinos. **Directions:** The hotel is signed from the Ctra Nacional 340, east of Marbella. Price guide: Single double/twin Pts15,500–26,000; suites Pts21,500–48,500.

MARBELLA CLUB HOTEL

BOULEVARD PRINCIPE ALFONSO VON HOHENLOHE, S/N, 29600 MARBELLA, SPAIN
TEL: +34 95 282 22 11 FAX: +34 95 282 98 84

This elite hotel was the inspiration of Prince Alfonso von Hohenlohe, who in 1954 extended and transformed his family home, so founding the Marbella Club Hotel. It immediately acquired a sophisticated clientele and has retained its exclusive reputation ever since. The hotel is an elegant traditional Andalusian residence, standing in a vast expanse of sub-tropical gardens and olive groves, reaching down to the sea. Apart from the luxurious bedrooms and suites with their opulent bathrooms and private terraces, there are clusters of cottages and bungalows, each with private gardens and some with their own pools. Discreet staff provide 24hr room service. The salons are charming and cool and there are delightful courtyards and patios in which to relax. In summer, guests sip aperitifs to live music in the Summer Bar, sample the superb seafood buffet by the pool and dine under the stars in the terrace restaurant. During cooler months the chef demonstrates his skills in the Grill Restaurant. The hotel has two pools one of them heated, while the Beach Club offers water sports. Many fine golf courses and tennis courts are close by. At night the nearby casino, discos and clubs are vibrant. **Directions:** Marbella Club Hotel is on the Golden Mile beach road between Marbella and Puerto Banús. Price guide: Single Pts26,000–58,000; double/twin Pts33,000–70,000, suites Pts11,000 175,000.

LAS DUNAS SUITES

CRTA. DE CADIZ, KM163.5, 29689 MARBELLA/ESTEPONA (MALAGA)
TEL: +34 95 279 4345 FAX: +34 95 279 4825 E-MAIL: lasdunas@senda.ari.es

This exciting complex is almost an annex to the luxurious Las Dunas Beach Hotel & Spa (illustrated above), as residents in the suites have the benefit of the many fine facilities of the hotel and yet they can enjoy the freedom of an apartment. The stylish residences feature "Designers Guild" furnishings and vary from one to three bedrooms – including one duplex, each having fully equipped modern kitchen, bathrooms, air conditioning, private terrace or balcony, daily cleaning – and access to the pool (heated) and beach. Entrée to the luxurious hotel opens the doors of one of the best cuisines in the locality – the Lido restaurant, supervised by Michelin star chef Heinz Winkler – featuring his "Cuisine Vitale Mediterranéenne". More informal meals are served at the "Piano Bar and Bistro Félix" specializing in Haute European Cuisine, inspired by Asiatic flavours, with live music and is open until 3am every day. Room service is also available. The Spa has a Jacuzzi, sauna, gym, therapist and beautician. This is a golfer's heaven, with reduced green fees for Las Dunas guests and resident golf-pro. A variety of watersports can be arranged. Sunbathing on the beach, exploring inland villages, visiting Granada and Seville are pleasant pastimes. Marbella offers a jet-set night life! **Directions:** Las Dunas is between Marbella and Estepona, on the coast road (Crta de Cadiz). Parking facilities. Price guide(+VAT): Garden level suites Pts22,000–110,000.

HOTEL BYBLOS ANDALUZ

MIJAS GOLF, APT. 138, 29640 FUENGIROLA, (MALAGA), SPAIN
TEL: +34 95 246 02 50 FAX: +34 95 247 67 83

Set in the heart of Andalusia, the luxurious Hotel Byblos offers glorious panoramic views over the surrounding mountains, gardens and golf courses. Although mainly Andalusian in style, the Moorish influences are clearly evident in the superb patios with tiled pools and fountains. The sybaritic bedrooms are the essence of comfort and have excellent en suite facilities. The rooms are decorated in various styles such as Arabian, Andalusian, Roman and Rustic and may be accessed through the distinctive courtyards of the hotel. The three restaurants have their own characteristic atmosphere but all offer an impeccable service. La Fuente, with its relaxing ambience, is renowned for its informal buffet meals comprising of local and international cuisine. The Andalusian restaurant, El Andaluz, has a fine Sevillian interior courtyard with colourful mosaics and offers daily specialities and an extensive dinner menu whilst the sophisticated Le Nailhac is a gastronomic delight. The Louison Bobet Institute of thalassotherapy, the largest of its kind in Europe, is equipped with swimming pools, subaquatic massages, solarium, La Prairie beauty centre and many other health facilities. Sport enthusiasts will enjoy the 18-hole golf courses and tennis courts. **Directions:** Hotel is signposted from exit 'Fuengirola (coin)' on the main Malaga to Cadiz coast road. Price guide: Single Pts28,000–34,000; double/twin Pts33,000–40,100; suite Pts38,200–185,000.

HOTEL DE LA RECONQUISTA

**GIL DE JAZ, 16, 33004 OVIEDO, PRINCIPADO DE ASTURIAS, SPAIN
TEL: +34 9 8 524 11 00 FAX: +34 9 8 524 11 66**

Oviedo in the Principado de Asturias is one of the few parts of Spain which the Moors failed to conquer and influence. The Hotel de la Reconquista is a delightful blend of history and sophistication. An archway in the baroque façade leads to the dramatic Patio de la Reina. The galleried Hall is impressive – with the famous Comida Campestre painting a focal point – indeed a fine collection of art is displayed throughout the hotel. Ornate period furniture adds interest to the spacious and comfortable bedrooms, all with grand marble bathrooms. The graceful salons have an aura of tranquillity – guests relax listening to the pianist most evenings. In the cafeteria light meals and tapas are served all day in an informal atmosphere. The Bar Americano is ideal for a drink before or after dinner. The Florencia Restaurant offers superb regional and cosmopolitan dishes accompanied by the finest Spanish wines. Visiting industrialists appreciate the efficient services of the excellent Business Club, eight well-equipped meeting rooms and the Ancient Chapel, suitable for conferences or special occasions. Golf, sailing, tennis, winter sports, salmon fishing, riding and mountaineering are all accessible. **Directions:** In the heart of Oviedo, close to the Parque de San Francisco, with private car parking. Price guide: Single Pts23,500; double/twin Pts29,500; suites Pts45,000–80,000. (Excl. VAT)

HOTEL LA COSTA

AVENIDA ARENALES DE MAR 3, 17256 PLATJA DE PALS, (COSTA BRAVA) SPAIN
TEL: +34 972 66 77 40 FAX: +34 972 66 77 36 E-MAIL: hlacosta@grn.es

Hotel La Costa is situated in the heart of the Costa Brava, adjoining the Pals Golf Club, one of the leading courses on the Spanish circuit. This comfortable and friendly hotel is a golfer's paradise – guests can take advantage of special green fees for playing at the Pals course, or at seven clubs nearby. All 120 bedrooms are comfortable and well-equipped and there are also 57 apartments, overlooking the sea. A choice of three bars includes the Tropical Bar which is situated beside the swimming pool and offers a bar and snack service. In the two restaurants the traditional dishes of Pals can be sampled, as well as exquisite Mediterranean and international cuisine. Featured among the excellent leisure facilities are an exotic multi-dimensional swimming pool, gymnasium, saunas, Jacuzzi, tennis courts and a private discotheque. Other attractive options available due to the hotel's wonderful location are catamaran sailing, windsurfing, scuba diving, microlite flying and ballooning. There are many varied tourist attractions within easy reach – most notably the medieval quarters in Pals and Peratallada, the Islas Medes Nature Reserve, the Empuries ruins and the Jewish quarter in Girona. **Directions:** Leave the A–7 at Girona Nord exit following the signs to La Bisbal, after 4km watch for signs to Pals. Price guide (per person): Single Pts12,950–19,200; double/twin Pts8,700–12,600; suites Pts10,125–14,700.

HOTEL MONASTERIO SAN MIGUEL

CALLE LARGA, 27, 11500 PUERTO DE SANTA MARIA (CADIZ), SPAIN
TEL: +34 956 540 440 FAX: +34 956 542 604 E-MAIL: monasterio@omeganet.es

Monasterio San Miguel is a fine baroque building with all its original features carefully conserved during its transformation from the Monastery San Miguel Arcangel to a hotel. The Monastery was built in 1727 to house the Clarisas Capuchinas nuns and today, an atmosphere of tranquillity still prevails throughout. It is set in a magnificent garden, complete with tropical plants and swimming pool. The 150 bedrooms are furnished in either classical or modern style and all offer an excellent level of comfort and a full range of amenities. A generous buffet breakfast is provided and the à la carte restaurant, "Las Bovedas" serves exquisite dishes, based on fresh produce of the region and a variety of fish from the Bay of Cádiz. The Auditorium, situated in the old church, is an ideal place to hold conventions, congresses and meeting of all kinds. Monasterio San Miguel is well-situated for those wishing to explore some of the most interesting cities of Andalucia including Seville, Jerez, Cádiz and Gibraltar. Guests must visit the world-famous Sherry wine cellars and the internationally renowned Royal Andalusian Equestrian School. El Puerto Santa Maria has 22km of beaches and golf, horse-riding, fishing and sailing are just some of the leisure activities within easy reach. **Directions**: The hotel is set in the centre of El Puerto Santa Maria. It is well signed after El Puerto De Santa Maria. Price guide: Single Pts14,800–18,000; double/twin Pts18,500–25,000; suites Pts30,000–40,000.

RESIDENCIA RECTOR

RECTOR ESPERABÉ, 10–APARTADO 399, 37008 SALAMANCA, SPAIN
TEL: +34 923 21 84 82 FAX: +34 923 21 40 08

This exclusive hotel, with its elegant façade, stands by the walls of the citadel, looking up to the Cathedral – a magnificent golden vision at night when floodlit. Indeed this is a golden city, much of Salamanca being built in a soft yellow stone. The interior looks cool and elegant, with archways between the spacious reception hall and the welcoming bar. Unique features in the main salon, with its big leather furniture and tapestries on the walls, are two exquisite modern stained glass windows. Beyond these there is a courtyard garden. There are just 13 bedrooms, of ample size, all air-conditioned and double-glazed. The furnishings are delightful and facilities in the marble bathrooms include a telephone. The hotel only serves breakfast, but it is easy to find restaurants serving traditional Spanish dishes or gastronomic experiences. It is possible to communicate in English in the hotel. There are many wonderful historical buildings in this city, including the Cathedral and the university and the city guide has two recommended routes and the first of these starts close to the hotel. **Directions:** Arriving on the main road from Madrid, drive up Avenida De Los Reyes Espana and turn left onto Pa de Rector Esperabé, finding the hotel approximately 300 metres on the left. Price guide: Single Pts12,000; double/twin Pts17,000; suites Pts21,000.

CASA DE CARMONA

PLAZA DE LASSO 1, 41410 CARMONA, SEVILLE, SPAIN
TEL: +34 954 19 10 00 FAX: +34 954 19 01 89

Brilliant restoration of the 16th century Lasso de la Vega palace has ensured that today guests, upon entering, feel impressed that they may actually stay in such a fine palace. It is very exclusive, in that it is only open to residents and their friends, not to the casual passer-by. The staff are wonderful, the concierge conducts arrivals to their rooms, explaining how everything works, and the chambermaids will unpack bags and take away laundry. Then it is time to explore the Casa. The exterior is in warm golden stone and the venerable door leads into spacious terracotta-tinted courtyards, the loggia terrace, an Arabian garden and an enchanting pool, surrounded by exotic plants. The salons are very regal, in wonderful harmonising colours and containing many fine antiques. The cool traditional bedrooms are delightful, with pristine linen, and the suites are luxurious. The wines and delicious dishes served in the handsome restaurant are Spanish. Conferences and seminars take place in four meeting rooms, furnished with the latest presentation equipment. Archaeologists appreciate Italica, other guests explore Seville, visit Andalucia, taste sherry in Jerez, enjoy the beaches at Cadiz or play golf nearby. **Directions:** From Seville NIV towards Cordoba, take the exit signed Carmona and follow signs to the hotel. Price guide: Single Pts17,000–29.000; double/twin Pts18,000–39,000; grand suite Pts80,000–120,000.

The Leading Hotels of the World®

HACIENDA BENAZUZA

41800 SANLÚCAR LA MAYOR, SEVILLE, SPAIN
TEL: +34 95 570 33 44 FAX: +34 95 570 34 10

Steeped in history, the Hacienda Benazuza dates back to the 10th century. The estate was founded by the Moors and its fascinating past includes a spell in the hands of the crusading order of the Knights of Santiago. It later became the seat of a succession of noblemen. Today's estate has been lovingly restored, with a luxurious hotel gracing its idyllic surroundings. Set amongst the old olive trees, it stands on a hill overlooking the Guadiamar river valley. By sensitively combining the original building with modern additions, a select and intimate hotel has been created – an ideal setting for a relaxing holiday, incentive trips, conventions or business meetings. The spirit of Benazuza is enhanced by the lavish decoration of its public rooms and opulent bedrooms with magnificent works of art and valuable antiques. Additionally, the bedrooms boast a range of facilities including satellite television and a minibar. Some have Jacuzzis. Three restaurants offer a choice of cuisine for luncheon and dinner. La Alquería specialises in international cuisine, while El Patio cultivates the art of traditional Andalusian cooking. La Alberca, an outdoor restaurant next to the pool, prepares snacks and barbecues. A host of activities are available on site or close by. **Directions**: From airport follow signs to Seville, then take A–49 towards Huelva. Take Sanlucar exit and follow signs to hotel. Price guide: Single Pts29,000–44,000; double/twin Pts37,000–54,000; suites Pts49,000–160,000.

SUITES HOTEL SAN ROQUE CLUB

CN340, KM126.5, 11360 SOTOGRANDE/SAN ROQUE (CÁDIZ), SPAIN
TEL: +34 956 613030 FAX: +34 956 613012

The San Roque Club is the perfect setting for a golfing or summer holiday, far enough away from the busy resorts to guarantee a relaxing break, but still within easy reach of Gibraltar and other places of interest. The accommodation is excellent – there are 100 large and sumptuously furnished bedrooms, arranged in individual club suites set on the hillside, surrounded by gardens. Guests have a choice of dining experiences, either sampling the delicious cuisine served in the elegant Japanese restaurant, enjoying the summer barbecues on the terrace or in the international restaurant. The Club prides itself on being a family hotel with excellent leisure facilities, including a very big swimming pool. The Equestrian Centre, tennis courts and sauna are all within the hotel grounds. The 6440 metre, par 72 championship course has played host to a number of major tournaments, and both the USA and European teams stayed here during the 1997 Ryder Cup. There are two other linking nine-hole circuits, reflecting the different character of the landscape and providing challenge and variety for players at all levels. The area does have some good restaurants and a night-life, although it remains quieter than the more cosmopolitan Marbella which lies within 45 minutes' drive. **Directions**: On CN340 Malaga-Cadiz road, hotel is signed from Urb. San Roque exit. Price guide (+7% VAT): Single Pts15,500–20,000; double/twin Pts19,500; suites Pts27,500.

HOTEL TERMES MONTBRIO RESORT, SPA & PARK

CARRER NOU, 38, 43340 MONTBRIO DEL CAMP (TARRAGONA), SPAIN
TEL: +34 977 81 40 00 FAX: +34 977 82 62 51 E-MAIL: Termes@ctv.es

The Hotel Termes Montbrió Resort, Spa and Park is a unique example of modern architecture at its best. Set in a tranquil location, this stylish complex is designed to please the discerning traveller, evoking both elegance and comfort throughout the buildings. The 140 en suite bedrooms are beautifully appointed. Situated in a spacious annex, all are well-equipped and decorated in a modernist style with yellow and pink colour schemes. There are various relaxing lounges in which to recline and enjoy an apéritif. The two restaurants are delightfully individual, with La Sequoia serving exquisite international cuisine and l'Horta Florida specialising in à la carte Mediterranean food. For health and fitness enthusiasts, the Thermal Centre is the highlight of any visit to the resort. The wide range of facilities include a hot spring swimming pool, giant Jacuzzi, panoramic gymnasium, Beauty hall and ultra violet rays and hydrotherapy and electrotherapy equipment. Those seeking a peaceful retreat will enjoy relaxing in the spacious courtyards, enhanced by enchanting fountains and impeccable gardens. Nearby distractions include the Port Aventura theme park, Roman amphitheatre and the glorious beaches of Costa Daurada. **Directions:** Leave the A7 motorway, in the direction of Tarragona, at exit 37 Cambrils. Follow signs to Montbrio del Camp. Price guide: Single Pts17,900; double/twin Pts22,400; suites Pts33,900.

GRAN HOTEL BAHIA DEL DUQUE

38660 ADEJE, COSTA ADEJE, TENERIFE SOUTH, CANARY ISLANDS, SPAIN
TEL: +34 922 74 69 00 FAX: +34 922 74 69 25

Gran Hotel Bahia Del Duque is a private romantic village created on a gentle hill sloping down to the sea. Nineteen houses in turn-of-the-century Canarian architecture form this prestigious complex in a large estate with sculptured terraces and pools. Corinthian columns flank the entrance, staff in period costume greet guests. There is a well-equipped conference and exhibition area. The bedrooms are in low colour-washed buildings, many with terraces facing the sea. The furniture has been specially designed, the floors are cool Spanish tiles, the bathrooms are luxurious. The Casas Ducales – Manor houses – have a separate reception area, breakfast room and butler service. Descending towards the coast guests find a fountain-filled patio surrounded by several restaurants – French, Spanish, Italian and the à la carte restaurant 'El Duque'. There are two bars and a reading room. Below are four swimming pools, further bars and restaurants. Floodlighting makes these even more spectacular. Leisure activities include strolling among the tropical trees, a beach club, tennis, putting and a fully equipped gym. Golf, windsurfing and diving are nearby. Visiting La Gomera by ferry or the Tenerife National Park is a fascinating experience. **Directions:** The hotel will meet guests at Reina Sofia Airport – there is parking for those hiring a car. Price guide: Single Pts33,500–60,000; double/twin Pts36,500–65,000; suites Pts60,000–210,000 (Plus 4.5% IGIC).

The Leading Hotels of the World®

HOTEL BOTÁNICO

AVDA. RICHARD J. YEOWARD, URB. BOTANICO, 38400 PUERTO DE LA CRUZ, TENERIFE, CANARY ISLANDS
TEL: +34 922 38 14 00 FAX: +34 922 38 15 04

The Botánico stands in extensive gardens filled with tropical plants, lush green foliage, bridges over lakes with fountains playing and shady places for those wishing to escape the sun. This is an opulent 21st century hotel, with marble much in evidence. The dramatic foyer is filled with light and colour. There are ten luxurious penthouse suites in addition to many lavish bedrooms, provided with every 'extra' imaginable, and glamorous bathrooms. Twenty-four hour room service is available. The Botánico has spectacular views of the Atlantic, Mount Teide and the Orotava Valley. Guests often meet in the arcade, at one of the pool bars by day or at night in the piano bar. They can choose between three delightful restaurants offering grills, Thai or Italian dishes. The wine list is superb. Tennis (floodlit), two pools, a driving range (good golf nearby also an 18 hole putting-green which is free to guests is adjacent to the hotel) and going out on the hotel launch occupy the day; alternatives are being pampered in the beauty centre or exploring old towns and villages up in the cool mountains. The Botánico also has a shuttle bus to the town centre which has intriguing shops and a vibrant night-life. **Directions:** The hotel will meet guests at the airport on request. Parking for those with a car. Price guide: Single Pts17,000–33,000; double/twin Pts23,000–53,000; suites Pts42,000–300,000.

HOTEL JARDIN TROPICAL

CALLE GRAN BRETAÑA, 38670 COSTA ADEJE, TENERIFE, CANARY ISLANDS
TEL: +34 922 746000 FAX: +34 922 746060

This sensational hotel was built just ten years ago, a magnificent Moorish palace embellished with domed towers, its white walls contrasting brilliantly with its setting of exotic green foliage – there are 300 types of trees and 16,000 plants in the tropical garden after which it is named – interspersed with blue pools and colourful flowers. The interior rooms display cool luxury, tiled floors, big windows, attractive fabrics, every bedroom having a terrace, and the exclusive Las Adelfas Suites are phenomenal, spacious and furnished in great style. Guests have a choice of five restaurants: Las Mimosas with its splendid buffets, Los Cucurucho poolside snack bar, Las Cuevas à la carte restaurant, Las Rocas specialising in seafood and El Patio for gourmet feasts. There is a piano in the Lobby Bar, dancing in the Café de Paris and a champagne room for sybarites. This part of Tenerife has no beach, but Las Rochas Beach Club adjacent to the hotel offers a seawater pool and sunbathing terraces with bar service, a health spa and fabulous restaurant. Golfers will appreciate special fees arranged with five local golf clubs. Deep sea fishing and exploring the island are other popular activities. **Directions:** Drivers follow signs to San Eugenio. Price guide: Single Pts25,000; double/twin Pts38,000; suites Pts73,000.

Sweden

KIRUNA

GÄLLIVARE

BODEN

LULEA

HOTING

UMEA

310

ÖSTERSUND

321

SÖDERHAMN

320

GÄVLE

FALUN

LUDVIKA

319

314

318

STOCKHOLM

NORRKÖPING

322

311

317

315 GÖTEBORG

GOTLAND

JÖNKÖPING

316

KALMAR

313

312

HELSINGBORG KALSKRONA

MALMO

HOTELL ÅREGÅRDEN

BOX 6, 83013 ÅRE, SWEDEN

TEL: +46 647 178 00 FAX: +46 647 17960 E-MAIL: info@diplomat–hotel–se

This lovely fin-de-siècle century house has been a hotel for some 100 years. Standing in the centre of Åre, it is in a fantastic position, close to the ski-lifts, shops and other local attractions, with a background of snow-clad mountains. The interior is traditional, with fine pine panelling much in evidence and the friendly staff contribute to the warm ambience of this excellently-run hotel. The charming bedrooms are light and colourful, the furnishings comfortable. There are pleasant apartments for 4-8 people in adjacent small houses. Hotell Åregården has a convivial bar and two excellent restaurants where delicious Swedish specialities are served. Guests also enjoy themselves in its popular Country Club, with famous live bands performing. A recent addition is a conference complex of seven meeting rooms, all having the latest communication and presentation equipment. Visitors relax in the splendid pool, saunas and sunbeds, ideal after a long winter day's skiing (the discounts on ski rental are appreciated). In summer, guests explore the countryside on bikes, walk among the mountains, or fish and play golf. **Directions:** Årefjällen is off the E14 between Trondheim and Östersund. Price Guide (per person): Single Skr595–895; double/twin Skr495–795; suite Skr795–995.

Aspa Herrgård

69693 ASPA BRUK, ASKERSUND, SWEDEN
TEL: +46 583 50210 FAX: +46 583 50150

Aspa Bruk is a very special place in Sweden, much admired by the 1916 Nobel Prize winning poet, Verner von Heidenstam and he used to stay at Aspa Herrgård, an enchanting 18th century manor house on the shores of Lake Vättern, by the verdant Tiveden National Park. The hotel has a marvellous tranquil ambience, created by the decorations in muted colours, the graceful period furniture, the bowls of flowers, beautiful objets d'art and memorabilia, fine paintings, views over the lake and park and, of course, the immaculate staff. The bedrooms are charming, comfortable and peaceful – some for non-smokers. The salons and library are traditional and there is a pleasant bar. The elegant dining room, with its exquisite table-settings, is the pièce de résistance, having won many accolades including that of the unique Relais Gourmand, while superb wines can be found in the 15th century cellar. The former stables are a museum to the Swedish poet, Bellman and the Manor hosts various cultural events, including art exhibitions and musical soirées, throughout the year. There are facilities for boules, croquet, golf and canoeing at hand. **Directions:** From Stockholm drive E20 towards Örebro, then take road 50 towards Akersund. Take right road 49 towards Skövde/Karlsborg. Price guide: Single Skr990–1290; double/twin Skr1380–2090; suite Skr2500.

SWEDEN (Båstad)

HOTEL BUENA VISTA

TARRAVÄGEN 5, 26935 BÅSTAD, SWEDEN
TEL: +46 431 760 00 FAX: +46 431 791 00

This is an unusual hotel to find on the coast of Southern Sweden – built during the last fin de siècle, Buena Vista is in the style of a grand Spanish villa It stands in the centre of Båstad, sufficiently elevated to have spectacular views of Laholm's Bay. The hotel is surrounded by pleasant gardens. The décor is immaculate, the ambience welcoming. The Hall at the bottom of the impressive galleried staircase is the heart of the villa – here guests rendezvous to have a drink and discuss their day. The bedrooms are charming and have well-designed bathrooms. There are several elegant dining rooms – small and romantic or somewhat bigger, with views over the waterfront – all serving beautifully presented regional and seasonal dishes. The wine list is splendid. In fine weather, the spacious open-air restaurant is popular. Buena Vista enjoys catering for meetings, seminars and special celebrations. It has a pristine chapel, enchanting for weddings or christenings. This is a mecca for golfers, with five good courses nearby. Excellent tennis facilities are within easy reach. The coast is 200m away for strolls along the beach and sea swimming is fantastic. **Directions:** From Malmö or Gothenburg take E6 motorway to picturesque Båstad, finding the hotel in the town centre. The nearest airports are Halmstad and Angelholm. Parking. Price guide: Single Skr660–750; double/twin Skr850–990; suites Skr1295.

HALLTORPS GÄSTGIVERI

38792 BORGHOLM, SWEDEN
TEL: +46 485 85000 FAX: +46 485 85001

The Halltorps Inn is one of the oldest manors recorded on the Viking island of Öland and it was only in 1975, following major reconstruction, that it became a hotel. In 1991 the extensive annex was completed, blending carefully with the original house. The position is superb, overlooking the spectacular Kalmar Sound. The eleven guest rooms in the original mansion are romantic and traditional, but the hotel is also very proud of its 25 rooms in the extension, each personalised by designers from different Swedish provinces. The spacious bathrooms have high-tec showers. The welcoming reception rooms have comfortable leather furniture and guests enjoy sampling the house speciality, spiced Aquavit, in the friendly bar! This is a hotel for gourmets, the inspired menu incorporating many local delicacies such as fish from the Baltic and wine lovers will appreciate the selection available. Guests relax on the sun terrace, play boules or croquet on the lawn, use the saunas or 'springcool' and in winter appreciate the three open fires, perhaps after cross-country skiing. Golf is just 1km away. The hotel arranges bird-watching safaris, wild flower excursions, wine tasting, and fishing tours. **Directions:** From the mainland E22, then the country road 136. Price guide: Single Skr810–880; double/twin Skr990–1170; suite Skr1300–1520.

HOTEL SUNDBYHOLMS SLOTT

63508 ESKILSTUNA, SWEDEN
TEL: +46 16 96500 FAX: +46 16 96578

Not all buildings called 'castles' have battlements. This graceful dwelling, built in 1640, is reminiscent of a château. It stands in its own extensive parkland, leading down to the shores of lovely Lake Malaren. There is a famous painting of Sundbyholm, by Prince Eugen, who had a studio on the second floor. The enchanting castle has undergone sympathetic restoration. The bedroom accommodation is, however, in other various areas, most having views of the lake. All rooms have modern showers. The superior suites are outstanding. The restaurant is in the castle, in the Knights Hall, which is famed for its brilliant cuisine and fine wines. Sparkling crystal, gleaming silver, beautiful flowers and brilliant chandeliers enhance the ambience. The Old Bailiff's House has been transformed into a modern conference complex. Another important feature is the Sundbyholm Country Club, with its magnificent championship golf course. Additionally it has teaching and practice grounds. Residents enjoy the local harbour – some even arrive by boat – and beautiful beaches on the lakeside. Others stroll through the beech groves, seeking the famous Sigurd runic rock. **Directions:** From Stockholm leave the E20 at Eskilstuna, follow signs. Sundbyholm is situated 12km north of Eskilstuna. Price guide: Single Skr600–1100; double/twin Skr850–1520.

HOTEL EGGERS

DROTTINGTORGET, BOX 323, 40125 GOTHENBURG, SWEDEN
TEL: +46 31 80 60 70 FAX: +46 31 15 42 43

Gothenburg is a delightful city to visit and it can be reached by air, rail or sea, for it is an important port, playing a significant part in the Scandinavian shipping industry as well as having cruise ships calling in. The Eggers is a fine traditional hotel, the second oldest in Sweden. It has a big foyer which has tall pillars, a graceful staircase and is pleasantly furnished. It is popular with the nearby business community because it has excellent meeting facilities with audio visual and other communication equipment available. Each bedroom differs from the next in style or colour, but all are extremely comfortable, thoughtfully equipped with modern amenities and have efficient bathrooms. The bar is an ideal rendezvous, decorated in warm colours and leading into the elegant "Eggers Restaurant", which has lovely wall coverings and brilliant chandeliers. While Swedish specialities are served, especially at the splendid breakfast buffet, the menu includes cosmopolitan favourites. It is also possible to hold receptions or small banquets here during conventions. Cruises round the islands are enjoyable; Gothenburg also has ten excellent golf courses. Additionally it is an ideal base for touring. The pedestrian shopping area is splendid and the maritime museum is fascinating. At night visitors enjoy the opera. **Directions:** Follow signs to centre of Gothenberg. Hotel is next to Centralstation. Price guide: Single Skr1115–1295; double/twin Skr1420; suite Skr1510–1660.

TOFTAHOLM HERRGÅRD

TOFTAHOLM PA, 34014 LAGAN, SWEDEN
TEL: +46 370 440 55 FAX: +46 370 440 45

This splendid manor house, with a history dating back over 600 years and a secret tunnel through which a king escaped from marauders in the sixteenth century, is in a magnificent position right on the shores of Lake Vidostern yet sheltered by forests of fragrant pine trees. This elegant hotel is timeless, old fashioned courtesies prevail, yet it meets the demands of today's travellers, who share it with a gentle ghost. The salons are elegant, peaceful and beautifully decorated and the traditional meeting room has plenty of natural light from the many windows. The quiet bedrooms, each individually styled, are charming, with delicate colour schemes and they look out over the countryside. Powerful hot showers are a feature of the bathrooms. Aperitifs are served on the terrace on warm evenings; otherwise there is a convivial corner next to Reception. Swedish cooking at its best is offered in the attractive restaurant with a wonderful array of tempting dishes. Hidden in the gardens is an authentic old inn serving tankards of frothy lager! Energetic guests appreciate the lakeside beach, the proximity of two superb golf courses, fishing, cycling, rowing, canoeing, cycling, jogging trails and skiing – and afterwards the sauna. Others relax on the lawn watching the boats. **Directions:** From Stockholm follow E4 to sign to Toftaholm. Price guide: Single Skr830–1030; double/twin Skr1200–1260; suites Skr1650.

ROMANTIK HOTEL SÖDERKÖPINGS BRUNN

SKÖNBERGAGATAN 35, BOX 44, 61421 SÖDERKÖPING
TEL: +46 121 10900 FAX: +46 121 13941 E-MAIL: info@soderkopingsbrunn.se

In 1719 it was discovered that the water from St Ragnhilds had medicinal properties and the Söderköping spa was built. It became a famous health resort in the 19th century and it is still possible to 'take the water' from a spring in Reception. Following considerate restoration, which has not disturbed the style of the original buildings – an important feature of the town – Söderköpings Brunn is now an impeccable modern hotel. The light and airy bedrooms are delightful, overlooking the gardens. Some are designated non-smoking and four are suitable for those with mobility problems. The bedrooms are divided between two houses. Guests gather in the lounge and bar before enjoying good food and wine, perhaps on the verandah in summer, otherwise in the spacious restaurant. Outside is a small bandstand with an open-air dance floor. The recent extensions included topical conference facilities and corporate entertaining can take place in the legendary 'Society Parlour'. The hotel has its own boats for trips along the Göta Canal and the River Storån or guests can take out a canoe. Active visitors can climb the Ramunder mountain, play tennis or enjoy golf alongside Lake Asplången, cycle, fish or explore the old town. **Directions:** Söderköping is near the E22, 15km south of Norrköping with its airport and railway station. Price guide. Single Skr600–975; double/twin Skr850–1175.

SWEDEN (Stockholm)

HOTELL DIPLOMAT

STRANDVÄGEN 7 C, BOX 14059, 104 40, STOCKHOLM, SWEDEN
TEL: +46 8 459 68 00 FAX: +46 8 459 68 20 E-MAIL: info@diplomat–hotel–se

It is always a joy to stay at a hotel overlooking a harbour and The Diplomat is magnificently positioned on the water's edge yet close to centre of Stockholm. Both the exterior and interior are fine examples of the Art Nouveau era, from the little tower and style of the windows to the spectacular bronze lift and delightful stained glass windows. Nonetheless, it is a sophisticated and modern hotel. It has been beautifully decorated, even the corridors having brilliant harmonious colour schemes and fine period furniture. These lead to attractive, spacious and well-equipped bedrooms. The elegant lounge is an ideal meeting place, an alternative rendezvous being the stylish bar, with its leather chairs and old prints on the walls. Buffet breakfasts, appetising lunches and dinners are served in the Diplomat Tea House. Private dining can be arranged in the smart Board Room. If not attending meetings in the nearby commercial centre, guests explore the fascinating Old Town, visit the museums or shopping centre. Boat trips round the harbour. Golf and tennis are not far away. **Directions:** The hotel is on Strandvägen, close to the Nybroviken Ferry terminal. Parking facilities can be arranged. Price guide: Single Skr1495–2095; double/twin Skr1995–2295; suite Skr3295–5690.

SVARTÅ HERRGÅRD

69393 SVARTÅ, SWEDEN
TEL: +46 585 500 03 FAX: +46 585 503 03

In the centre of Sweden, east of Stockholm, in the glorious wooded countryside surrounding Svartå, there is a magnificent manor house built in 1782. It has been lovingly restored and discreetly modernised and today it is an immaculate, romantic hotel standing in well-kept gardens stretching down to a sparkling lake. The fascinating history of the Svartå Herrgård is reflected in the elegant decorations, fine antiques, graceful chairs, brilliant chandeliers and handsome portraits. The wonderfully peaceful guest rooms are exquisite, with delicate colour schemes, period furniture and views over the countryside. The bathrooms are modern. The lounge bar has a splendid vaulted ceiling and grand snooker table; the breakfast room is refreshing in blue and white. Dining in the handsome restaurant, with its lovely frescoes, is memorable – inspired interpretations of Swedish specialities and cosmopolitan favourites are offered and the wine list is excellent. The adjacent Villa Lugnsbo is a self-contained conference centre, with various sized meeting rooms, excellent equipment and its own cafeteria. Boating on the lake, exploring Svartå and playing golf and tennis nearby are summer sports; in winter good skiing is accessible. **Directions:** E18 from Stockholm, then Road 204 to Svartå, watching for signs to the hotel. Price guide: Single Skr 800; double/twin Skr 1000–1600.

ROMANTIK HOTEL ÅKERBLADS

79370 TÄLLBERG, SWEDEN
TEL: +46 247 50800 FAX: +46 247 50652

This charming traditional farmhouse, now extended and modernised without detracting from the original buildings, has been the home of the Åkerblad family since the 16th century. It is on a hillside in the village of Tällberg and has spectacular views over the Siljan Lake. Today, most of the bedrooms are separate from the main building, being in three adjacent houses. They are wonderfully light, with big windows, pine furnishings and soft harmonising colour schemes. The bathrooms are more inclined to have showers than baths. There is a spacious Skänrummet, with lovely stone walls, which is very convivial – sometimes enlivened further by folk-dancing – and a cosy,

colourful, small bar. The traditional dining room offers a wonderful array of Smörgåsbord in addition to a delicious evening menu based on grandmother's cooking! The cellar holds many splendid wines. A larger salon transforms into a superb banqueting hall. Excellent conference facilities are also available. In winter, skiing and sleigh-rides are on the programme, in summer there are boat trips on the lake, museums and crafts shops and even gold washing at nearby Orsa. Nightlife can be found in most of the neighbouring villages. **Directions:** From Stockholm the E70 leads all the way to Tällberg. Price guide: Single Skr350–600; double/twin Skr500–1200.

HOTEL TÄNNDALEN

84098 TÄNNDALEN, SWEDEN
TEL: +46 684 220 20 FAX: +46 684 224 24

To reach Tänndalen you fly to Norway, for it is close to the border, high up in the Swedish mountains. In reality this is much more than a hotel, it is almost a village in itself – a complex of attractive wooden buildings set against magnificent scenery. Created by the hospitable Mortberg family, its reputation is for fine living and good sport! Many of the comfortable bedrooms and self-catering apartments (with paintings and ornaments by local artists) are in charming rustic chalets and houses just minutes walk from the hotel itself, where guests relax in the congenial halls before open fires, investigate the shop stocked by nearby craftsmen, fraternise in the coffee shop and bar or dive into the swimming pool. The restaurant has a reputation for delicious food – including regional specialities such as reindeer, trout and cloudberries – and for excellent wines. There are also superb conference facilities. In winter there is fantastic skiing, both down hill and cross country. The Mortbergs organise dog sledging and snowmobile safaris. Summer brings alpine flora and fauna – reindeers, elks and bears! Activities are hiking, climbing, tennis, golf, fishing and canoeing. Local markets are fascinating. The Tänndalen arranges evening entertainments. **Directions:** Road 84: 12 miles west of Funasdalen, 18km from the border. Røros in Norway is the nearest airport. Parking. Price guide: Single Skr695–995; double/twin Skr 900–1200; suites Skr1200–1600.

TANUMS GESTGIFVERI

45700 TANUMSHEDE, SWEDEN
TEL: +46 525 290 10 FAX: +46 525 295 71

There has been an inn at Tanumshede for over 300 years, for it was on 6th July 1663 that Bjørn of Hee received the right to become an innkeeper, on condition that he built a stable for travellers' horses. Offering fine hospitality has therefore been a long tradition at this unique small hotel. The Öster family, after considerable research and restoration work, have resurrected the 17th century spirit of the Inn, especially in the Butler's Pantry and the dining rooms. Guests stay in the Old Doctor's Villa, where comfortable suites and bedrooms, each differing from the next, have flowery or velvet upholstery, period furniture and all modern comforts. Visitors with mobility problems have not been overlooked. The

rustic bar serves snacks and the fine restaurant menu features fresh fish from the nearby coast and Bohuslan archipeligo, game and berries from the hinterland. The ancient cellars hold fine wines. The Gestgifveri has a sauna and residents enjoy a game of billiards in the evening. The balmy climate is perfect for exploring the unspoilt countryside. The region is known for ancient rock paintings, Viking graves and old churches. The fishing ports are fascinating. Golf and sailing are in the vicinity. **Directions:** Route E6, Tanumshede Grebbestad exit, take Route 163 to Tanumshede. Price guide: Single Skr 650; double/twin Skr 910; suites Skr 1410–1910.

Switzerland

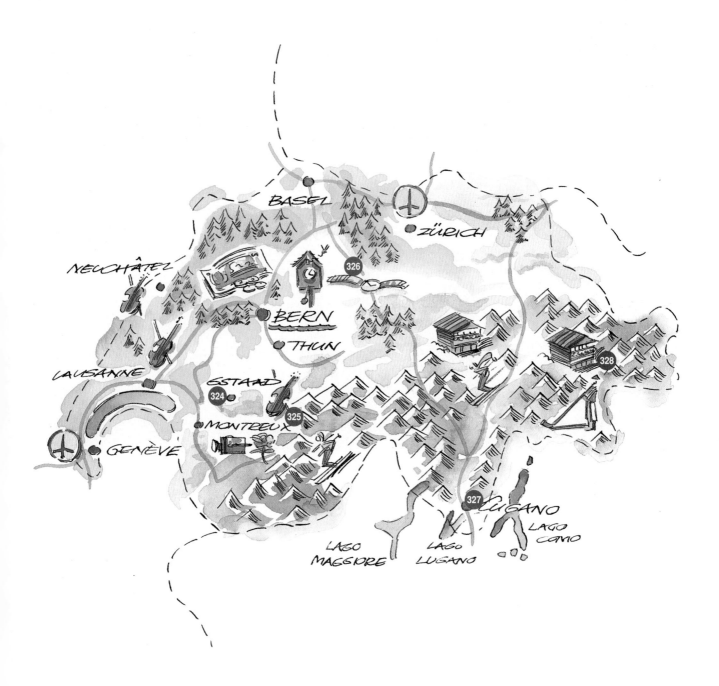

HOSTELLERIE BON ACCUEIL

1837 CHÂTEAU D'OEX, SWITZERLAND
TEL: +41 26 924 6320 FAX: +41 26 924 5126

In the region known as Pays d'Enhaut, 1000m above sea level, there is an 18th century chalet, cleverly and discreetly transformed into the pretty Hostellerie Bon Accueil, on the outskirts of Château d'Oex, famed for its cheese-making. The hotel is in a sunny position, surrounded by mountains, forests and meadows. The reception rooms are traditionally furnished and have big windows looking out across to the peaks. The bedrooms are delightful and decorated in pretty floral fabrics. A few are in the new annex, adjacent to the hotel. Happy evenings can be spent in the rustic Cellar-Bar, with its big fire and old stone walls. The cuisine is of the highest standards, with a French influence, enjoyed in the romantic candle-lit dining room or, in summer, on the splendid terrace with its spectacular views. This is serious winter-sports territory, with runs for all standards, being close to the Gstaad Super Ski Region. In summer, walkers appreciate the wild flowers and mountain streams. Others participate in river-rafting, golf, tennis, canoeing and hot-air ballooning. **Directions:** Leave E27 at Bulle or Aigle. Follow signs to Chateau d'Oex, turn left, crossing the railway track, watching for signs for the hotel. Price guide: Single SF90–125; double/twin SF145–210.

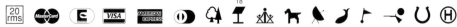

ROYAL HOTEL BELLEVUE

3718 KANDERSTEG, SWITZERLAND
TEL: +41 33 675 88 88 FAX: +41 33 675 88 80 TOLL FREE +41 800 700 600 88

This distinguished country house hotel, one of the Leading Hotels of the World, lies in a small unspoiled village resort in the middle of the Bernese Oberland. Surrounded by its own spacious gardens and lawns (12,000 square meters), the hotel offers an exceptional variety of leisure activities, summer and winter sports: easy alpine skiing and cross country skiing, open-air and indoor pools, fitness, beauty parlour, tennis and riding (both with instructors), golf practice areas, golf Interlaken 38km, yacht sailing and a 350HP motorboat, waterskiing, mountain-bikes and superb walking. In the classic restaurant, candlelight dinners are served in impeccable style with piano music. The Taverna rustic restaurant is ideal for meals in informal or sport dress. Light lunch is served near the poolside, overlooking the private park with magnificent views of mountains and glaciers. The bright and cheerful interior, furnished in antiques with elegantly fashionable soft colours, creates an atmosphere of comfort and refinement. All rooms and suites are luxuriously decorated in individual styles, all with bathrooms providing the highest comfort. **Directions:** N6 Bern to Interlaken, take Spiez exit, 20km to Kandersteg. Direct trains from Zurich Airport. From Bern Airport trains every hour, Limousine at Kandersteg station. Internal trains IC and EC stop in Kandersteg. Price guide: Single Sf200–350; double/twin Sf300–440; suites Sf450–700.

ROMANTIK HOTEL WILDEN MANN

BAHNHOFSTRASSE 30, 6000 LUCERNE 7, SWITZERLAND
TEL: +41 41 210 16 66 FAX: +41 41 210 16 29 E-MAIL: mail@wilden-mann.ch

This elegant hotel, whose history dates as far back as 1517, is a small jewel possessing incomparable charm of a medieval town house in the fascinating Old Town of Lucerne; its beautiful lake and woodland scenery immortalised in the story of William Tell. The hotel's façade with its arched doorway, bright window boxes, pretty blinds and balconies immediately tells arrivals that the Wilden Mann is special – the lobby is a joy with fine antiques and comfortable welcoming furniture. Each bedroom and junior suite is individually decorated and offers modern comfort. The salon is a delightful place for apéritifs before trying one of the three well-known restaurants. The "Wilden Mann Stube" is the connoisseurs' meeting point for French and International cuisine and fine wines. The light, airy "Geranium Terrace", where grill specialities are served, is perfect in summer weather, while the rustic "Burgerstube" is cosy and casual, serving local specialities. There are also handsome private dining rooms which can be used for meetings. The Wilden Mann is a "home from home" for the discerning traveller looking for small scale refinement and charm. **Directions:** In the heart of Lucerne, 200 metres to Chapel Bridge. 500 metres to railway station and lake. Parking 50 metres around the corner. Price guide: Single SF155–240; double/twin SF240–350; suites SF310–420.

VILLA PRINCIPE LEOPOLDO & RESIDENCE

Prima Hotels

VIA MONTALBANO, 6900 LUGANO, SWITZERLAND
TEL: 41 91 985 8855 FAX: 41 91 985 8825 E-MAIL: info@leopoldo.ch

This villa – a graceful example of neo-classicism era – was built for Prince Leopoldo of Hohenzollern who forsook his throne for the benign climate and undulating countryside of Ticino, the jewel of which is Lake Lugano. Today, following discreet transformation, the Villa is an élite hotel standing on the lower slopes of Collina d'Oro, with a distinguished Visitors' Book. While adjacent to Lugano it also offers seclusion. The bedrooms are luxurious, with lovely fabric covered walls and classical furnishings, balconies and lavish marble bathrooms. Several are designated non-smoking. The salons and lobby are spacious and elegant, evocative of the Villa's past. Guests appreciate cocktails in the inviting piano bar while selecting succulent dishes from the menu, many of which have a Mediterranean origin. Some fine Italian wines are suggested. In summer the restaurant is doubled in size by the addition of a series of enchanting gazebos on the garden terrace with its glorious outlook. There are also several stylish meeting and private dining rooms. The hotel pool is floodlit at night. Other recreations are tennis, fishing in the lake and golf nearby, boat trips on Lake Lugano, exploring the city and enjoying its varied night life. **Directions:** N2 from Zurich, exiting at Lugano South. The hotel is signed in the valley entering Lugano. Single SF210–500; double/twin SF290–700; suites SF700–1800.

POSTHOTEL ENGIADINA

VIA MAISTRA, 7524 ZUOZ, SWITZERLAND
TEL +41 81 85 41 021 FAX: +41 81 85 43 303

This traditional Swiss manor house, for over 120 years an immaculate hotel, is in Zuoz, a village that has kept much of its 16th century architectural charm. In winter, the snow-covered Engadine provides superb skiing and in summer it offers wonderful walks among the flower-filled meadows, lakes and forests of the Swiss National Park. The Posthotel reception hall is spacious with graceful vaulted ceilings. The attractive lounges have lovely tiled fireplaces, period furniture and a peaceful ambience. The bedrooms all look across to the Alps. Energetic visitors start the day with a breakfast from the extensive buffet in the colourful Sela Verda and Sela Melna dining rooms, to which they return later in the day for the table d'hôte dinner. Two other handsome restaurants, La Posta Veglia and La Prüveda offer haute cuisine and marvellous Swiss, French and Italian wines. Evenings often end in the La Chamanna bar. In summer, the hotel pool, tennis court and bicycles are popular. Europe's highest golf course is nearby, trout fishing can be arranged and surfboarders go to the Engadine lakes. Winter sports enthusiasts appreciate the sauna to relax their weary muscles. **Directions:** By road or rail, through Chur. Zuoz is signed from St. Moritz, just 15km away. Price guide: Single SF128–160; double/twin SF176–300.

Turkey

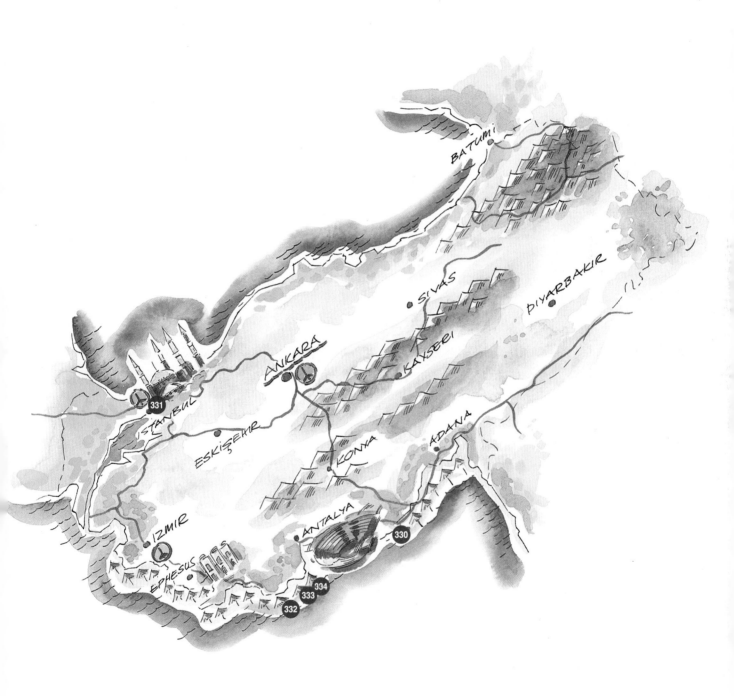

HOTEL GRAND KAPTAN

OBA, GÖL MEVKII, 07400 ALANYA, TURKEY
TEL: +90 242 514 0101 FAX: +90 242 514 0092

This large, modern hotel offers so many amenities that it is virtually a self-contained complex which guests need never leave throughout their stay. Its position is marvellous, right on the Mediterranean shore. Many of the bright, air-conditioned bedrooms have terraces with wonderful views of the sun setting over the water, a spectacular alternative to international TV channels. The bathrooms have all today's extras. Children are well catered for, with their own play areas while adults can sample the Lobby Bar, the romantic Terrace Bar overlooking the sea, the Beach Bar, Vitamin Bar and the unique Pool Bar with its seats actually in the water. The Kaptan specialises in extensive buffets for breakfast and again later in the day when the range of dishes offered is very cosmopolitan. There is an à la carte menu available, and a good wine list. The café offers lighter dishes. Most meals are enjoyed out of doors and there are occasional barbecues. Dress is extremely informal. Sporting activities include a freshwater pool, floodlit tennis, and many water sports including the Seabike. The hotel has an extensive private beach, a fitness room, sauna, billiards and table tennis and at night a casino and cabarets to entertain guests. There is also a shopping arcade. **Directions:** From Antalya airport take the coast road, following signs to Alanya. Price guide: Single US$50–US$103; double/twin US$55–US$138.

BOSPHORUS PASHA

YALIBOYU CADDESI NO. 64, BEYLERBEYI, 80210 ISTANBUL, TURKEY
TEL: +90 216 422 0003 FAX: +90 216 422 0012

Visitors to the elegant Bosphorus Pasha have the best of all worlds. They have the advantage of being close to the bustling centre of ancient Istanbul while enjoying all the comforts of a modern top class luxury hotel in a setting which reflects a peaceful culture dating back hundreds of years. Standing in beautifully manicured grounds, this elegant, white, three storey hotel, on the shores of the Bosphorous Strait, is steeped in history starting from the early 18th century. In its original residence form it featured a harem. Severely damaged by a fire in 1983, it was completely rebuilt during 1993–96 using previous drawings and photographs. The interior is as grand as the façade with guests experiencing traditional welcoming Turkish

hospitality in a rich and luxurious setting. The 14 bedrooms are each beautifully appointed with care having been given to every detail. Many of them look out onto the deep blue hues of the Bosphorus. The former boathouse of the historical residence has been converted into a relaxing, romantic, picture-windowed restaurant where diners can enjoy excellent international cuisine, which includes a wide variety of fish and meat dishes together with numerous pasta dishes and an extensive wine list. **Directions**: The hotel is situated in the village of Beylerbeyi which is reached by crossing the Bosphorous Bridge out of Istanbul. Price guide: Single US$275–315; double/twin US$330–370; suite US$750.

TURKEY (Kalkan)

HOTEL VILLA MAHAL

P.K. 4 KALKAN, 07960 ANTALYA, TURKEY
TEL: +90 242 844 32 68 FAX: +90 242 844 21 22

This intimate hotel stands on a hillside, overlooking the spectacular Bay of Kalkan. It is surrounded by olive trees and is perfect for a secluded holiday away from the stresses of the twentieth century. Villa Mahal has a private beach, however, because of its position, there are a number of steps to go down to the beach platforms and it is not recommended for those with any mobility problems. The villa is built round a delightful courtyard and with a maximum of 17 guests, the ambience is more like that of a private house than a hotel. The bedrooms are bright and airy, cooled by individually remote controlled air conditioning units and have roof terraces. The bathrooms have showers. Breakfast consists of a delicious buffet, served on the rooftop terrace and light lunches are served at the beach bar. Evening apéritifs are enjoyed on the terrace before dining under the stars, feasting on succulent Turkish specialities. Sometimes there are barbecues. The hotel's boat takes guests across the bay to Kalkan, a fascinating town with its harbour, market, tavernas and cafés – an opportunity to meet the locals! Water sports and cruises can be arranged. Recommended expeditions include exploring the mountains, ancient ruins at Xanthos and other historic sites. Closed 1 Nov–30 April. **Directions:** Taking main road from the Dalaman airport towards Kas, turn left 700m after the Kalkan sign, driving towards the beach. Price guide: Single $50–70; double/twin $70–90; suites $90–110.

CLUB SAVILE

CUKURBAG YARIMADASI, KAS, ANTALYA, TURKEY
TEL: +90 242 836 1393 UK TEL: +44 171 625 3001

This unique collection of 11 apartments, located on one of the country's most picturesque peninsulas, offers the perfect combination of modern comfort and Turkish style. There are two apartment buildings – Pasha's House and Vizier's House. Each comprise two penthouses and four one-bedroom self-contained and self-catering apartments. Inside, the décor is light and the furnishings elegantly contemporary to create a feeling of cool spaciousness. A full range of modern facilities is provided. Waiting for guests as they enter their accommodation for the first time is an exclusive Club Savile hamper, monogrammed bathrobes and soft towelling slippers to add a touch of luxury. Several of the apartments have large terraces, offering wonderful views of the bay and peninsula. A large freshwater swimming pool available for the private use of residents lies within the grounds. Pool attendants are on hand to supply beach towels and cushions for the sun loungers. At the end of the day, after a relaxing drink in the bar, guests can sample the mouth-watering cuisine, served in the à la carte restaurant overlooking the bay. For those wishing to stay within the privacy of their apartment, the excellent menus can still be enjoyed courtesy of room service. **Directions**: Kas is signposted from Dalaman. In Kas, follow signs for the peninsula and then those for Club Savile. Price guide: (per week) 1 bed apt £350–£600; 2 bed apt £550 900; 3 bed apt £750–£1200.

SAVILE RESIDENCE

CUKURBAG YARIMADASI, KAS/ANTALYA, TURKEY
TEL: +90 242 836 2300 UK TEL: +44 171 625 3001

This charming new country house hotel enjoys a superb location on the beautiful Kas peninsula. Reflecting the exotic character of Turkey, while matching the fine standards of accommodation and hospitality offered by the best English country house, it boasts wonderful views from every room. While each of the standard rooms is tastefully decorated and air-conditioned, more than a touch of luxury is evident throughout the suites. As well as being beautifully furnished and appointed, these are equipped with every modern comfort, including a hi-fi player, satellite television, minibar and tea and coffee-making facilities. They also include a shaded balcony, an ideal place to relax and absorb the beauty of the surroundings. Residents have a private freshwater swimming pool, use of a spacious lounge and a choice of bars – including one adjacent to the pool and another close to the sea. A delicious Mediterranean breakfast is included in the price of a stay at The Savile Residence, while other culinary delights are prepared in the à la carte restaurant. A guilty conscience can soon be soothed by making use of the purpose-built fitness centre! Beyond this haven of peace lie many attractions, including Kas and the ancient city of Myra. **Directions**: Kas is signposted from Dalaman. In Kas follow signs for the peninsula and then for Savile Residence. Price guide: Single: £40–£50; double/twin £50–£60; suite £70–£150.

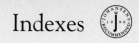

Hayfield	The Waltzing Weasel	01663 743402
Helmsley	The Feathers Hotel	01439 770275
Helmsley	The Feversham Arms Hotel	01439 770766
Hindon, Nr Salisbury	The Lamb at Hindon	01747 820573
Honiton	Home Farm Hotel	01404 831278
King's Lynn	The Rose & Crown	01485 541382
Kingsbridge	The Kings Arms Hotel	01548 852071
Kingskerswell	The Barn Owl Inn	01803 872130
Knutsford	Longview Hotel And Restaurant	01565 632119
Ledbury	Feathers Hotel	01531 635266
Leek	The Three Horseshoes Inn & Restaurant	01538 300296
Lincoln	Hare & Hounds	01400 272090
Long Melford	The Countrymen	01787 312356
Long Sutton	The Devonshire Arms Hotel	01458 241271
Ludlow	Mr Underhill's	01584 874431
Lymington	Hotel Gordleton Mill	01590 682219
Lynmouth	The Rising Sun	01598 753223
Maidstone	The Harrow At Warren Street	01622 858727
Maidstone	Ringlestone Inn	01622 859900
Malmesbury	The Horse And Groom Inn	01666 823904
Market Weighton	The Londesborough	01430 872214
Mells	The Talbot Inn at Mells	01373 812254
Milton Keynes	The Different Drummer	01908 564733
Montacute	The King's Arms Inn & Restaurant	01935 822513
Newbury	The Swan Inn	01488 668271
Newby Bridge	The Swan Hotel	015395 31681
North Walsham	Elderton Lodge Hotel & Restaurant	01263 833547
Norwich	The Stower Grange	01603 860210
Nottingham	Hotel Des Clos	01159 866566
Onneley	The Wheatsheaf Inn At Onneley	01782 751581
Oundle	The Talbot	01832 273621
Oxford	Holcombe Hotel	01869 338274
Oxford	The Jersey Arms	01869 343234
Oxford	The Mill & Old Swan	01993 774441
Padstow	The Old Custom House Hotel	01841 532359
Pelynt,Nr Looe	Jubilee Inn	01503 220312
Penistone	The Fountain Inn & Rooms	01226 763125
Petworth	Badgers	01798 342651
Petworth	The Stonemason's Inn	01798 342510
Petworth	White Horse Inn	01798 869 221
Port Gaverne	The Port Gaverne Hotel	01208 880244
Preston	Ye Horn's Inn	01772 865230
Reading	The Bull at Streatley	01491 875231
Romsey	Dukes Head	01794 514450
Ross-on-Wye	Cottage of Content	01432 840242
Rothley	The Rothley Court	0116 237 4141
Rugby	The Golden Lion Inn of Easenhall	01788 832265
Rutland Water	Normanton Park Hotel	01780 720315
Rye	The George Hotel	01797 222144
Saddleworth	The Old Bell Inn Hotel	01457 870130
St. Ives	Olivers Lodge Hotel & Restaurant	01480 463252
Salisbury	The Old Mill Hotel & Restaurant	01722 327517
Salisbury	The White Horse	01725 510408
Sevenoaks	The Royal Oak	01732 451109
Sheffield	The Old Vicarage	0114 247 5814
Sherborne	The Walnut Tree	01935 851292
Shifnal	Naughty Nell's	01952 411412
Shipton Under Wychwood	The Shaven Crown Hotel	01993 830330
Shipton-Under-Wychwood	The Lamb Inn	01993 830465
Southport	Tree Tops Country House Hotel	01704 879651
Stafford	The Dower House	01889 270707
Stow-on-the-Wold	The Horse and Groom Inn & Restaurant	01451 830584
Stow-On-The-Wold	The Kings Head Inn & Restaurant	01608 658365
Stow-on-the-Wold	The Unicorn Hotel & Restaurant	01451 830257
Stratford-upon-Avon	The Coach House Hotel	01789 204109 / 299468
Stroud	The Bear of Rodborough Hotel	01453 878522
Sudbury	The Bull Hotel	01787 378494
Telford	The Hundred House Hotel	01952 730353
Tenterden	The White Lion Hotel	01580 765077
Tetbury	The Close Hotel	01666 502272
Thelbridge	Thelbridge Cross Inn	01884 860316
Thornham	The Lifeboat Inn	01485 512236
Thornham Magna	Four Horseshoes	01379 678777
Thorpe Market	Green Farm Restaurant And Hotel	01263 833602
Tintagel	The Port William	01840 770230
Totnes	The Sea Trout Inn	01803 762274
Totnes	The Watermans Arms	01803 732214
Troutbeck	The Mortal Man Hotel	015394 33193
Upton-Upon-Severn	The White Lion Hotel	01684 592551
Walberswick	The Bell Inn	01502 723109
Weobley	Ye Olde Salutation Inn	01544 318443
West Witton	The Wensleydale Heifer Inn	01969 622322
Whitewell	The Inn At Whitewell	01200 448222
Wooler	The Tankerville Arms Hotel	01668 281581
Worcester	The Old Schoolhouse	01905 371368
Worthing	The Old Tollgate Restaurant And Hotel	01903 879494
Wroxham	The Barton Angler Country Inn	01692 630740
York	The George at Easingwold	01347 821698

WALES

Chepstow	The Castle View Hotel	01291 620349
Llanarmon Dyffryn Ceiriog	The West Arms Hotel	01691 600665
Llandeilo	The Plough Inn	01558 823431
Welshpool	The Lion Hotel And Restaurant	01686 640452

SCOTLAND

Aboyne	Birse Lodge Hotel	01339 886253
Blair Atholl	The Loft Restaurant	01796 481377
Blairgowrie	The Glenisla Hotel	01575 582223
Cullen	The Seafield Arms Hotel	01542 840791
Inverness	Grouse & Trout	01808 521314
Isle Of Skye	Hotel Eilean Iarmain or Isle Ornsay Hotel	01471 833332
Isle Of Skye	Uig Hotel	01470 542205
Kenmore	The Kenmore Hotel	01887 830205
Killearn	The Black Bull	01360 550215
Loch Ness	The Foyers Hotel	01456 486216
Moffatt	Annandale Arms Hotel	01683 220013
Pitlochry	The Moulin Hotel	01796 472196
Plockton	The Plockton Hotel & Garden Restaurant	01599 544274
Poolewe	Pool House Hotel	01445 781272
Powmill	The Gartwhinzean	01577 840595
St Andrews	The Grange Inn	01334 472670

CHANNEL ISLANDS

Jersey	Sea Crest Hotel And Restaurant	01534 46353

Country Houses & Small Hotels

ENGLAND

Alcester	Arrow Mill Hotel And Restaurant	01789 762419
Appleton-Le-Moors	Appleton Hall	01751 417227
Arundel	Burpham Country House Hotel	01903 882160
Ashbourne	The Beeches Farmhouse	01889 590288
Atherstone	Chapel House	01827 718949
Badminton	Petty France	01454 238361
Bakewell	East Lodge Country House Hotel	01629 734474
Bakewell	The Peacock Hotel at Rowsley	01629 733518
Bamburgh	Waren House Hotel	01668 214581
Bath	Apsley House	01225 336966
Bath	Bath Lodge Hotel	01225 723040
Bath	Bloomfield House	01225 420105
Bath	Duke's Hotel	01225 463512
Bath	Eagle House	01225 859946
Bath	Oldfields	01225 317984
Bath	Paradise House	01225 317723
Bath	Widbrook Grange	01225 864750 / 863173
Bath	Woolverton House	01373 830415
Belper	Dannah Farm Country Guest House	01773 550273 / 630
Beverley	The Manor House	01482 881645
Bibury	Bibury Court	01285 740337
Bideford	Yeoldon House Hotel	01237 474400
Biggin-By-Hartington	Biggin Hall	01298 84451
Blockley	Lower Brook House	01386 700286
Bolton	Quarlton Manor Farm	01204 852277
Bridgnorth	Cross Lane House Hotel	01746 764887
Brighton	The Granville	01273 326302
Broadway	Collin House Hotel	01386 858354
Broadway	The Old Rectory	01386 853729
Brockenhurst	Thatched Cottage Hotel & Restaurant	01590 623090
Brockenhurst	Whitley Ridge & Country House Hotel	01590 622354
Bury St. Edmunds	The Priory	01284 766181
Cambridge	Melbourn Bury	01763 261151
Carlisle	Crosby Lodge Country House Hotel	01228 573618
Cartmel	Aynsome Manor Hotel	015395 36653
Chagford	Easton Court Hotel	01647 433469
Cheltenham	Charlton Kings Hotel	01242 231061
Cheltenham	Halewell	01242 890238
Chichester	Crouchers Bottom Country Hotel	01243 784995
Chichester	Woodstock House Hotel	01243 811666
Chipping Campden	The Malt House	01386 840295
Church Stretton	Mynd House Hotel & Restaurant	01694 722212
Clearwell	Tudor Farmhouse Hotel & Restaurant	01594 833046
Clovelly	Foxdown Manor	01237 451325
Coalville	Abbots Oak	01530 832 328
Combe Martin	Ashelford	01271 850469
Crediton	Coombe House Country Hotel	01363 84487
Crewe	Pear Tree Lake Farms	01270 820307
Dartmoor	Bel Alp House	01364 661217
Dartmoor	Prince Hall Hotel	01822 890403
Dartmouth	Broome Court	01803 834275
Dartmouth	Nonsuch House	01803 752829
Diss	Chippenhall Hall	01379 588180 / 586733
Dorchester	Yalbury Cottage Hotel	01305 262382
Dover	Wallett's Court	01304 852424
Dover	The Woodville Hall	01304 825256
Dulverton	Ashwick Country House Hotel	01398 323868
Enfield	Oak Lodge Hotel	0181 360 7082
Epsom	Chalk Lane Hotel	01372 721179
Evershot	Rectory House	0193583 273
Evesham	The Mill At Harvington	01386 870688
Exeter	The Lord Haldon Hotel	01392 832483
Exford	The Crown Hotel	01643 831554/5
Exmoor	The Beacon Country House Hotel	01643 703476
Fakenham	Vere Lodge	01328 838261
Falmouth	Trelawne Hotel-The Hutches Restaurant	01326 250226
Fenny Drayton	White Wings	01827 716100
Gatwick	Stanhill Court Hotel	01293 862166
Golant by Fowey	The Cormorant Hotel	01726 833426
Grasmere	White Moss House	015394 35295
Great Snoring	The Old Rectory	01328 820597
Hampstead Village	Sandringham Hotel	0171 435 1569
Hampton Court	Chase Lodge	0181 943 1862
Hamsterley Forest	Grove House	01388 488203
Harrogate	The White House	01423 501388
Hawes	Rookhurst Georgian Country House Hotel	01969 667454
Helmsley	Ryedale Country Lodge	01439 748246
Helston	Nansloe Manor	01326 574691
Hereford	The Bowens Country House	01432 860430
Hereford	The Steppes	01432 820424
Holt	Felbrigg Lodge	01263 837588
Hope	Underleigh House	01433 621372
Ilminster	The Old Rectory	01460 54364
Isle of Wight	Rylstone Manor	01983 862806
Keswick	Dale Head Hall Lakeside Hotel	017687 72478
Keswick	Swinside Lodge Hotel	017687 72948
Kingsbridge	The White House	01548 580580
Kirkby Lonsdale	Hipping Hall	015242 71187
Lavenham	Lavenham Priory	01787 247404
Leominster	Lower Bache House	01568 750304
Lifton	The Thatched Cottage Country Hotel	01566 784224
Lincoln	Washingborough Hall	01522 790340
Looe	Allhays Country House	01503 272434
Looe	Coombe Farm	01503 240223
Loughborough	The Old Manor Hotel	01509 211228
Ludlow	Delbury Hall	01584 841267
Ludlow	Overton Grange Hotel	01584 873500
Luton	Little Offley	01462 768243
Lydford	Moor View House	01822 820220
Lyme Regis	Thatch Lodge Hotel	01297 560407
Lynton	Hewitt's Hotel	01598 752293
Maidstone	Tanyard	01622 744705
Malton	Newstead Grange	01653 692502
Matlock	The Manor Farmhouse	01629 534246
Matlock	Sheriff Lodge Hotel	01629 760760
Middlecombe	Periton Park Hotel	01643 706885
Middleham	Millers House Hotel	01969 622630
Minchinhampton	Burleigh Court	01453 883804
Minehead	Channel House Hotel	01643 703229
Morchard Bishop	Wigham	01363 877350
Morpeth	Eshott Hall	01670 787777
New Polzeath	The Cornish Cottage Hotel	01208 862213
New Romney	Romney Bay House	01797 364747
North Walsham	Beechwood Hotel	01692 403231
Norwich	The Beeches Hotel & Victorian Gardens	01603 621167
Norwich	Catton Old Hall	01603 419379
Norwich	Norfolk Mead Hotel	01603 737531
Norwich	The Old Rectory	01603 700772
Nottingham	The Cottage Country House Hotel	01159 846882
Nottingham	Langar Hall	01949 860559
Oswestry	Pen-y-Dyffryn Country Hotel	01691 653700
Ottery St. Mary	Venn Ottery Barton	01404 812733
Owlpen	Owlpen Manor	01453 860261
Oxford	Fallowfields	01865 820416
Padstow	Cross House Hotel	01841 532391
Penrith	Temple Sowerby House Hotel	017683 61578
Petersfield	Langrish House	01730 266941
Porlock Weir	The Cottage Hotel	01643 863300
Porthleven	Tye Rock Hotel	01326 572695
Portsmouth	The Beaufort Hotel	01705 823707
Pulborough	Chequers Hotel	01798 872486
Redditch	The Old Rectory	01527 523000
Ringwood	Moortown Lodge	01425 471404
Rock	The St Enodoc Hotel	01208 863394
Ross-On-Wye	Glewstone Court	01989 770367
Rye	White Vine House	01797 224748
Saham Toney	Broom Hall	01953 882125
St. Ives	Boskerris Hotel	01736 795295
St Ives	The Countryman At Trink Hotel	01736 797571
St Mawes	The Hundred House Hotel	01872 501336
Salcombe	The Lyndhurst Hotel	01548 842481
Saunton	Preston House Hotel	01271 890472
Seavington St Mary	The Pheasant Hotel	01460 240502
Sheffield	Staindrop Hotel & Restaurant	0114 284 6727
Sherborne	The Eastbury Hotel	01935 813131
Shipton-Under-Wychwood	The Shaven Crown Hotel	01993 830330
Simonsbath	Simonsbath House Hotel	01643 831259
South Molton	Marsh Hall Country House Hotel	01769 572666
Staverton	Kingston House	01803 762 235
Stevenage	Redcoats Farmhouse Hotel & Restaurant	01438 729500
Stonor	The Stonor Arms	01491 638866
Stow-On-The-Wold	Conygree Gate Hotel	01608 658389
Stratford-upon-Avon	Glebe Farm House	01789 842501
Tewkesbury	Upper Court	01386 725351
Tintagel	Trebrea Lodge	01840 770410
Truro	The Royal Hotel	01872 270345
Uckfield	Hooke Hall	01825 761578
Wadebridge	Trehellas House	01208 72700
Wareham	Kemps Country House Hotel & Restaurant	01929 462563
Warwick	The Ardencote Manor Hotel	01926 843111
Wells	Beryl	01749 678738
Wells	Coxley Vineyard	01749 670285
Wells	Glencot House	01749 677160
Whitby	Dunsley Hall	01947 893437
Wimborne Minster	Beechleas	01202 841684
Wincanton	Holbrook House Hotel	01963 32377
Windermere	Fayrer Garden House Hotel	015394 88195
Windermere	Quarry Garth Country House Hotel	015394 88282
Windermere	Storrs Hall	015394 47111
Witherslack	The Old Vicarage Country House Hotel	015395 52381
Woodbridge	Wood Hall Hotel & Country Club	01394 411283
Worthing	Findon Manor	01903 872733
York	The Parsonage Country House Hotel	01904 728111
Yoxford	Hope House	01728 668281

WALES

Aberdovey	Plas Penhelig Country House Hotel	01654 767676
Abergavenny	Glangrwyney Court	01873 811288
Abergavenny	Llanwenarth House	01873 830289
Abergavenny	Penyclawdd Court	01873 890719
Betws-y-Coed	Tan-y-Foel	01690 710507
Brecon	Old Gwernyfed Country Manor	01497 847376
Caernarfon	Ty'n Rhos Country House	01248 670489
Cardigan	The Pembrokeshire Retreat	01239 841387
Conwy	Berthlwyd Hall Hotel	01492 592409
Conwy	The Old Rectory	01492 580611
Dolgellau	Plas Dolmelynllyn	01341 440273
Monmouth	The Crown At Whitebrook	01600 860254
Pwllheli	Plas Bodegroes	01758 612363
Tenby	Waterwynch House Hotel	01834 842464
Tintern	Parva Farmhouse and Restaurant	01291 689411
Welshpool	Buttington House	01938 553351

SCOTLAND

Ballater,Royal Deeside	Balgonie Country House	013397 55482
By Huntly	The Old Manse of Marnoch	01466 780873
Castle Douglas	Longacre Manor	01556 503576
Comrie	The Royal Hotel	01764 679200
Drumnadrochit	Polmaily House Hotel	01456 450343
Dumfries	Trigony House Hotel	01848 331211
Dunkeld	The Pend	01350 727586
Edinburgh	No 22 Murrayfield Gardens	0131 337 3569
Fintry	Culcreuch Castle Hotel & Country Park	01360 860555
Helmsdale	Navidale House Hotel	01431 821 258
Inverness	Culduthel Lodge	01463 240089
Isle Of Harris	Ardvourlie Castle	01859 502307
Isle of Mull	Highland Cottage	01688 302030
Isle Of Mull	Killiechronan	01680 300403
Isle of Skye	Bosville Hotel	01478 612846
Kentallen Of Appin	Ardsheal House	01631 740227
Killiecrankie,By Pitlochry	The Killiecrankie Hotel	01796 473220
Kinlochbervie	The Kinlochbervie Hotel	01971 521275
Kinross	Nivingston Country House	01577 850216
Lockerbie	The Dryfesdale Hotel	01576 202427
Moffat	Well View Hotel	01683 220184
Nairn	Boath House	01667 454896
Oban	Dungallen House Hotel	01631 563799
Oban	The Manor House Hotel	01631 562087
Perth	Newmiln Country House	01738 552364
Pitlochry	Dunfallandy House	01796 472648
Port Appin	Druimneil	01631 730228
Port Of Menteith	The Lake Hotel	01877 385258
Rhu	Aldonaig	01436 820863
St. Boswell By Melrose	Clint Lodge	01835 822027
Strathtummel	Queen's View Hotel	01796 473291

IRELAND

Bantry	Ballylickey Manor House	00 353 27 50071
Caragh Lake Co Kerry	Ard-na-Sidhe	00 353 66 69105
Caragh Lake Co Kerry	Caragh Lodge	00 353 66 69115
Cashel Co Tipperary	Cashel Palace Hotel	00 353 62 62707
Connemara	Ross Lake House Hotel	00 353 91 550109
Dublin	Aberdeen Lodge	00 353 1 2838155
Dublin	The Fitzwilliam Park	00 353 1 6628 280
Killadeas	The Inishclare Restaurant	013656 28550
Kilkee Co Clare	Halpins Hotel & Vittles Restaurant	00 353 65 56032
Killarney Co Kerry	Earls Court House	00 353 64 34009
Kilmeaden	The Old Rectory - Kilmeaden House	00 353 51 384254
Letterkenny	Castle Grove Country House	00 353 745 1118
Riverstown,Co Sligo	Coopershill House	00 353 71 65108
Skibbereen Co.Cork	Liss Ard Lake Lodge	00 353 28 22365
Sligo,Co Sligo	Markree Castle	00 353 71 67800
Wicklow,Co Wicklow	The Old Rectory	00 353 404 67048

CHANNEL ISLANDS

Guernsey	Bella Luce Hotel & Restaurant	01481 38764
Guernsey	La Favorita Hotel	01481 35666
Guernsey	The White House	01481 722159
Jersey	Hotel La Tour	01534 43770

Hotels – North America, Bermuda, The Caribbean

BERMUDA

Paget	Harmony Club	1 441 236 3500
Paget	The Newstead Hotel	1 441 236 6060
Warwick	Surf Side Beach Club	1 441 236 7100

CANADA

Sidney	Seaside Luxury Resort	1 250 598 1000
Vancouver	The Wedgewood Hotel	1 604 689 7777
Vancouver	The West End Guest House	1 604 681 2889/1302
Victoria	Dashwood Manor	1 250 385 5517
Whistler	Durlacher Hof	1 604 932 1924

CARIBBEAN

St Vincent	Petit St. Vincent Resort	1 787 458 8801

NORTH AMERICA

Arizona (Flagstaff)	Inn at 410	1 520 774 0088
Arizona (Phoenix)	Maricopa Manor	1 602 274 6302
Arizona (Sedona)	Canyon Villa Inn	1 520 284 1226
Arizona (Sedona)	The Inn On Oak Creek	1 520 282 7896
Arizona (Tucson)	The Lodge on the Desert	1 520 325 3366
Arizona (Tucson)	Tanque Verde Ranch	1 520 296 6275
Arizona (Tucson)	White Stallion Ranch	1 520 297 0252
California (Beverly Hills)	Beverly Hills Hotel and Bungalows	1 310 276 2251
California (Carmel)	Pine Inn	1 408 624 3851
California (Eureka)	Carter House	1 707 444 8062
California (Ferndale)	Gingerbread Mansion Inn	1 707 786 4000
California (Healdsburg)	Madrona Manor	1 707 433 4231
California (Hollywood)	Château Marmont	1 213 656 1010
California (Hollywood)	Le Parc Suite Hotel	1 310 855 8888
California (Hopland)	Thatcher Inn	1 707 744 1890
California (Inverness)	Manka's Inverness Lodge	1 415 669 1034
California (Mill Valley)	Mountain Home Inn	1 415 381 9000
California (Monterey Peninsula)	The Martine Inn	1 831 373 3388
California (Muir Beach)	Pelican Inn	1 415 383 6000
California (Nevada City)	Red Castle Inn Historic Lodging	1 530 265 5135
California (Sacramento)	The Sterling Hotel	1 916 448 1300
California (San Francisco)	The Archbishop's Mansion	1 415 563 7872
California (San Francisco)	The Maxwell Hotel	1 415 986 2000
California (San Francisco)	Nob Hill Lambourne	1 415 433 2287
California (Santa Monica)	Shutters on the Beach	1 310 458 0300
California (Shasta)	Brigadoon Castle	1 530 396 2785
Colorado (Denver)	Castle Marne	1 303 331 0621
Connecticut (Deep River)	Riverwind Inn	1 860 526 2014
Connecticut (Greenwich)	The Homestead Inn	1 203 869 7500
Connecticut (New Preston)	The Boulders	1 860 868 0541
Delaware (Montchanin)	The Inn at Montchanin Village	1 302 888 2133
Florida (Cumberland Island)	Greyfield Inn	1 904 261 6408
Florida (Fort Lauderdale)	Lago Mar	1 954 523 6511
Florida (Key West)	Curry Mansion	1 305 294 5349
Florida (Key West)	Heron House	1 305 294 9227
Florida (Lake Wales)	Chalet Suzanne	1 941 676 6011
Florida (Miami Beach)	Ocean Front Hotel	1 305 672 2579
Florida (Miami Beach)	The Richmond	1 305 538 2331
Georgia (Macon)	1842 Inn	1 912 741 1842
Georgia (Perry)	Henderson Village	1 912 988 8696
Georgia (St. Simons Island)	The Lodge on Little St. Simons Island	1 912 638 7472
Georgia (Savannah)	The Eliza Thompson House	1 912 236 3620
Georgia (Savannah)	Foley House Inn	1 912 232 6622
Georgia (Savannah)	The Gastonian	1 912 232 2869
Georgia (Savannah)	The Jesse Mount House	1 912 236 1774
Georgia (Savannah)	Presidents Quarters	1 912 233 1600
Georgia (Thomasville)	Melhana Plantation	1 912 266 2290
Hawaii (Volcano Village, Big Island)	Chalet Kilauea	1 808 967 7786
Louisiana (Napoleonville)	Madewood Plantation House	1 504 369 7151
Louisiana (New Orleans)	The Claiborne Mansion	1 504 949 7327
Louisiana (New Orleans)	Windsor Court	1 504 523 6000
Louisiana (Thibodaux)	The Dansereau House	1 504 447 1002
Maine (Greenville)	The Lodge at Moosehead Lake	1 207 695 4400
Maine (Kennebunkport)	Kennebunkport Inn	1 207 967 2621
Maryland (Frederick)	Tyler Spite Inn	1 301 831 4455
Maryland (Taneytown)	Antrim 1844	1 410 756 6812
Massachusetts (Boston Area)	A Cambridge House	1 617 491 6300
Massachusetts (Cape Cod)	Wedgewood Inn	1 508 362 9178
Massachusetts (Chatham)	The Captain's House Inn	1 508 945 0127
Massachusetts (Chatham)	Pleasant Bay Village Resort	1 508 945 1133
Massachusetts (Deerfield)	Deerfield Inn	1 413 774 5587
Massachusetts (Eastham)	The Whalewalk Inn	1 508 255 0617
Massachusetts (Lenox)	Wheatleigh	1 413 637 0610
Michigan (Harbor Springs)	Notley Kimberly Country Estate	1 616 526 7646
Michigan (Petoskey)	Staffords Perry Hotel	1 616 347 4000
Mississippi (Jackson)	Fairview Inn	1 601 948 3429
Mississippi (Natchez)	Monmouth Plantation	1 601 442 5852
Mississippi (Vicksburg)	Duff Green Mansion	1 601 636 6968
New Hampshire (Henniker)	Colby Hill Inn	1 603 428 3281
New Hampshire (Jackson)	Inn at Thorn Hill	1 603 383 4242
New Hampshire (Jackson)	Nestlenook Farm	1 603 383 9101
New Jersey (Cape May)	The Queens Hotel	1 609 884 1613
New Jersey (Hope)	The Inn at Millrace Pond	1 908 459 4884
New Jersey (Spring Lake)	Sea Crest By The Sea	1 732 449 9031
New York (Cazenovia)	The Brewster Inn	1 315 655 9232
New York (Clarence)	Asa Ransom House	1 716 759 2315
New York (East Aurora)	The Roycroft Inn	1 716 652 5552
New York (East Hampton)	Centennial House	1 516 324 2681
New York (Ithaca)	The Rose Inn	1 607 533 7905
New York (New York)	The Kitano New York	1 212 885 7000
New York (New York)	The Lowell	1 212 838 1400
North Carolina (Asheville)	Richmond Hill Inn	1 828 252 7313
North Carolina (Lake Toxaway)	The Greystone Inn	1 704 966 4700
North Carolina (Pittsboro)	The Fearrington House	1 919 542 2121
North Carolina (Tryon)	Pine Crest	1 828 859 9135
North Carolina (Waynesville)	The Swag Country Inn	1 828 926 0430
Oregon (Depoe Bay)	Channel House Inn	1 541 765 2140
Oregon (Eugene)	Campbell House	1 541 343 1119
Oregon (Hood River)	Columbia Gorge Hotel	1 541 386 5566
Pennsylvania (Hawley)	The Settlers Inn	1 717 226 2993
Pennsylvania (Milford)	Cliff Park Inn	1 717 296 6491
Pennsylvania (South Sterling)	The French Manor	1 717 676 3244
Rhode Island (Newport)	Cliffside Inn	1 401 847 1811
Rhode Island (Newport)	Vanderbilt Hall	1 401 846 6200
Rhode Island (Westerly)	The Villa	1 401 596 1054
South Carolina (Beaufort)	The Rhett House Inn	1 843 524 9030
South Carolina (Charleston)	Two Meeting Street Inn	1 803 723 7322
South Carolina (Charleston)	Wentworth Mansion	1 843 853 1886
Vermont (Brandon)	Churchill House Inn	1 802 247 3078
Vermont (Chittenden)	Mountain Top Inn & Resort	1 802 483 2311
Vermont (Dorset)	Cornucopia of Dorset	1 802 867 5751
Vermont (Lower Waterford)	Rabbit Hill Inn	1 802 748 5168
Vermont (Manchester Village)	1811 House	1 802 362 1811
Vermont (Mendon)	Red Clover Inn	1 802 775 2290
Vermont (Shelburne)	The Inn at Shelburne Farms	1 802 985 8498
Vermont (Stowe)	The Mountain Road Resort	1 802 253 4566
Vermont (Vergennes)	Basin Harbor	1 802 475 2311
Washington (Kirkland)	The Woodmark Hotel	1 425 803 5563
Washington (Orcas Island)	Turtleback Farm Inn	1 360 376 4914
Washington (Port Angeles)	Domaine Madeleine	1 360 457 4174
Washington (Port Townsend)	Ann Starrett Mansion	1 300 385 3205
Washington (Seattle)	Sorrento Hotel	1 206 622 6400
Washington (Winthrop)	Sun Mountain Lodge	1 509 996 2211
Wisconsin (Fish Creek)	The White Gull Inn	1 920 868 3517
Wisconsin (Sturgeon Bay)	Inn at Cedar Crossing	1 920 743 4200
Wisconsin (Sturgeon Bay)	White Lace Inn	1 920 743 1105
Wyoming (Jackson Hole)	The Alpenhof Lodge	1 307 733 3242

Hotels in Europe accepting Johansens Privilege Card

AUSTRIA

Hotel Auersperg	Salzburg	33
Kur-Sport & Gourmethotel Moser	Bad Hofgastein	20
Romantik Hotel im Weissen Rössl	St Wolfgang am See	39
Romantik Hotel Schwarzer Adler	Innsbruck	26
Schlosshotel Igls	Igls	24
Sporthotel Igls	Igls	25

BELGIUM

Hotel de Orangerie	Bruges	48
The Stanhope	Brussels	55

CYPRUS

The Four Seasons Hotel	Limassol	97

CZECH REPUBLIC

Hotel Hoffmeister	Prague	100

FRANCE

Château des Vigiers	Monestier	135
Grand Hôtel du Domaine de Divonne	Divonne-les-Bains	122
Grand Hôtel Vista Palace	Roquebrune Cap-Martin/Monaco	151
Hôtel du Louvre	Paris	142
Hôtel Le Tourville	Paris	144
Hôtel Square	Paris	145
Mas d'Artigny	Saint Paul	152

GERMANY

Hôtel Eisenhut	Rothenburg Ob der Tauber	170
Hotel Königshof	Munich	167

ITALY

Albergo Pietrasanta-Palazzo Bonetti-Barsanti	Pietrasanta	211
Albergo Terminus	Como	190
Hotel Auriga	Milan	207
Hotel Terme Di Saturnia	Saturnia	224
Hotel Villa Flori	Como	191
Posthotel Weisses Rössl	Nova Levante	209
Romantic Hotel Oberwirt	Marling-Meran	205

LUXEMBOURG

Hotel Saint Nicolas	Remich	248

NETHERLANDS

Hotel De Arendshoeve	Bergambacht	251
Hotel de Wiemsel	Ootmarsum	255
Hotel Restaurant de Swaen	Oisterwijk	254

SPAIN

Hacienda El Santiscal	Arcos De La Frontera	283
Hotel de la Reconquista	Oviedo	298
Hotel La Costa	Pals	299
Hotel Rigat Park	Lloret de Mar	287
Monasterio de San Miguel	Puerto de Santa Maria-Cádiz	300

SWITZERLAND

Romantik Hotel Wilden Mann	Lucerne/ Luzern	326
Villa Principe Leopoldo & Residence	Lugano	327

Guest Survey Report

Your own Johansens 'inspection' gives reliability to our guides and assists in the selection of Award Nominations

Name/location of hotel: _____ Page No: _____

Date of visit: _____

Name & address of guest: _____

_____ Postcode: _____

Please tick one box in each category below:	Excellent	Good	Disappointing	Poor
Bedrooms				
Public Rooms				
Restaurant/Cuisine				
Service				
Welcome/Friendliness				
Value For Money				

PLEASE return your Guest Survey Report form!

Occasionally we may allow other reputable organisations to write with offers which may be of interest.
If you prefer not to hear from them, tick this box ☐

To: Johansens, FREEPOST (CB264), 43 Millharbour, London E14 9BR

Guest Survey Report

Your own Johansens 'inspection' gives reliability to our guides and assists in the selection of Award Nominations

Name/location of hotel: _____ Page No: _____

Date of visit: _____

Name & address of guest: _____

_____ Postcode: _____

Please tick one box in each category below:	Excellent	Good	Disappointing	Poor
Bedrooms				
Public Rooms				
Restaurant/Cuisine				
Service				
Welcome/Friendliness				
Value For Money				

PLEASE return your Guest Survey Report form!

Occasionally we may allow other reputable organisations to write with offers which may be of interest.
If you prefer not to hear from them, tick this box ☐

To: Johansens, FREEPOST (CB264), 43 Millharbour, London E14 9BR

ORDER FORM

Call our 24hr credit card hotline FREEPHONE +44 800 269 397

Simply indicate which title(s) you require by putting the quantity in the boxes provided. Choose your preferred method of payment and return this coupon (NO STAMP REQUIRED) to: Johansens, FREEPOST (CB264), 43 Millharbour, London E14 9BR. Your FREE gifts will automatically be dispatched with your order.
Fax orders welcome on +44 171 537 3594

PRINTED GUIDES

	Qty	Total £
A Hotels – Great Britain & Ireland 1999 ....£19.95		
B Country Houses and Small Hotels – Great Britain & Ireland 1999 ....£10.95		
C Traditional Inns, Hotels and Restaurants – Great Britain & Ireland 1999 ......£10.95		
D Hotels – Europe & The Mediterranean 1999 ....£14.95		
E Hotels – North America, Bermuda, Caribbean 1999 ....£9.95		
F Historic Houses Castles & Gardens 1999 *published & mailed to you in March '99* £4.99		
G Museums & Galleries 1999 *published & mailed to you in April '99* £8.95		
H Business Meeting Venues 1999 *published & mailed to you in March '99* £20.00		
I Japanese Edition 1999 ....£9.95		
J Privilege Card 1999 ....£20.00 *You get one free card with your order, please mention here the number of additional cards you require*		
TOTAL 1		

CD-ROMs

	Qty	Total £
K The Guide 1999 – Great Britain & Ireland *published and mailed to you in Nov 98* £29.95		
L The Guide 1999 – Europe & North America *published and mailed to you in Nov 98* ..£19.95		
M Business Meeting Venues 1999 *published and mailed to you in April '99* £20.00		
TOTAL 2		

SPECIAL OFFERS

	Qty	Total £
SAVE £7.85 3 Johansens guides A+B+C .. £41.85 ..£34		
In a presentation box set add £5		
SAVE £12.80 4 Johansens guides A+B+C+D ....£56.80 ..£44		
In a presentation box set add £5		
SAVE £14.75 5 Johansens guides A+B+C+D+E ....£66.75 ..£52		
In a presentation box set add £5		
+Johansens Suit Cover	FREE	
+P&P	FREE	
SAVE £10.90 2 Johansens CD-ROMS K+L .£49.90 ..£39		
SAVE £10 Business Meeting Pack H+M.....£40 ..£30		
TOTAL 3		

Postage & Packing

UK: £4.50 or £2.50 for single orders and CD-ROMs
Ouside UK: Add £5 or £3 for single orders and CD-ROMs.

TOTAL 4

One Privilege Card
10% discount, room upgrade when available,
VIP service at participating establishments

FREE

TOTAL 1+2+3+4

Name (Mr/Mrs/Miss)

Address

Postcode

Prices Valid Until 31 August 1999
Please allow 21 days for delivery

Occasionally we may allow other reputable organisations to write to you with offers which may be of interest. If you prefer not to hear from them, tick this box. ☐

☐ I enclose a cheque for £ _____ payable to Johansens
☐ I enclose my order on company letterheading, please invoice (UK only)
☐ Please debit my credit/charge card account (please tick).
☐ MasterCard ☐ Diners ☐ Amex ☐ Visa ☐ Switch (Issue Number)

Card No

Signature

Exp date

J16

------------------------------✂------------------------------

ORDER FORM

Call our 24hr credit card hotline FREEPHONE +44 800 269 397

Simply indicate which title(s) you require by putting the quantity in the boxes provided. Choose your preferred method of payment and return this coupon (NO STAMP REQUIRED) to: Johansens, FREEPOST (CB264), 43 Millharbour, London E14 9BR. Your FREE gifts will automatically be dispatched with your order.
Fax orders welcome on +44 171 537 3594

PRINTED GUIDES

	Qty	Total £
A Hotels – Great Britain & Ireland 1999 ....£19.95		
B Country Houses and Small Hotels – Great Britain & Ireland 1999 ....£10.95		
C Traditional Inns, Hotels and Restaurants – Great Britain & Ireland 1999 ......£10.95		
D Hotels – Europe & The Mediterranean 1999 ....£14.95		
E Hotels – North America, Bermuda, Caribbean 1999 ....£9.95		
F Historic Houses Castles & Gardens 1999 *published & mailed to you in March '99* £4.99		
G Museums & Galleries 1999 *published & mailed to you in April '99* £8.95		
H Business Meeting Venues 1999 *published & mailed to you in March '99* £20.00		
I Japanese Edition 1999 ....£9.95		
J Privilege Card 1999 ....£20.00 *You get one free card with your order, please mention here the number of additional cards you require*		
TOTAL 1		

CD-ROMs

	Qty	Total £
K The Guide 1999 – Great Britain & Ireland *published and mailed to you in Nov 98* £29.95		
L The Guide 1999 – Europe & North America *published and mailed to you in Nov 98* ..£19.95		
M Business Meeting Venues 1999 *published and mailed to you in April '99* £20.00		
TOTAL 2		

SPECIAL OFFERS

	Qty	Total £
SAVE £7.85 3 Johansens guides A+B+C .. £41.85 ..£34		
In a presentation box set add £5		
SAVE £12.80 4 Johansens guides A+B+C+D ....£56.80 ..£44		
In a presentation box set add £5		
SAVE £14.75 5 Johansens guides A+B+C+D+E ....£66.75 ..£52		
In a presentation box set add £5		
+Johansens Suit Cover	FREE	
+P&P	FREE	
SAVE £10.90 2 Johansens CD-ROMS K+L .£49.90 ..£39		
SAVE £10 Business Meeting Pack H+M.....£40 ..£30		
TOTAL 3		

Postage & Packing

UK: £4.50 or £2.50 for single orders and CD-ROMs
Ouside UK: Add £5 or £3 for single orders and CD-ROMs.

TOTAL 4

One Privilege Card
10% discount, room upgrade when available,
VIP service at participating establishments

FREE

TOTAL 1+2+3+4

Name (Mr/Mrs/Miss)

Address

Postcode

Prices Valid Until 31 August 1999
Please allow 21 days for delivery

Occasionally we may allow other reputable organisations to write to you with offers which may be of interest. If you prefer not to hear from them, tick this box. ☐

☐ I enclose a cheque for £ _____ payable to Johansens
☐ I enclose my order on company letterheading, please invoice (UK only)
☐ Please debit my credit/charge card account (please tick).
☐ MasterCard ☐ Diners ☐ Amex ☐ Visa ☐ Switch (Issue Number)

Card No

Signature

Exp date

J16

Guest Survey Report

Your own Johansens 'inspection' gives reliability to our guides and assists in the selection of Award Nominations

Name/location of hotel: _____ Page No: _____

Date of visit: _____

Name & address of guest: _____

_____ Postcode: _____

Please tick one box in each category below:	Excellent	Good	Disappointing	Poor
Bedrooms				
Public Rooms				
Restaurant/Cuisine				
Service				
Welcome/Friendliness				
Value For Money				

PLEASE return your Guest Survey Report form!

Occasionally we may allow other reputable organisations to write with offers which may be of interest.
If you prefer not to hear from them, tick this box ☐

To: Johansens, FREEPOST (CB264), 43 Millharbour, London E14 9BR

Guest Survey Report

Your own Johansens 'inspection' gives reliability to our guides and assists in the selection of Award Nominations

Name/location of hotel: _____ Page No: _____

Date of visit: _____

Name & address of guest: _____

_____ Postcode: _____

Please tick one box in each category below:	Excellent	Good	Disappointing	Poor
Bedrooms				
Public Rooms				
Restaurant/Cuisine				
Service				
Welcome/Friendliness				
Value For Money				

PLEASE return your Guest Survey Report form!

Occasionally we may allow other reputable organisations to write with offers which may be of interest.
If you prefer not to hear from them, tick this box ☐

To: Johansens, FREEPOST (CB264), 43 Millharbour, London E14 9BR

ORDER FORM

Call our 24hr credit card hotline FREEPHONE +44 800 269 397

Simply indicate which title(s) you require by putting the quantity in the boxes provided. Choose your preferred method of payment and return this coupon
(NO STAMP REQUIRED) to: Johansens, FREEPOST (CB264), 43 Millharbour, London E14 9BR. Your FREE gifts will automatically be dispatched with your order.
Fax orders welcome on +44 171 537 3594

PRINTED GUIDES

		Qty	Total £
A	Hotels – Great Britain & Ireland 1999 ....£19.95		
B	Country Houses and Small Hotels – Great Britain & Ireland 1999 ....£10.95		
C	Traditional Inns, Hotels and Restaurants – Great Britain & Ireland 1999 ......£10.95		
D	Hotels – Europe & The Mediterranean 1999 ....£14.95		
E	Hotels – North America, Bermuda, Caribbean 1999 ....£9.95		
F	Historic Houses Castles & Gardens 1999 *published & mailed to you in March '99* £4.99		
G	Museums & Galleries 1999 *published & mailed to you in April '99*............£8.95		
H	Business Meeting Venues 1999 *published & mailed to you in March '99* £20.00		
I	Japanese Edition 1999 ....£9.95		
J	Privilege Card 1999 ....£20.00 *You get one free card with you order, please mention here the number of additional cards you require*		

TOTAL 1 [ ]

CD-ROMs

		Qty	Total £
K	The Guide 1999 – Great Britain & Ireland *published and mailed to you in Nov 98* £29.95		
L	The Guide 1999 – Europe & North America *published and mailed to you in Nov 98* ..£19.95		
M	Business Meeting Venues 1999 *published and mailed to you in April '99* £20.00		

TOTAL 2 [ ]

SPECIAL OFFERS

		Qty	Total £
SAVE £7.85	3 Johansens guides A+B+C .£41.85 .£34		
	In a presentation box set add £5		
SAVE £12.80	4 Johansens guides A+B+C+D ....£56.80 .£44		
	In a presentation box set add £5		
SAVE £14.75	5 Johansens guides A+B+C+D+E ....£66.75 ..£52		
	In a presentation box set add £5		
	+*Johansens Suit Cover*	FREE	
	+*P&P*	FREE	
SAVE £10.90	2 Johansens CD-ROMS K+L £49.90 .£39		
SAVE £10	Business Meeting Pack H+M......£40 .£30		

TOTAL 3 [ ]

Postage & Packing
UK: £4.50 or £2.50 for single orders and CD-ROMs
Ouside UK: Add £5 or £3 for single orders and CD-ROMs.

TOTAL 4 [ ]

One Privilege Card [FREE]
10% discount, room upgrade when available,
VIP service at participating establishments

TOTAL 1+2+3+4 [ ]

Name (Mr/Mrs/Miss)

Address

Postcode

Prices Valid Until 31 August 1999
Please allow 21 days for delivery

Occasionally we may allow other reputable organisations to write to you with offers which may be of interest. If you prefer not to hear from them, tick this box. [ ]

☐ I enclose a cheque for £ _____ payable to Johansens
☐ I enclose my order on company letterheading, please invoice (UK only)
☐ Please debit my credit/charge card account (please tick).
☐ MasterCard ☐ Diners ☐ Amex ☐ Visa ☐ Switch (Issue Number) [ ]

Card No [ ][ ][ ][ ]

Signature _____ Exp date [ ]

J16

✂ ···

ORDER FORM

Call our 24hr credit card hotline FREEPHONE +44 800 269 397

Simply indicate which title(s) you require by putting the quantity in the boxes provided. Choose your preferred method of payment and return this coupon
(NO STAMP REQUIRED) to: Johansens, FREEPOST (CB264), 43 Millharbour, London E14 9BR. Your FREE gifts will automatically be dispatched with your order.
Fax orders welcome on +44 171 537 3594

PRINTED GUIDES

		Qty	Total £
A	Hotels – Great Britain & Ireland 1999 ....£19.95		
B	Country Houses and Small Hotels – Great Britain & Ireland 1999 ....£10.95		
C	Traditional Inns, Hotels and Restaurants – Great Britain & Ireland 1999 ......£10.95		
D	Hotels – Europe & The Mediterranean 1999 ....£14.95		
E	Hotels – North America, Bermuda, Caribbean 1999 ....£9.95		
F	Historic Houses Castles & Gardens 1999 *published & mailed to you in March '99* £4.99		
G	Museums & Galleries 1999 *published & mailed to you in April '99*............£8.95		
H	Business Meeting Venues 1999 *published & mailed to you in March '99* £20.00		
I	Japanese Edition 1999 ....£9.95		
J	Privilege Card 1999 ....£20.00 *You get one free card with you order, please mention here the number of additional cards you require*		

TOTAL 1 [ ]

CD-ROMs

		Qty	Total £
K	The Guide 1999 – Great Britain & Ireland *published and mailed to you in Nov 98* £29.95		
L	The Guide 1999 – Europe & North America *published and mailed to you in Nov 98* ..£19.95		
M	Business Meeting Venues 1999 *published and mailed to you in April '99* £20.00		

TOTAL 2 [ ]

SPECIAL OFFERS

		Qty	Total £
SAVE £7.85	3 Johansens guides A+B+C .£41.85 .£34		
	In a presentation box set add £5		
SAVE £12.80	4 Johansens guides A+B+C+D ....£56.80 .£44		
	In a presentation box set add £5		
SAVE £14.75	5 Johansens guides A+B+C+D+E ....£66.75 ..£52		
	In a presentation box set add £5		
	+*Johansens Suit Cover*	FREE	
	+*P&P*	FREE	
SAVE £10.90	2 Johansens CD-ROMS K+L £49.90 ..£39		
SAVE £10	Business Meeting Pack H+M......£40 .£30		

TOTAL 3 [ ]

Postage & Packing
UK: £4.50 or £2.50 for single orders and CD-ROMs
Ouside UK: Add £5 or £3 for single orders and CD-ROMs.

TOTAL 4 [ ]

One Privilege Card [FREE]
10% discount, room upgrade when available,
VIP service at participating establishments

TOTAL 1+2+3+4 [ ]

Name (Mr/Mrs/Miss)

Address

Postcode

Prices Valid Until 31 August 1999
Please allow 21 days for delivery

Occasionally we may allow other reputable organisations to write to you with offers which may be of interest. If you prefer not to hear from them, tick this box. [ ]

☐ I enclose a cheque for £ _____ payable to Johansens
☐ I enclose my order on company letterheading, please invoice (UK only)
☐ Please debit my credit/charge card account (please tick).
☐ MasterCard ☐ Diners ☐ Amex ☐ Visa ☐ Switch (Issue Number) [ ]

Card No [ ][ ][ ][ ]

Signature _____ Exp date [ ]

J16

Guest Survey Report

Your own Johansens 'inspection' gives reliability to our guides and assists in the selection of Award Nominations

Name/location of hotel: _____ Page No: _____

Date of visit: _____

Name & address of guest: _____

_____ Postcode: _____

Please tick one box in each category below:	Excellent	Good	Disappointing	Poor
Bedrooms				
Public Rooms				
Restaurant/Cuisine				
Service				
Welcome/Friendliness				
Value For Money				

PLEASE return your Guest Survey Report form!

Occasionally we may allow other reputable organisations to write with offers which may be of interest.
If you prefer not to hear from them, tick this box ☐

To: Johansens, FREEPOST (CB264), 43 Millharbour, London E14 9BR

Guest Survey Report

Your own Johansens 'inspection' gives reliability to our guides and assists in the selection of Award Nominations

Name/location of hotel: _____ Page No: _____

Date of visit: _____

Name & address of guest: _____

_____ Postcode: _____

Please tick one box in each category below:	Excellent	Good	Disappointing	Poor
Bedrooms				
Public Rooms				
Restaurant/Cuisine				
Service				
Welcome/Friendliness				
Value For Money				

PLEASE return your Guest Survey Report form!

Occasionally we may allow other reputable organisations to write with offers which may be of interest.
If you prefer not to hear from them, tick this box ☐

To: Johansens, FREEPOST (CB264), 43 Millharbour, London E14 9BR

ORDER FORM

Call our 24hr credit card hotline FREEPHONE +44 800 269 397

Simply indicate which title(s) you require by putting the quantity in the boxes provided. Choose your preferred method of payment and return this coupon (NO STAMP REQUIRED) to: Johansens, FREEPOST (CB264), 43 Millharbour, London E14 9BR. Your FREE gifts will automatically be dispatched with your order.
Fax orders welcome on +44 171 537 3594

PRINTED GUIDES

		Qty	Total £
A	Hotels – Great Britain & Ireland 1999 ....£19.95		
B	Country Houses and Small Hotels – Great Britain & Ireland 1999 ....£10.95		
C	Traditional Inns, Hotels and Restaurants – Great Britain & Ireland 1999 ......£10.95		
D	Hotels – Europe & The Mediterranean 1999 ....£14.95		
E	Hotels – North America, Bermuda, Caribbean 1999 ....£9.95		
F	Historic Houses Castles & Gardens 1999 *published & mailed to you in March '99* £4.99		
G	Museums & Galleries 1999 *published & mailed to you in April '99* £8.95		
H	Business Meeting Venues 1999 *published & mailed to you in March '99* £20.00		
I	Japanese Edition 1999 ....£9.95		
J	Privilege Card 1999 ....£20.00		
	You get one free card with you order, please mention here the number of additional cards you require		

TOTAL 1 [ ]

CD-ROMs

		Qty	Total £
K	The Guide 1999 – Great Britain & Ireland *published and mailed to you in Nov 98* £29.95		
L	The Guide 1999 – Europe & North America *published and mailed to you in Nov 98* ..£19.95		
M	Business Meeting Venues 1999 *published and mailed to you in April '99* £20.00		

TOTAL 2 [ ]

SPECIAL OFFERS

		Qty	Total £
SAVE £7.85	3 Johansens guides A+B+C £41.85 ..£34		
	In a presentation box set add £5		
SAVE £12.80	4 Johansens guides A+B+C+D ....£56.80 ..£44		
	In a presentation box set add £5		
SAVE £14.75	5 Johansens guides A+B+C+D+E ....£66.75 ..£52		
	In a presentation box set add £5		
	+Johansens Suit Cover	FREE	
	+P&P	FREE	
SAVE £10.90	2 Johansens CD-ROMS K+L £49.90 ..£39		
SAVE £10	Business Meeting Pack H+M.....£40 .£30		

TOTAL 3 [ ]

Postage & Packing

UK: £4.50 or £2.50 for single orders and CD-ROMs
Ouside UK: Add £5 or £3 for single orders and CD-ROMs.

TOTAL 4 [ ]

One Privilege Card [FREE]
10% discount, room upgrade when available,
VIP service at participating establishments

TOTAL 1+2+3+4 [ ]

Name (Mr/Mrs/Miss)
Address
Postcode

Prices Valid Until 31 August 1999
Please allow 21 days for delivery

Occasionally we may allow other reputable organisations to write to you with offers which may be of interest. If you prefer not to hear from them, tick this box. [ ]

☐ I enclose a cheque for £ _____ payable to Johansens
☐ I enclose my order on company letterheading, please invoice (UK only)
☐ Please debit my credit/charge card account (please tick).
☐ MasterCard ☐ Diners ☐ Amex ☐ Visa ☐ Switch (Issue Number)

Card No
Signature
Exp date

J16

✂ ··

ORDER FORM

Call our 24hr credit card hotline FREEPHONE +44 800 269 397

Simply indicate which title(s) you require by putting the quantity in the boxes provided. Choose your preferred method of payment and return this coupon (NO STAMP REQUIRED) to: Johansens, FREEPOST (CB264), 43 Millharbour, London E14 9BR. Your FREE gifts will automatically be dispatched with your order.
Fax orders welcome on +44 171 537 3594

PRINTED GUIDES

		Qty	Total £
A	Hotels – Great Britain & Ireland 1999 ....£19.95		
B	Country Houses and Small Hotels – Great Britain & Ireland 1999 ....£10.95		
C	Traditional Inns, Hotels and Restaurants – Great Britain & Ireland 1999 ......£10.95		
D	Hotels – Europe & The Mediterranean 1999 ....£14.95		
E	Hotels – North America, Bermuda, Caribbean 1999 ....£9.95		
F	Historic Houses Castles & Gardens 1999 *published & mailed to you in March '99* £4.99		
G	Museums & Galleries 1999 *published & mailed to you in April '99* £8.95		
H	Business Meeting Venues 1999 *published & mailed to you in March '99* £20.00		
I	Japanese Edition 1999 ....£9.95		
J	Privilege Card 1999 ....£20.00		
	You get one free card with you order, please mention here the number of additional cards you require		

TOTAL 1 [ ]

CD-ROMs

		Qty	Total £
K	The Guide 1999 – Great Britain & Ireland *published and mailed to you in Nov 98* £29.95		
L	The Guide 1999 – Europe & North America *published and mailed to you in Nov 98* ..£19.95		
M	Business Meeting Venues 1999 *published and mailed to you in April '99* £20.00		

TOTAL 2 [ ]

SPECIAL OFFERS

		Qty	Total £
SAVE £7.85	3 Johansens guides A+B+C £41.85 ..£34		
	In a presentation box set add £5		
SAVE £12.80	4 Johansens guides A+B+C+D ....£56.80 ..£44		
	In a presentation box set add £5		
SAVE £14.75	5 Johansens guides A+B+C+D+E ....£66.75 ..£52		
	In a presentation box set add £5		
	+Johansens Suit Cover	FREE	
	+P&P	FREE	
SAVE £10.90	2 Johansens CD-ROMS K+L £49.90 ..£39		
SAVE £10	Business Meeting Pack H+M.....£40 .£30		

TOTAL 3 [ ]

Postage & Packing

UK: £4.50 or £2.50 for single orders and CD-ROMs
Ouside UK: Add £5 or £3 for single orders and CD-ROMs.

TOTAL 4 [ ]

One Privilege Card [FREE]
10% discount, room upgrade when available,
VIP service at participating establishments

TOTAL 1+2+3+4 [ ]

Name (Mr/Mrs/Miss)
Address
Postcode

Prices Valid Until 31 August 1999
Please allow 21 days for delivery

Occasionally we may allow other reputable organisations to write to you with offers which may be of interest. If you prefer not to hear from them, tick this box. [ ]

☐ I enclose a cheque for £ _____ payable to Johansens
☐ I enclose my order on company letterheading, please invoice (UK only)
☐ Please debit my credit/charge card account (please tick).
☐ MasterCard ☐ Diners ☐ Amex ☐ Visa ☐ Switch (Issue Number)

Card No
Signature
Exp date

J16

Guest Survey Report

Name/location of hotel: _____   Page No: _____

Date of visit: _____

Name & address of guest: _____

_____   Postcode: _____

Please tick one box in each category below:	Excellent	Good	Disappointing	Poor
Bedrooms				
Public Rooms				
Restaurant/Cuisine				
Service				
Welcome/Friendliness				
Value For Money				

PLEASE return your Guest Survey Report form!

Occasionally we may allow other reputable organisations to write with offers which may be of interest.
If you prefer not to hear from them, tick this box ☐

To: Johansens, FREEPOST (CB264), 43 Millharbour, London E14 9BR

Guest Survey Report

Your own Johansens 'inspection' gives reliability to our guides and assists in the selection of Award Nominations

Name/location of hotel: _____   Page No: _____

Date of visit: _____

Name & address of guest: _____

_____   Postcode: _____

Please tick one box in each category below:	Excellent	Good	Disappointing	Poor
Bedrooms				
Public Rooms				
Restaurant/Cuisine				
Service				
Welcome/Friendliness				
Value For Money				

PLEASE return your Guest Survey Report form!

Occasionally we may allow other reputable organisations to write with offers which may be of interest.
If you prefer not to hear from them, tick this box ☐

To: Johansens, FREEPOST (CB264), 43 Millharbour, London E14 9BR

ORDER FORM

Call our 24hr credit card hotline FREEPHONE +44 800 269 397

Simply indicate which title(s) you require by putting the quantity in the boxes provided. Choose your preferred method of payment and return this coupon (NO STAMP REQUIRED) to: Johansens, FREEPOST (CB264), 43 Millharbour, London E14 9BR. Your FREE gifts will automatically be dispatched with your order.
Fax orders welcome on +44 171 537 3594

PRINTED GUIDES

	Qty	Total £
A Hotels – Great Britain & Ireland 1999 ....£19.95		
B Country Houses and Small Hotels – Great Britain & Ireland 1999 ....£10.95		
C Traditional Inns, Hotels and Restaurants – Great Britain & Ireland 1999 ......£10.95		
D Hotels – Europe & The Mediterranean 1999 ....£14.95		
E Hotels – North America, Bermuda, Caribbean 1999 ....£9.95		
F Historic Houses Castles & Gardens 1999 *published & mailed to you in March '99* £4.99		
G Museums & Galleries 1999 *published & mailed to you in April '99* £8.95		
H Business Meeting Venues 1999 *published & mailed to you in March '99* £20.00		
I Japanese Edition 1999 ....£9.95		
J Privilege Card 1999 ....£20.00 *You get one free card with you order, please mention here the number of additional cards you require*		
TOTAL 1		

SPECIAL OFFERS

	Qty	Total £
SAVE £7.85 3 Johansens guides A+B+C ..£41.85 ..£34		
In a presentation box set add £5		
SAVE £12.80 4 Johansens guides A+B+C+D ....£56.80 ..£44		
In a presentation box set add £5		
SAVE £14.75 5 Johansens guides A+B+C+D+E ....£66.75 ..£52		
In a presentation box set add £5		
+*Johansens Suit Cover*	FREE	
+*P&P*	FREE	
SAVE £10.90 2 Johansens CD-ROMS K+L £49.90 ..£39		
SAVE £10 Business Meeting Pack H+M......£40 ..£30		
TOTAL 3		

CD-ROMs

	Qty	Total £
K The Guide 1999 – Great Britain & Ireland *published and mailed to you in Nov 98* £29.95		
L The Guide 1999 – Europe & North America *published and mailed to you in Nov 98* ..£19.95		
M Business Meeting Venues 1999 *published and mailed to you in April '99* £20.00		
TOTAL 2		

Postage & Packing

UK: £4.50 or £2.50 for single orders and CD-ROMs
Ouside UK: Add £5 or £3 for single orders and CD-ROMs.

TOTAL 4 | |

One Privilege Card | FREE
10% discount, room upgrade when available,
VIP service at participating establishments

TOTAL 1+2+3+4 | |

Name (Mr/Mrs/Miss)

Address

Postcode

☐ I enclose a cheque for £ _____ payable to Johansens
☐ I enclose my order on company letterheading, please invoice (UK only)
☐ Please debit my credit/charge card account (please tick).
☐ MasterCard ☐ Diners ☐ Amex ☐ Visa ☐ Switch (Issue Number) _____

Card No

Signature

Exp date

Prices Valid Until 31 August 1999
Please allow 21 days for delivery

Occasionally we may allow other reputable organisations to write to you with offers which may be of interest. If you prefer not to hear from them, tick this box ☐

J16

✂ ....

ORDER FORM

Call our 24hr credit card hotline FREEPHONE +44 800 269 397

Simply indicate which title(s) you require by putting the quantity in the boxes provided. Choose your preferred method of payment and return this coupon (NO STAMP REQUIRED) to: Johansens, FREEPOST (CB264), 43 Millharbour, London E14 9BR. Your FREE gifts will automatically be dispatched with your order.
Fax orders welcome on +44 171 537 3594

PRINTED GUIDES

	Qty	Total £
A Hotels – Great Britain & Ireland 1999 ....£19.95		
B Country Houses and Small Hotels – Great Britain & Ireland 1999 ....£10.95		
C Traditional Inns, Hotels and Restaurants – Great Britain & Ireland 1999 ......£10.95		
D Hotels – Europe & The Mediterranean 1999 ....£14.95		
E Hotels – North America, Bermuda, Caribbean 1999 ....£9.95		
F Historic Houses Castles & Gardens 1999 *published & mailed to you in March '99* £4.99		
G Museums & Galleries 1999 *published & mailed to you in April '99* £8.95		
H Business Meeting Venues 1999 *published & mailed to you in March '99* £20.00		
I Japanese Edition 1999 ....£9.95		
J Privilege Card 1999 ....£20.00 *You get one free card with you order, please mention here the number of additional cards you require*		
TOTAL 1		

SPECIAL OFFERS

	Qty	Total £
SAVE £7.85 3 Johansens guides A+B+C ..£41.85 ..£34		
In a presentation box set add £5		
SAVE £12.80 4 Johansens guides A+B+C+D ....£56.80 ..£44		
In a presentation box set add £5		
SAVE £14.75 5 Johansens guides A+B+C+D+E ....£66.75 ..£52		
In a presentation box set add £5		
+*Johansens Suit Cover*	FREE	
+*P&P*	FREE	
SAVE £10.90 2 Johansens CD-ROMS K+L £49.90 ..£39		
SAVE £10 Business Meeting Pack H+M......£40 ..£30		
TOTAL 3		

CD-ROMs

	Qty	Total £
K The Guide 1999 – Great Britain & Ireland *published and mailed to you in Nov 98* £29.95		
L The Guide 1999 – Europe & North America *published and mailed to you in Nov 98* ..£19.95		
M Business Meeting Venues 1999 *published and mailed to you in April '99* £20.00		
TOTAL 2		

Postage & Packing

UK: £4.50 or £2.50 for single orders and CD-ROMs
Ouside UK: Add £5 or £3 for single orders and CD-ROMs.

TOTAL 4 | |

One Privilege Card | FREE
10% discount, room upgrade when available,
VIP service at participating establishments

TOTAL 1+2+3+4 | |

Name (Mr/Mrs/Miss)

Address

Postcode

☐ I enclose a cheque for £ _____ payable to Johansens
☐ I enclose my order on company letterheading, please invoice (UK only)
☐ Please debit my credit/charge card account (please tick).
☐ MasterCard ☐ Diners ☐ Amex ☐ Visa ☐ Switch (Issue Number) _____

Card No

Signature

Exp date

Prices Valid Until 31 August 1999
Please allow 21 days for delivery

Occasionally we may allow other reputable organisations to write to you with offers which may be of interest. If you prefer not to hear from them, tick this box ☐

J16

Guest Survey Report

Your own Johansens 'inspection' gives reliability to our guides and assists in the selection of Award Nominations

Name/location of hotel: _____ Page No: _____

Date of visit: _____

Name & address of guest: _____

_____ Postcode: _____

Please tick one box in each category below:	Excellent	Good	Disappointing	Poor
Bedrooms				
Public Rooms				
Restaurant/Cuisine				
Service				
Welcome/Friendliness				
Value For Money				

PLEASE return your Guest Survey Report form!

Occasionally we may allow other reputable organisations to write with offers which may be of interest.
If you prefer not to hear from them, tick this box ☐

To: Johansens, FREEPOST (CB264), 43 Millharbour, London E14 9BR

Guest Survey Report

Your own Johansens 'inspection' gives reliability to our guides and assists in the selection of Award Nominations

Name/location of hotel: _____ Page No: _____

Date of visit: _____

Name & address of guest: _____

_____ Postcode: _____

Please tick one box in each category below:	Excellent	Good	Disappointing	Poor
Bedrooms				
Public Rooms				
Restaurant/Cuisine				
Service				
Welcome/Friendliness				
Value For Money				

PLEASE return your Guest Survey Report form!

Occasionally we may allow other reputable organisations to write with offers which may be of interest.
If you prefer not to hear from them, tick this box ☐

To: Johansens, FREEPOST (CB264), 43 Millharbour, London E14 9BR

ORDER FORM

Call our 24hr credit card hotline FREEPHONE +44 800 269 397

Simply indicate which title(s) you require by putting the quantity in the boxes provided. Choose your preferred method of payment and return this coupon (NO STAMP REQUIRED) to: Johansens, FREEPOST (CB264), 43 Millharbour, London E14 9BR. Your FREE gifts will automatically be dispatched with your order. Fax orders welcome on +44 171 537 3594

PRINTED GUIDES

		Qty	Total £
A Hotels – Great Britain & Ireland 1999 ....£19.95			
B Country Houses and Small Hotels – Great Britain & Ireland 1999 ....£10.95			
C Traditional Inns, Hotels and Restaurants – Great Britain & Ireland 1999 ......£10.95			
D Hotels – Europe & The Mediterranean 1999 ....£14.95			
E Hotels – North America, Bermuda, Caribbean 1999 ....£9.95			
F Historic Houses Castles & Gardens 1999 *published & mailed to you in March '99* £4.99			
G Museums & Galleries 1999 *published & mailed to you in April '99* £8.95			
H Business Meeting Venues 1999 *published & mailed to you in March '99* £20.00			
I Japanese Edition 1999 ....£9.95			
J Privilege Card 1999 ....£20.00 *You get one free card with you order, please mention here the number of additional cards you require*			

TOTAL 1

SPECIAL OFFERS

		Qty	Total £
SAVE £7.85 3 Johansens guides A+B+C . £41.85 ..£34			
In a presentation box set add £5			
SAVE £12.80 4 Johansens guides A+B+C+D ....£56.80 ..£44			
In a presentation box set add £5			
SAVE £14.75 5 Johansens guides A+B+C+D+E ....£66.75 ..£52			
In a presentation box set add £5			
+Johansens Suit Cover			**FREE**
+P&P			**FREE**
SAVE £10.90 2 Johansens CD-ROMS K+L £49.90 ..£39			
SAVE £10 Business Meeting Pack H+M......£40 .£30			

TOTAL 3

CD-ROMs

		Qty	Total £
K The Guide 1999 – Great Britain & Ireland *published and mailed to you in Nov 98* £29.95			
L The Guide 1999 – Europe & North America *published and mailed to you in Nov 98* ..£19.95			
M Business Meeting Venues 1999 *published and mailed to you in April '99* £20.00			

TOTAL 2

Postage & Packing

UK: £4.50 or £2.50 for single orders and CD-ROMs
Ouside UK: Add £5 or £3 for single orders and CD-ROMs.

TOTAL 4

One Privilege Card **FREE**
10% discount, room upgrade when available,
VIP service at participating establishments

TOTAL 1+2+3+4

Name (Mr/Mrs/Miss)
Address
Postcode

☐ I enclose a cheque for £ _____ payable to Johansens
☐ I enclose my order on company letterheading, please invoice (UK only)
☐ Please debit my credit/charge card account (please tick).
☐ MasterCard ☐ Diners ☐ Amex ☐ Visa ☐ Switch (Issue Number)

Prices Valid Until 31 August 1999
Please allow 21 days for delivery

Occasionally we may allow other reputable organisations to write to you with offers which may be of interest. If you prefer not to hear from them, tick this box. ☐

Card No
Signature
Exp date

J16

✂ ....

ORDER FORM

Call our 24hr credit card hotline FREEPHONE +44 800 269 397

Simply indicate which title(s) you require by putting the quantity in the boxes provided. Choose your preferred method of payment and return this coupon (NO STAMP REQUIRED) to: Johansens, FREEPOST (CB264), 43 Millharbour, London E14 9BR. Your FREE gifts will automatically be dispatched with your order. Fax orders welcome on +44 171 537 3594

PRINTED GUIDES

		Qty	Total £
A Hotels – Great Britain & Ireland 1999 ....£19.95			
B Country Houses and Small Hotels – Great Britain & Ireland 1999 ....£10.95			
C Traditional Inns, Hotels and Restaurants – Great Britain & Ireland 1999 ......£10.95			
D Hotels – Europe & The Mediterranean 1999 ....£14.95			
E Hotels – North America, Bermuda, Caribbean 1999 ....£9.95			
F Historic Houses Castles & Gardens 1999 *published & mailed to you in March '99* £4.99			
G Museums & Galleries 1999 *published & mailed to you in April '99* £8.95			
H Business Meeting Venues 1999 *published & mailed to you in March '99* £20.00			
I Japanese Edition 1999 ....£9.95			
J Privilege Card 1999 ....£20.00 *You get one free card with you order, please mention here the number of additional cards you require*			

TOTAL 1

SPECIAL OFFERS

		Qty	Total £
SAVE £7.85 3 Johansens guides A+B+C .. £41.85 ..£34			
In a presentation box set add £5			
SAVE £12.80 4 Johansens guides A+B+C+D ....£56.80 ..£44			
In a presentation box set add £5			
SAVE £14.75 5 Johansens guides A+B+C+D+E ....£66.75 ..£52			
In a presentation box set add £5			
+Johansens Suit Cover			**FREE**
+P&P			**FREE**
SAVE £10.90 2 Johansens CD-ROMS K+L £49.90 ..£39			
SAVE £10 Business Meeting Pack H+M......£40 .£30			

TOTAL 3

CD-ROMs

		Qty	Total £
K The Guide 1999 – Great Britain & Ireland *published and mailed to you in Nov 98* £29.95			
L The Guide 1999 – Europe & North America *published and mailed to you in Nov 98* ..£19.95			
M Business Meeting Venues 1999 *published and mailed to you in April '99* £20.00			

TOTAL 2

Postage & Packing

UK: £4.50 or £2.50 for single orders and CD-ROMs
Ouside UK: Add £5 or £3 for single orders and CD-ROMs.

TOTAL 4

One Privilege Card **FREE**
10% discount, room upgrade when available,
VIP service at participating establishments

TOTAL 1+2+3+4

Name (Mr/Mrs/Miss)
Address
Postcode

☐ I enclose a cheque for £ _____ payable to Johansens
☐ I enclose my order on company letterheading, please invoice (UK only)
☐ Please debit my credit/charge card account (please tick).
☐ MasterCard ☐ Diners ☐ Amex ☐ Visa ☐ Switch (Issue Number)

Prices Valid Until 31 August 1999
Please allow 21 days for delivery

Occasionally we may allow other reputable organisations to write to you with offers which may be of interest. If you prefer not to hear from them, tick this box. ☐

Card No
Signature
Exp date

J16

Guest Survey Report

Name/location of hotel: _____ Page No: _____

Date of visit: _____

Name & address of guest: _____

_____ Postcode: _____

Please tick one box in each category below:

	Excellent	Good	Disappointing	Poor
Bedrooms				
Public Rooms				
Restaurant/Cuisine				
Service				
Welcome/Friendliness				
Value For Money				

PLEASE return your Guest Survey Report form!

Occasionally we may allow other reputable organisations to write with offers which may be of interest.
If you prefer not to hear from them, tick this box ☐

To: Johansens, FREEPOST (CB264), 43 Millharbour, London E14 9BR

Guest Survey Report

Your own Johansens 'inspection' gives reliability to our guides and assists in the selection of Award Nominations

Name/location of hotel: _____ Page No: _____

Date of visit: _____

Name & address of guest: _____

_____ Postcode: _____

Please tick one box in each category below:

	Excellent	Good	Disappointing	Poor
Bedrooms				
Public Rooms				
Restaurant/Cuisine				
Service				
Welcome/Friendliness				
Value For Money				

PLEASE return your Guest Survey Report form!

Occasionally we may allow other reputable organisations to write with offers which may be of interest.
If you prefer not to hear from them, tick this box ☐

To: Johansens, FREEPOST (CB264), 43 Millharbour, London E14 9BR

ORDER FORM

Call our 24hr credit card hotline FREEPHONE +44 800 269 397

Simply indicate which title(s) you require by putting the quantity in the boxes provided. Choose your preferred method of payment and return this coupon (NO STAMP REQUIRED) to: Johansens, FREEPOST (CB264), 43 Millharbour, London E14 9BR. Your FREE gifts will automatically be dispatched with your order. Fax orders welcome on +44 171 537 3594

PRINTED GUIDES

	Qty	Total £
A Hotels – Great Britain & Ireland 1999 ....£19.95		
B Country Houses and Small Hotels – Great Britain & Ireland 1999 ....£10.95		
C Traditional Inns, Hotels and Restaurants – Great Britain & Ireland 1999 ......£10.95		
D Hotels – Europe & The Mediterranean 1999 ....£14.95		
E Hotels – North America, Bermuda, Caribbean 1999 ....£9.95		
F Historic Houses Castles & Gardens 1999 *published & mailed to you in March '99* £4.99		
G Museums & Galleries 1999 *published & mailed to you in April '99* £8.95		
H Business Meeting Venues 1999 *published & mailed to you in March '99* £20.00		
I Japanese Edition 1999 ....£9.95		
J Privilege Card 1999 ....£20.00		
You get one free card with you order, please mention here the number of additional cards you require		
TOTAL 1		

CD-ROMs

	Qty	Total £
K The Guide 1999 – Great Britain & Ireland *published and mailed to you in Nov 98* £29.95		
L The Guide 1999 – Europe & North America *published and mailed to you in Nov 98* ..£19.95		
M Business Meeting Venues 1999 *published and mailed to you in April '99* £20.00		
TOTAL 2		

SPECIAL OFFERS

	Qty	Total £
SAVE £7.85 3 Johansens guides A+B+C ..£41.85..£34		
In a presentation box set add £5		
SAVE £12.80 4 Johansens guides A+B+C+D ....£56.80..£44		
In a presentation box set add £5		
SAVE £14.75 5 Johansens guides A+B+C+D+E ....£66.75..£52		
In a presentation box set add £5		
+Johansens Suit Cover		FREE
+P&P		FREE
SAVE £10.90 2 Johansens CD-ROMS K+L £49.90..£39		
SAVE £10 Business Meeting Pack H+M.....£40..£30		
TOTAL 3		

Postage & Packing

UK: £4.50 or £2.50 for single orders and CD-ROMs
Ouside UK: Add £5 or £3 for single orders and CD-ROMs.

TOTAL 4		

One Privilege Card
10% discount, room upgrade when available,
VIP service at participating establishments

TOTAL 1+2+3+4 [ ]

Name	(Mr/Mrs/Miss)
Address	
	Postcode

☐ I enclose a cheque for £ _____ payable to Johansens
☐ I enclose my order on company letterheading, please invoice (UK only)
☐ Please debit my credit/charge card account (please tick).
☐ MasterCard ☐ Diners ☐ Amex ☐ Visa ☐ Switch (Issue Number)

Card No
Signature
Exp date

Prices Valid Until 31 August 1999
Please allow 21 days for delivery

Occasionally we may allow other reputable organisations to write to you with offers which may be of interest. If you prefer not to hear from them, tick this box. ☐

J16

✂ ....

ORDER FORM

Call our 24hr credit card hotline FREEPHONE +44 800 269 397

Simply indicate which title(s) you require by putting the quantity in the boxes provided. Choose your preferred method of payment and return this coupon (NO STAMP REQUIRED) to: Johansens, FREEPOST (CB264), 43 Millharbour, London E14 9BR. Your FREE gifts will automatically be dispatched with your order. Fax orders welcome on +44 171 537 3594

PRINTED GUIDES

	Qty	Total £
A Hotels – Great Britain & Ireland 1999 ....£19.95		
B Country Houses and Small Hotels – Great Britain & Ireland 1999 ....£10.95		
C Traditional Inns, Hotels and Restaurants – Great Britain & Ireland 1999 ......£10.95		
D Hotels – Europe & The Mediterranean 1999 ....£14.95		
E Hotels – North America, Bermuda, Caribbean 1999 ....£9.95		
F Historic Houses Castles & Gardens 1999 *published & mailed to you in March '99* £4.99		
G Museums & Galleries 1999 *published & mailed to you in April '99* £8.95		
H Business Meeting Venues 1999 *published & mailed to you in March '99* £20.00		
I Japanese Edition 1999 ....£9.95		
J Privilege Card 1999 ....£20.00		
You get one free card with you order, please mention here the number of additional cards you require		
TOTAL 1		

CD-ROMs

	Qty	Total £
K The Guide 1999 – Great Britain & Ireland *published and mailed to you in Nov 98* £29.95		
L The Guide 1999 – Europe & North America *published and mailed to you in Nov 98* ..£19.95		
M Business Meeting Venues 1999 *published and mailed to you in April '99* £20.00		
TOTAL 2		

SPECIAL OFFERS

	Qty	Total £
SAVE £7.85 3 Johansens guides A+B+C ..£41.85..£34		
In a presentation box set add £5		
SAVE £12.80 4 Johansens guides A+B+C+D ....£56.80..£44		
In a presentation box set add £5		
SAVE £14.75 5 Johansens guides A+B+C+D+E ....£66.75..£52		
In a presentation box set add £5		
+Johansens Suit Cover		FREE
+P&P		FREE
SAVE £10.90 2 Johansens CD-ROMS K+L £49.90..£39		
SAVE £10 Business Meeting Pack H+M.....£40..£30		
TOTAL 3		

Postage & Packing

UK: £4.50 or £2.50 for single orders and CD-ROMs
Ouside UK: Add £5 or £3 for single orders and CD-ROMs.

TOTAL 4		

One Privilege Card
10% discount, room upgrade when available,
VIP service at participating establishments

TOTAL 1+2+3+4 [ ]

Name	(Mr/Mrs/Miss)
Address	
	Postcode

☐ I enclose a cheque for £ _____ payable to Johansens
☐ I enclose my order on company letterheading, please invoice (UK only)
☐ Please debit my credit/charge card account (please tick).
☐ MasterCard ☐ Diners ☐ Amex ☐ Visa ☐ Switch (Issue Number)

Card No
Signature
Exp date

Prices Valid Until 31 August 1999
Please allow 21 days for delivery

Occasionally we may allow other reputable organisations to write to you with offers which may be of interest. If you prefer not to hear from them, tick this box. ☐

J16